Theatre and Political Process

Theatre and Political Process

STAGING IDENTITIES IN TOKELAU AND
NEW ZEALAND

Ingjerd Hoëm

Berghahn Books
New York • Oxford

First published in 2004 by

Berghahn Books
www.berghahnbooks.com

© 2004 Ingjerd Hoëm

Library of Congress Cataloging-in-Publication Data

Hoem, Ingjerd.
Theatre and political process : staging identities in Tokelau and New
Zealand / Ingjerd Hoëm.
    p. cm.
Includes bibliographical references.
ISBN 1-57181-583-X (alk. paper) -- ISBN 1-57181-584-8 (pbk. : alk. paper)
    1. Tokelauans--Politics and government. 2. Tokelauans--Ethnic
identity. 3. Tokelauans--Social life and customs. 4. Tokelau--Politics and
government. 5. Tokelau--Economic conditions. 6. Tokelau--Foreign
relations. I. Title.

DU424.5.T65H64 2004
306.44'089'9946—dc22

2004043743

British Library Cataloguing in Publication Data

A catalogue record for this book is available
from the British Library.

Printed in Canada

ISBN 1-57181-583-X (hardback)

Contents

Preface

ɞ৵⭒৵ɞ

My work in Tokelau began in 1985, when I was a graduate student in Social Anthropology at the University of Oslo, Norway. Since then I have spent 25 months altogether doing fieldwork, including 7 months in the Tokelau communities in New Zealand, mainly in the Hutt Valley area outside of Wellington. When I was first introduced to the field of Pacific studies, I had the opportunity to participate in a course in linguistic fieldwork technique, arranged by Professor Even Hovdhaugen at the Department of Linguistics, University of Oslo. This course included a short field trip to Hawaii, Samoa and Fiji with a small group of students. During the stay in Samoa, arrangements were made with the then Office for Tokelau Affairs in Apia (now Tokelau Apia Liaison Office), to instigate a research project in Tokelau the following year. This project initially involved three researchers: two linguists – Hovdhaugen and Arnfinn Muruvik Vonen – and myself. By request of the then Director of the Tokelau Education Department, Falani Aukuso, and with the help of the teacher, and later Minister of Education, Consulata Mahina Iosefo (her assistance even came to include a visit to Norway), we eventually produced a handbook and a grammar of the Tokelau language. The books were written and published in Tokelauan and English (Hovdhaugen *et al.* 1989). During this period, I undertook two field trips to Tokelau, from July to December 1986, and from March to July 1988 (see Hoëm 1995 for a further description of this research).

My work at the time was on the relationship between language, culture and society, and documents some of the main characteristics and typical speech genres of Tokelau discourse. In particular, it relates common communicative patterns, found in 'men's talk' and 'women's talk', to locally held conceptions of knowledge and morality. This work, for my MA thesis (Magistergrad), called *Sharing a Language – Sharing a Way of Life?*, was presented in 1990 and was later published in a revised version as *A Way With Words. Language and Culture in Tokelau Society* (Hoëm 1995). Hovdhaugen and Vonen have subsequently published extensively on various aspects of Tokelau grammar, while I have continued to concentrate on the relationship between indigenous concepts, communicative practices and sociocultural change. Macro- and micropolitical issues came to constitute a large proportion of the material of the above-mentioned work, and my focus on language, cognition and communication was naturally coloured by this fact.

At the University of Oslo, Hovdhaugen continued to introduce various aspects of Polynesian languages as part of his undergraduate courses in linguistics. Yet another student, Mari Myksvoll, completed her MA thesis in linguistics (in 1995), having carried out fieldwork in Tokelau. In 1992, the Oceania-Group, consisting of Professor E. Hovdhaugen, senior lecturer H.G. Simonsen, researcher A.M. Vonen, and myself, won a prize for 'excellence in research' (fremragende forskning) from the Research Council for the Humanities for our work in Oceania. This award allowed us, among other things, to invite John Pedro, a Tokelau student of linguistics at Victoria University of Wellington, New Zealand, to study Tokelauan in Norway.

My fieldwork has been funded mainly by The Institute for Comparative Research in Human Culture; I and many others have had the unique opportunity to conduct research in the Pacific, thanks to the Board's decision to support research in the Oceanic region for a five-year period. My main supervisor in Social Anthropology has been Professor Axel Sommerfelt, who taught me how to formulate and follow a research procedure in such a way as not to unduly prejudice the results. In principle, it may sound easy to adopt an empirically-oriented interpretative practice and to pose open-ended questions and to be attentive to the information thus engendered. In practice, however, this is not an easy discipline to follow, as it frequently leads to the often relatively uncomfortable experience of having to reconsider one's ideas of what the world is like and also of one's place in it. If I have not always been able to practice what he taught me, this is certainly not through any fault of his.

After a year working as a Research Assistant (Vit. Ass.) at the Department of Linguistics, preparing and editing a volume on Tokelau oral literature (Hoëm, Ed. 1992), I applied for a doctoral fellowship at the Faculty of Humanities at the University of Oslo. This four-year fellowship allowed yet another period of fieldwork in the Pacific. I went to Samoa, Tokelau and New Zealand, and worked there from June 1992 to May 1993. Subsequently I returned to Samoa, Tokelau and New Zealand, from November to February 1993–94, to document some events of central importance to this work. My most recent visits to the Pacific and New Zealand were in 1997 (Solomon Islands, New Zealand), 2002 (New Zealand) and 2003 (Samoa and New Zealand).

During the periods of fieldwork in New Zealand, I was generously offered an office at the Stout Research Centre at Victoria University of Wellington. This gave me a base to work from, and provided a very useful point of connection with the field of Pacific studies at the university, as well as making contact with the New Zealand Tokelau administration easier. Tokelau's political counterparts in Wellington, the Ministry of Foreign Affairs and Trade, the SSC (State Services Commission), and various other bodies, such as the Tokelau Law Project, also generously opened their doors to me, and came to be included in the scope of my fieldwork.

It is important to note that the dimension of ethnicity, in the sense of the politicisation of identity typically associated with majority: minority situations,[1] had already emerged and was visible in Tokelau at the time of my first fieldwork in 1986. In this context of the politicisation of identity, which is not a dominant aspect of all interactions, but rather results from an increased interaction with the outside world, symbolic markers of identity, such as 'language', 'history', and 'tradition', emerge. As markers of identity, they carry qualitatively different values and interpretations from references that deal with the semantic fields associated with, for example, 'language', 'history', and 'culture' outside of the majority: minority context. This aspect of what may be called 'the politics of representation' will be described and discussed in greater detail in this work. Here, I introduce it only to explain how I – sitting in my office in Oslo talking on the phone with Vonen who was in Wellington doing research – was fascinated to learn that a group of Tokelauans had gathered in New Zealand to produce a play about Tokelau's history. As far as I knew, this was an unprecedented event, and I was curious to learn more about what this new addition to the repertoire of Tokelau performative genres signified. This intriguing piece of information reached me as I was in the process of formulating my research project, and as a direct result of this phone call, I came to spend the major part of my fieldwork following members of this group. I knew some individuals central to this social network from previous fieldwork, and I was eager to see what they were up to.

Notes

1. Comaroff and Comaroff (1992: 54).

Acknowledgements

I would like to take this opportunity to thank the many people and institutions who have made this work possible. First of all, I wish to express my gratitude to the people of Atafu, Fakaofo and Nukunonu, the Tokelau community in Samoa, and to members of the Tokelau communities in New Zealand, for making room for me and my research. In particular, I wish to thank Moana Rimoni, Tui and Ane Sopoaga, Vae and Feleti Lopa, Luiano and Juliana Peres, Manea Pasilio, Casimilo Peres, Tioni Vulu, Akata and Metale Tala, Susanna Lemisio, Falani and Sulu Aukuso, Akapito Pasikale, Sak Patelesio, Consy Iosefo, Hohe Lui and Epi Swan. I would also like to thank all members and associates of the song-group Tagi and the theatre group Tokelau te Ata. *Fakafetai lahi lele mo te alolofa mai.*

The Tokelau Administration, the Administrator for Tokelau for most of the period that this work covers, Lindsay Watt, and the Tokelau Law Project Professor, Tony Angelo, have been most helpful in introducing me to the world of Tokelau's external relations. I would also like to thank Dean David Mackay at the Victoria University of Wellington and the staff at the Stout Research Centre for facilitating my work there.

During the writing of this book, I have spent periods as a visiting fellow at the Max-Planck Institute (MPI) in Nijmegen. I would like to thank Professor Gunter Senft for inviting me, and the staff at the MPI for providing me with an excellent, challenging and friendly working environment. The members of the Oceania-Group at the Department of Linguistics, University of Oslo, Even Hovdhaugen, Hanne Gram Simonsen and Arnfinn M. Vonen, have been invaluable for this project. Eduardo Archetti, Fredrik Barth, Niko Besnier, Maurice Bloch, Alessandro Duranti, Jonathan Friedman, Antony Hooper, Robin Hooper, Signe Howell, Judith Huntsman, Edvard Hviding, Kjersti Larsen, Andrew Pawley, Arne Aleksej Perminow, Sidsel Roalkvam, Simon Schaffer, Andrew Strathern, Christina Toren, Jurg Wassman, Harvey Whitehouse, and numerous others at, or associated with, the Department of Social Anthropology at the University of Oslo have contributed in various ways to this work, and I thank them all for their help.

Finally, as mentioned earlier, the Institute for Comparative Research in Human Culture, The Norwegian Research Council, the Faculty of Arts at the University of Oslo and the Oceania-Group have all supported my work financially. I am very grateful to these bodies for granting me the opportunity to carry out long-term research.

Introduction

On Fieldwork Methodology

The fieldwork methodology I use involves following a select number of individuals, and their social networks, over a period of time and across the variety of social contexts their life-trajectories may take them. At least this is my recollection of how Prof. Fredrik Barth, during a discussion of how I should approach my second fieldwork, formulated it at the time.[1] I took this advice very seriously. This method, if followed through, is bound to result in a high degree of familiarity with the life-world encountered and experienced by the people one follows, with their interests and desires, conflicts and concerns. It also reveals the whole spectrum of culturally significant roles and statuses, institutions, arenas, and situations constituting the social field covered by the study.[2]

To the participant observer, the fieldwork process broadly takes the form of a gradual and partial assimilation of unfamiliar practices, to a degree where the new information is transformed into internalised knowledge, much of which exists in an embodied form. In this process, the unfamiliar routines, gestures, postures and expressions that one gradually adopts during fieldwork become unconscious habits; that is, they are reproduced automatically and without reflection. Illustrations of such embodied knowledge would, in my case, be to bow down, to walk in a crouching posture if I have to pass in front of a person of higher status, or to demonstrate my pleasure in a gift by lifting it over my head. These kinds of routines may be made the subject of reflection and may serve as a source of information (Bloch 1990). To subject oneself to such a socialisation process, to be an instrument in one's own research in this reflexive manner, means to create a new *social personae* for oneself (see also Hastrup 1989, and Goward 1984). To play with one's social identity in this way is bound to have some effect on one's post-fieldwork practices and attitudes – in short, to also have some influence on the researcher's life out of the field. During my first visit to Samoa, my host-family Aiono (in Fasitoouta) renamed me Ina. The Tokelau equivalent would be Hina, but even there, the name 'Ina' stuck and it has stayed with me ever since. It is as Ina that many people came to know me. It is as Ingjerd that I write this book. The two differ in that they are part of separate social networks, do different things and have, at least in part, different concerns. I recognise myself in both of them, and I have even had the experience of witnessing the occasional encounter between the two. For instance, when I was about to leave at the end of one of my longer stays in New Zealand, I had shifted my mental frame of reference without realising it – from 'Ina in the field' to 'Ingjerd going home'. In this state of departure, I made a phone-call to one of my Tokelau associates and introduced myself by saying 'This is Ingjerd, is Ina there?' instead of 'This is Ina, is [...] (the name of the woman I called) there?' It was a most concrete experience of role dilemma, and for me a very comic one at that moment. I laughed and laughed, and as I laughed I realised that I was very sad indeed to leave. Of course, the personal names of 'Ina' or 'Ingjerd' are in a sense only name-tags and labels, but the shifting references may serve to illustrate the role dilemmas that are a part of the role- and code switching that participant observation (but also other social situations) often requires (see for example, Blom and Gumperts 1972; Barth 1971).

However, the fact that my life so far has frequently presented me with opportunities to develop and manifest many, and sometimes widely different, social incarnations, is of little relevance to the events I describe in this book. In the following, therefore, I choose not to dwell on my own story in or out of the field, except in the very few places where it impinges on the interpretation of the material I present. The distancing process achieved through what may be called a double return, both from the field and from achieved embodiment back to externalised knowledge, in the form of writing or other media, is obviously more dominant towards the end of a research project, but a certain movement between closeness and distance is always present as part of any fieldwork experience. Learning always occurs in the gaps between the world, as one knows it from previous experience, and the world as it is encountered during fieldwork. In the attempt to establish an acceptable social persona, one tries on new roles and fails at fulfilling the role expectations that others have for you. In short, one learns in a constant movement, between more or less successful adaptation, and heroic or pathetic mistakes.

There are many competing metaphors for the role of the fieldworker and many of them are negative: s/he is like a spy; s/he is someone who betrays the confidence s/he has been entrusted with, by the shameless telling of other peoples secrets (Hastrup and Ramløv 1988). The more positive or self-congratulatory metaphors liken the anthropologist to Hermes, to a cultural translator, healer or broker, one who mediates between worlds and contributes knowledge as a common good (Crapanzano 1986; Tyler 1986).

In Tokelau terms, as in many other Pacific societies, there are, at least, two seemingly opposed models of knowledge. The dominant one is based on the conceptualisation of knowledge as a limited good, and as a personal or collective possession (see eds. Thomas, A., I. Tuia and J. Huntsman 1990, on the concept *taoga*, or treasures). It is ultimately genealogical in form (Charlot 1983; Hoëm 1994) and constitutes an important basis for leadership positions. To possess, and to be able to use, such knowledge to further the interests of one's extended family and allies, such as for example to substantiate claims to land rights, is of crucial importance in village life. This kind of knowledge is not something to share freely. To gather such knowledge is to take something away, and to disseminate it is threatening – doing so is easily perceived as undermining the established power structure. The Elders' position in the Village Councils (*Fono o Taupulega*), and their power to rule the village affairs (*pule*)[3] is based on a perception of them as knowledgeable persons (*poto*). Their deliberations are traditionally not made known to the villagers, only the outcome of their decisions, and the basis for the decisions is not usually openly questioned. To share 'the knowledge' is also undesirable from a local point of view, because it inevitably presents one version of current relationships, thus backing one group at the expense of the others. These attitudes are important to note, as they represent the rationale for the patterns of communication in the villages that the theatre group described later comes up against, and which they more or less deliberately set out to challenge (see, in particular, Chapter one).

I have been confronted with this conception of knowledge as personal property in many different ways during fieldwork. In some ways, this mirrors the professional accumulation of symbolic capital, where fieldwork sites are easily turned into academic turfs. I have thus been told that I am just like a *palagi*, meaning that I take what I learn away with me, rather than to stay and pool my resources with some Tokelauan group. In this context, I have had my fieldwork likened to the activities of the slave raiders who came to Tokelau and took most of the able-bodied men (i.e., their strength and productive power, *malohi*) away. In this light, I come, I take what I want, and then I go away and invest what I have received somewhere else. On the other hand, and according to the other part of the model, to take is to engage in a pattern of reciprocity. From this perspective, one is always a part of an exchange relationship, of give *and* take. This relationship is performative: as one cannot refuse another's right to take, one cannot avoid the obligation to give.[4] To choose not to participate is not an option. How the knowledge (or other resource) is provided, and concomitantly, whether breeches of etiquette are seen to be serious or not, depends very much on the context and the manner in which the 'taking' and 'giving' of it is conducted. I have asked about things which people didn't consider fitting for me to know, and have been brushed off, more or less politely. By these and other breeches of 'proper conduct' I have learned about patterns of communication and concomitant moral codes, and about different speech contexts.[5]

Knowledge that cannot be used or uttered in a political meeting without grave consequences may be playfully presented in a song. Such a performance may also have social, even political, consequences, but not necessarily of a fatal nature for the performer.[6] The dividing line between contexts of uttermost importance and seriousness and contexts of playfulness is very thin: clowning and fun is part and parcel of Tokelau life. In this light, then, the act of giving is also a moment of taking something away; however, at a later stage something is always returned – otherwise the relationship ceases to exist. Whether the return contribution will be accepted as *malie*, as a pleasing *mea alofa*, a thing of love, depends as much on the spirit in which the gift is offered as it does on the memories of the recipients of the interaction preceding the return. As the play, which is a central case in this work, eventually came to be presented as such a gift (see Chapter one), so my writing also represents a return contribution.

M. Hertzfeld (1997) draws our attention to what he calls areas of great sensitivity and self-stereotyping that exist in every society. He labels them areas of 'cultural intimacy', and observes that once a fieldworker enters into some degree of social intimacy, that is into the commensuality that members of a society regularly partake in, he or she is exposed to and included in reflections on areas of cultural intimacy. Writing within the context of the self-presentation of nation states, he observes that the images that the nation state (or local community) wishes to project to the outside world are a matter of great sensitivity and are always subject to editing and suppression. His position is that anthropologists inevitably, and with good reason, recount part of these 'intimacies', the narratives of local perspectives, to the public. He sees this as a politically important activity, as representing counter stories to the polished narratives that tend to accompany the nation state.

In other words, the description and analysis of social fields (Grønhaug 1974) emerging from the social networks encountered during fieldwork, and of the narratives people tell in the course of everyday life, is different in significant ways from the same people's self-presentation in highly sensitive and politicised contexts, such as when presenting Tokelau to the New Zealand public, either in the media, or through so-called cultural performances. The tensions and discrepancies between these two levels of representation will be explored further in this work. In this sense, the title of this work, *Staging Identities*, can be read in many ways. First of all, it points to the fact that self-presentation is always relationally situated. Furthermore, it points to the exposure to widely different representations of ways of life faced by the younger generation of Tokelau today – and to their responses to this situation. Finally and most concretely, it designates what the Tokelau theatre group, Tokelau Te Ata, attempted to achieve – that is, to present an alternative way of living to the Tokelau Communities in Tokelau and in New Zealand.[7]

Awareness of the situated character of cultural knowledge is heightened by the methodological approach to the field described above. The fact that one encounters most people involved in the social field under study, and experiences the main institutions and the array of significant arenas and contexts while following the people to whom one has attached oneself, provides – as all approaches do – only a partial view of the sociocultural system one describes. However, and in contrast to much other research, it gives an experience-near view of the workings of society, and of processes of structuration, as opposed to purely structural analyses. In the process of creating viable (or not so viable) ways of being in the Tokelau communities, the existence of new tools of expression, and of new media, such as newsletters, video recorders and TV sets, and of new genres such as written poetry and theatre, is central. Therefore, in this work I have set out to explore how new experiences and media enter into previously established communicative practices and affect patterns of identification.

Contemporary Argonauts

A special issue of *Pacific Studies*, devoted to the strategies developed by Pacific islanders 'for settling in new places', suggests that we leave the practice of drawing 'absolute boundaries around geographical and cultural areas'. Instead, they propose that we focus on 'movements and processes [...].' (2002: 03). Still, most scholars in the study of movement keep as their main focus the consequences that the conditions for migration have on the organisation of community life. In my work, I suggest that we leave the boundaries of community studies and instead explore trans-local networks, hence the subtitle 'Tokelau and New Zealand'. With the phrase 'contemporary argonauts', I point to the deep continuity that exists between present-day movements in the Pacific and the journeys of earlier periods. I wish to draw attention to contemporary movements back and forth between urban centres and village communities, to point to connections *and* also to discontinuities, following Sahlins' suggestion that we see Pacific communities as consisting of agentive networks expanding into new regions, rather than as passive victims of large-scale processes (Sahlins 1993). To the growing field of 'displacement' studies, we need to add ethnographic studies of contemporary movement of a different, perhaps more ordinary, kind. This is a kind of movement that cannot be adequately described as labour migration, nor as a direct result of large-scale economic factors, but perhaps rather should be treated as a part of an expansive form of sociality. The ethnographic material presented in this work may be read as illustrations of this kind of social practice.

A Lament

The song rendered below was first presented to the Tokelau communities in the Wellington area as part of the repertoire of a New Zealand Tokelau song group named Tagi. In the song, the group addresses the issue of growing up as first generation, New Zealand-born Tokelauans. They are living in a cultural setting where the dominant values are quite different from those associated with life in the atoll environment of Atafu, Nukunonu and Fakaofo – the three atoll communities comprising Tokelau. Later on, the song was included in a theatre play also called *Tagi*, or 'lament', produced with the explicitly stated intention of reflecting upon and confronting the communities with the situation that the Tokelau population in New Zealand faces. The play *Tagi*, and another play called *Mafine*, 'woman', will be described and discussed within the framework of this work as reflections of the shifting realities and processes of identification that present-day 'argonauts of the Pacific' may experience.

Taku Tama e	O My Child
Te leo kua he lagona	You don't understand the language anymore
ka ko na kupu koi manatua	but you recognise the words.
Taku tama e	O my child.
Te lumanaki o to ta nuku	The future of our village.
Tuku mai ko au ke fano	Let me move towards
hea nei ko na fakakupu mai ai koe.	what the words are that you speak to me.
Aua kua malama oku mata	Because my eyes have caught the light
ki lanu kehekehe o tenei olaga	of the different colours of this life.
Ko ai nei e ia mafaia te kavega	Who then is capable of bringing
te fatu ma te loto	the heart and the spirit
e teu e toku nuku	by which my village beautifies itself?
Ka ko (t)oku tino nei kua ola	So that my body here can be brought alive
i te huamalie o tenei olaga	by the sweetness of this life.
Te leo kua he lagona	You don't understand the language
ka ko na kupu koi manatua	but you still remember the words.
Taku tama e	O my child.
Te lumanaki o to ta nuku	The future of our village.

(From the cassette Lagi a Tokelau, produced by the Tokelau song group Tagi, New Zealand. Transcription and translation mine.)

As the words of the song *Taku Tama e* indicate, there is a big difference between the passive knowledge of a language and vague familiarity with a way of life, and the active mastery of the same. However, and as the song poignantly reflects, the process of learning about the unfamiliar life-world, whether Tokelau or New Zealand, can be reciprocal and of mutual benefit. In this view, an opposition between local mores and the experience of modernity, and between life in and outside of Tokelau, need not be irreconcilable. The suggestion that second-generation Tokelauans in New Zealand could learn from things pertaining to Tokelau, and that those familiar with Tokelau could benefit from seeing the different colours of life in New Zealand, is, however, not a vision that is unanimously shared.

Communicative Practices

The child addressed in the song (one of the new generation of New Zealand-born Tokelauans) is said to represent the future of the 'village' (*nuku*). The village or community, in common conceptions, is the foundation of a life lived 'the Tokelau way' (*faka-Tokelau*). To live a good life, and to ensure that this way of life continues in the future, it is essential to be in touch with 'the heart and the spirit' through which the village may 'beautify' (*teu*) itself. The narrator is searching for a means to convey to the child the experiences this implies. However, the narrator also expresses a wish to understand what it is that the child sees: to understand what the different experiences are that the child speaks of.

This last wish is somewhat unusual, expressed within a Tokelau context. As in other Austronesian societies, a main criterion for social differentiation is relative age (see J. Fox [1995: 223]; see also the ethnographic background later in this chapter). The concomitant communicative practice is expressed in a pattern where the senior person commands (*pule*) and the younger person obeys (*uhitaki*). That is, the older, knowledgeable person controls the flow of information, and the younger person assumes responsibility for carrying out an order – without being entitled to question the contents of the command. (For an illustration of this communicative pattern from Samoa, see E. Ochs 1988.) Therefore, the vision contained in the song is, at least partly, in violation of dominant communicative practices and principles of orientation.

In this connection, the expression 'to beautify' is of particular significance. It represents a key concept informing communicative practice. The terms (*teu, teuteu*), carry the additional meanings 'to decorate, to prepare, to resolve' and 'to settle differences'. In other words, what we find here is a reference to local ways of conflict management. The terms most specifically designate the actions needed to (re)establish social harmony (that is: *fealofani*, mutual love; *maopoopo*, harmony, consensus, collective coherence and cooperation) after a disruption. This is most commonly done through the deliberations of a *fono*, or meeting. *Kupu teuteu*, 'words to settle differences' are used at the end of such meetings (cf., TD 380). (See A. Duranti [1990: 647] for an illustration from Samoa.)

This semantic field points to a culturally close connection between violence and beauty and to the often precarious balance struck between them (E. Valentine Daniel 1994; Hoëm 2000). To establish a culturally acceptable balance between disruption and harmony, deliberate action is needed. To transform what is disgusting, ugly or bad (*mataga, kino*) into something beautiful, acceptable and good (*gali, lelei*) is a serious and important activity. As such it contrasts with so-called 'things of no account' (*mea tauanoa*), the unimportant, non-serious activities. Disciplining action may involve the use of force, and to do so in a socially acceptable manner requires and cultivates knowledge (*poto, iloa*). Uncontrolled eruptions of violence are strongly disapproved of. The goal of disciplining action is to achieve an aesthetically pleasing social harmony and cooperative spirit – that is, the smooth running of village and family affairs. Such social control is an aspect of most Tokelau activities, informing everyday as well as festive occasions.

A need for such harmony-generating action is expressed in the song, and true to Tokelau exegetical practice, the appeal may be interpreted on multiple levels. It speaks of the challenge involved in listening to the child, and transforming its message so that the message may benefit the village. It speaks of the work involved in bringing the child in touch with the heart and spirit of the village. The song may also be read as asking, in a self-abasing manner, the audience to bear with its potentially disruptive message in a way which ensures that harmonious relations prevail.

Matters of Life and Death

One important aspect of the activities associated with 'beautification' is what is commonly labelled face-work (cf., E. Goffman 1959). Tokelauans discuss and experience this culturally important part of life in terms of a rich vocabulary, centred around key concepts such as 'face' (*mata*), 'front'(*mua*) and 'back'(*muli, tua*). A marked characteristic of a main proportion of the terms employed in this connection is their spatial *reference*. Historically, these terms are linked conceptually through the pervasive pan-Polynesian dual cosmogonic concepts of *po* (night, nightside) and *ao* (day, dayside), the relationship between which is governed by the practices associated with the concepts of *tapu* (or *ha*) and *noa* (see Gell 1993, 1995; also Shore 1982, 1989; Thomas 1995, and Hoëm 2000). Through these practices, distinctions are established between formal and informal, restricted and unrestricted persons, things and situations, and between important and unimportant activities (see also Mageo 1998). The ultimate rationale for the continued importance (and semantic productivity) of such distinctions, currently co-existing in a syncretistic manner with various Christian beliefs and practices, lies in how they constitute a frame of reference for regulation and control of the fecundity of the human and the natural environment. In other words, this framework is part of the means by which Tokelauans relate to matters of life and death. A similar observation is made by N. Besnier based on his research in the atoll society Nukulaelae, in Tokelau's neighbour nation-state Tuvalu (see also Mageo 1998). In my analysis, in Tokelau conceptions fecundity is achieved through aesthetically and morally correct action, furthered by the exercise of legitimate authority. In other words, patterns of authority and leadership, of gender roles and everyday conduct, are informed by these underlying principles and patterns of differentiation.

To illustrate: in the atoll societies, any situation of scarcity of a vital resource (*oge*, 'famine'), such as water, is commonly interpreted as caused by somebody having acted in an anti-social fashion. To remedy the situation and bring about a state of abundance, the misdemeanour must be discovered and public redress must be made. Throughout this book, we shall see many illustrations of how such central conceptions manifest as particular expressions of the previously mentioned ancient cosmological patterns, coexisting with versions of Christianity and other, more recently adopted ideas. I shall draw attention to how local forms of sociality may be seen to constitute a pattern of orientation, or what I refer to as *a sense of place*.

Relationships and Representations of Agency

In language, these patterns of orientation are expressed in the most general manner through constructions of agency. Agency in common usage is used synonymously with freedom of action; that is, agency is perceived as a quality of action, most often associated with the individual subject. In this work, however, I approach agency in a more general sense that is also more applicable cross-culturally – namely agency will be used to mean locally held theories of causality (Duranti 1994). Through taking into account how relationships of causality are represented linguistically, we gain an additional and potentially very valuable intake to local cosmology and theories of self (Sahlins 1985; Rosaldo 1980, 1983, 1984; Tonkin 1992; Mageo 1998). All forms and levels of representation of relationships also colour our perceptions of the same. The relationships of command and responsibility, of authority and submission, may be expressed in many ways by employing a variety of resources (Duranti 1990; Keating 2000). For example, the spatial, kinetic and the linguistic dimension may all be drawn upon, and may work simultaneously to express the qualities of a particular relationship.

Thus, the relationship between a person summoned to appear before a meeting (*fono*) of the Council of Elders (*taupulega*), and the village authorities in Tokelau, is expressed in a very concrete manner through the spatial arrangements of the meeting house. The Elders are seated along the posts or walls of the house, in a row (or rows) according to relative status, and facing the offender. The person summoned sits in the middle of the floor, directly in front of the Elders. The character of the relationship is also expressed kinetically: the Elders sit cross-legged with straight backs, looking directly at the offender, while he or she sits, also cross-legged, but with a bowed neck, and with downcast eyes. Furthermore, the relationship is expressed in language. For example, the Elders might speak at length, and the person who has been summoned would respond in short sentences and with a barely audible voice. In addition, the relationship may be expressed linguistically by more subtle means.

For an illustration of the linguistic resources that may be employed, we can return to the songline presented earlier in this chapter: 'Who then is capable of bringing the heart and the spirit by which my village beautifies itself?' This sentence construction employs the strongest available grammatical means of expressing causal responsibility (the ergative marker, e). This choice of expression is of social consequence. The action of beautifying the village is explicitly represented as 'belonging to' the village, that is, by the ergative agent. An alternate way of expressing the responsibility as weaker would be to say, 'the village is beautified', but leaving the 'by whom' unstated. In the last case, no relationship of command and responsibility would be indicated.

In this manner, space, kinetics and language may equally function as resources, by means of which important aspects of social relationships (including social events) may be expressed. How relationships of different kinds are shaped in Tokelau society, and what philosophy of action people have developed, will be described in this book through a particular focus on how agency is represented, produced and experienced by differently positioned subjects.

Macropolitical Influences

Finally, in the most general sense, the song-text presents dilemmas inherent in the situation that the people of Tokelau presently face. A tension between the 'different colours of this life' and the 'sweetness' associated with the Tokelau way of life is perhaps most strongly felt within the Tokelau communities in New Zealand, but it is also a part of the realities of life in the villages in the three atolls comprising Tokelau. The search for contemporary ways and means of expression, how such a desire manifests itself, and what this project signifies in the light of common practices within the communities, both in Tokelau and in New Zealand, therefore constitutes the main proportion of the material presented in the following.

It is too early to say to what extent the more recent developments concerning Tokelau's political status will retrospectively come to be seen as representing radical change in the area of political institutions and leadership structure. However, from the material I present here, it is obvious that the local patterns of communication, hinging as they do on the exercise of gerontocratic, male authority in the village institutions, and on the complementary allocation of rights and responsibilities between the genders, and between *tamatane* (offspring of brothers) and *tamafafine* (offspring of sisters) sides within the extended kin groups, are affected by new work institutions, by the growing monetary economy, and by new tools of expression, in a manner which represents a qualitatively different situation to that which any previous generation has had to cope with. In this context, this book represents a study of micro-historical processes in the making (Handelman 1998). In the following chapters, the recent political developments and the concomitant infrastructural changes in the atoll societies will be described more fully in light of what little is known about Tokelau's pre-contact history, and of the comparatively well documented period following the advent of the papalagi[8] from the mid-eighteenth century.

Ethnographic Background

The three Tokelau atolls – Atafu, Nukunonu and Fakaofo – lie approximately 500 km. north of Samoa, in what is most commonly defined as the Polynesian part of the South Pacific. The fourth Tokelau atoll, Olohega, is currently American territory, but is still claimed by Tokelau. The atolls support a population of around 1600 people and are close to the Equator. Each atoll consists of hundreds of small islets that are connected by coral reef at low tide, and which surround relatively extensive lagoon areas. Anchorage is difficult, and there are no harbours. The main contact with the outside world is by freight ships which also carry passengers. These ships are chartered to run between Samoa and Tokelau, and when they reach the atolls they stand offshore, while cargo and passengers are transported through the reef channel in locally manned aluminium dinghies with outboard motors. At the time of writing, the inter-atoll vessel Tutolu had undergone structural modifications and run back and forth to Samoa every fortnight.

The total land area of Tokelau approaches 12 square kilometres. None of the islets rise above 5 feet. There is very little fertile soil and few sources of fresh water besides rain. Tokelau's fisheries zone covers a large area, about 290,000 sq. km, and is still abundant in fish, although foreign trawling vessels take their toll on the stocks. Coconuts and pandanus fruit, fish and other kinds of seafood, as well as pigs and chickens, constitute the main ingredients of Tokelau food (Hovdhaugen 1992a). In addition, the local cooperative stores provide oil, fat, sugar, flour, tinned food and other additions to the traditional staples. The mean daily temperature is 28° Centigrade (approximately 82° Fahrenheit), with seasonal variations with respect to rainfall and types of winds, ranging from calm to the increasingly frequent hurricanes accompanied by tidal waves.

In 1982, the total number of people living in Tokelau was approximately 1650, and it is about the same today. Due to overpopulation on the islands, a government-sponsored migration scheme to New Zealand was started in the mid-1960s, and there are now about 4000 to 5000 Tokelauans living more or less permanently in New Zealand and in smaller enclaves in places such as Australia, Hawaii and mainland U.S.A. On each of the three atolls, the population is concentrated on one islet on the western, leeward side of the atoll. On both Atafu and Nukunonu, the village islets are relatively large. On Fakaofo, the village covers the whole of a smaller islet of about eleven acres, Fale, which has been built up over the years and in part reclaimed from the reef and the lagoon bed.[9] Since 1966, the village has expanded to the larger adjacent island, Fenua Fala, where the school and hospital are located.[10]

There was sporadic contact between people living on the atolls and various visitors on seafaring vessels during the late eighteenth and early nineteenth centuries. Missionary activity, both Catholic and Protestant, arrived in the early 1860s. This activity coincided with the most tragic incident in the known history of Tokelau: in 1863, slavers engaged in the Peruvian slave trade raided the three atolls. More than 45 percent of the population, mainly adult males, was lost in this raid (Maude 1968). After this incident, the establishment of the missions met with little resistance (Hooper and Huntsman 1972). In 1889, Tokelau was declared a protectorate of Great Britain. In 1910, it was incorporated into the Gilbert and Ellice Island Protectorate, which in 1916 became the Gilbert and Ellice Islands colony. De-annexed in 1924, the islands came under the New Zealand Administration of Western Samoa in 1925. As a consequence of the dramatic decimation of the population (by the slave raiders and due to a dysentery epidemic coinciding with the period of first extensive contact with representatives from the world outside the Pacific), the pre-contact system of social stratification, of chiefly lines and of fights for ascendancy (Fox 1995),[11] was disrupted. Fakaofo's overlordship was formally ended by colonial decree in 1915 and with this, the until then chiefly form of leadership was transformed and retained in a new shape in the institutions of Village Councils (*Fono o Taupulega*) where, since then, the Elders (*Toeaina*, men from approximately their mid-sixties and above) have ruled (Hooper and Huntsman 1985).

Until the 1950s, contact with New Zealand was in the form of short-term visits by officials. The churches had representatives staying for longer periods, but these were selected from other parts of the Pacific, in the main from Samoa (Huntsman 1980). Apart from this, Tokelau was left largely to itself (Hooper 1982). Western Samoa became independent in 1962, and in 1964 Tokelau was given the choice of becoming affiliated with either Western Samoa or the Cook Islands. In response to this, Tokelau asked to be allowed to continue their association with New Zealand. In terms of UN classification, Tokelau is today a 'non self-governing territory', but it is currently assuming more responsibility for its own government and administration.

The mother tongue is the Tokelau language, which belongs to the Polynesian branch of the Austronesian language family. Linguistically classified as belonging to the Samoic Outlier Subgroup of Polynesian, it is closely related to the languages of its neighbouring countries, Tuvalu and Samoa, to the languages of its Polynesian speaking island neighbours in the east, Northern Cook Islands, Pukapuka, Manihiki and Rakahanga, and to the languages of the so-called Polynesian Outliers in the west, Sikaiana and Luangiua in the Solomon Islands (Hovdhaugen *et al.* 1989). As I have described elsewhere (Hoëm 1995), Tokelauan was long thought by outside observers to be on the verge of becoming extinct. This may be because most official communication in earlier decades was conducted in Samoan, the language of the church and the school, and later in English. Samoan was also used to some degree in formal, ritual speech in the Protestant congregations. However, Tokelauan has always been, and still is, the language of everyday speech in the villages and among the older generation in New Zealand. The young generation in New Zealand differ to what extent they are able to speak Tokelauan, but most are able to understand it (cf., the song presented above). Kindergartens where only Tokelauan is spoken, so-called language nests (*kohaga leo*), have been established to counter this tendency. This project is modelled on similar experiments among native Hawaiians in Hawaii and the Maori population in New Zealand. In Tokelau, Tokelauan is now the primary language of instruction, and English is taught as a second language. This is a radical break with school policy in the 1960s and 1970s where children were punished for speaking their native language at school.

All villagers either have rights to land on the island or else are married to someone who does. Land is inalienable in the sense that it is forbidden by law to sell it. The village councils mentioned above (*Fono o Taupulega*) still consist of male elders (*toeaina*) on Fakaofo and Nukunonu; on Atafu they also elect *matai* (titled male family heads) to sit in the councils. The village councils hold weekly meetings where they decide upon the 'timing of all major activities of the population, the days for village work, for communal fishing enterprises, village-wide games etc.' (Hooper 1982: 17).

In other words, the village councils have the right to order people to do jobs for the village, such as when the women are ordered to weave hats, mats and fans as gifts for guests to the village, or to prepare a feast for them, or when the men are ordered to clear the reef channel of stones, or to help construct a house. The Village Councils also adjudicate in village disputes, such as those concerning land rights. They have the power to settle conflicts, and decide on family internal affairs. such as cases of extra-marital pregnancies. In recent years, the councils have had to work in closer cooperation with the Tokelau Public Service, and they elect representatives to partake in the Inter-atoll Assembly: the General Fono.

Describing the position of the Village Councils and the dominant leadership structure in the late 1960's and throughout the 1970's, A. Hooper comments that, at the time, 'this centralised direction is one of the keystones of Tokelau community structure, and it is not called into question by any notion of "individual rights"' (ibid.: 19). As we shall see in the following, this pattern is currently undergoing some changes, particularly in connection with the transition to a market economy.

The Tokelau kinship system is cognatic (Huntsman 1969: 220), and its internal workings have been studied extensively. Huntsman describes how the extended family (*kaiga*, *kau kaiga*) is divided into two sides: the *tamatane* side, which consists of the offspring of the sons of the original founding couple of the estate; and the *tamafafine* side, who are the offspring of the daughters of the founding couple. She presents the *tamatane:tamafafine* relationship as being modelled on the relationship between brothers and sisters. The relationship between brothers and sisters is said to be highly dignified (*mamalu*) and there are clear interactional restrictions (*tapu* or *ha*) on this relationship, which is called *va* ('respect', or literally, 'space between', 'distance'). The interactional pattern between brothers and sisters (after puberty) is one of avoidance and mutual deference. They are bound together in the vital relationship regulating the flow of goods and services within the extended family group, *kaukaiga*. This relationship takes place between the brother (or most commonly, group of brothers) who provides for his natal family (not the one he has moved into upon marriage) and offers his collected share of food to his sister who resides in the family homestead and who is responsible for distributing his goods to the extended family. The *tamatane* have the power and authority, *pule*, over productive property and its use – that is, the right to control land, and agricultural and fishing equipment and its use. *Tamafafine* have the right to live on the land and to control and distribute the produce of cooperative enterprises and other property associated with the *kaiga* homestead (Hooper 1968: 239). The senior male *tamatane*, the *pule*, or 'ruler', supervises the activities of the tamatane, and represents the *kaiga* members in the Council of Elders (Huntsman 1971: 330). The *fatupaepae*, literally the 'foundation stone', defined as 'the senior female *tamafafine* residing on the *kaiga* homestead' (ibid: 330) supervises the activities of the *tamafafine*, and may call meetings in the family – or ask the senior male *tamatane* or *matai* to do so. The members of a *kaiga* use the land areas they hold together. Earlier, these estates were in principle broken up approximately every fourth generation, as a result of strict rules against marrying closer than third or ideally fourth cousins: since people who hold land in common are per definition counted as kinsmen, and the cognatic nature of kinship implies that everybody has kinship relations, however distant, to everybody else, in difficult cases this dilemma is solved by dividing up land areas when distantly related cousins marry (Hooper and Huntsman 1976). Briefly then, this demonstrates how, ideally, a Tokelau extended family is organised internally, in terms of task allocation and respective positions and domains of power.[12]

The economy of the village's subsistence sphere is run through the institution of *inati*, that is, a system which dictates an equal share distribution of any major catch of fish, or of any other major collective food resource, to all members of the villages, and in the main regardless of age and social status. One man is appointed by the village council to work as a distributor (*tauvaega*) of *inati* shares. When there is a major distribution, he collects the goods to be distributed on the village *laulau* (a word referring to a plate or table, which in this case denotes a raised concrete platform) and he calls out the names of the share groups. The share groups, commonly represented by a child, come and receive their share and take it to their *kaiga* homestead to be distributed among its members. Young children, in general, serve as errand boys and girls, and go as messengers between adults in different households. The goods prototypically distributed in an inati are the *ika ha*, sacred fish. This category includes such species as turtles, swordfish and shark, and is an interesting category, in that, by definition, it is a kind of fish that must be shared with all (but which is taboo for some families). It is explicitly forbidden to keep such a catch within the family group. This restriction on consumption also applies to any large catch of fish (for example if the catch counts over twenty skipjack, it must also be shared with the village). Other goods are also distributed to the village in this manner: it happens that the surplus from the village cooperative store, or the remains from some public project, is divided out.

In this very fundamental sense, according to its system of redistribution of subsistence goods, Tokelau is an egalitarian society. This is in contrast to other, more stratified Pacific societies, such as Samoa, where distribution of subsistence goods serves a marker of social differentiation. In particular, food distributions at *feasts* epitomise allocation of difference (Keating 2000). In Tokelau, this is also the case to a certain degree, in that prominent elders, village leaders, the pastor, and other visiting dignitaries frequently receive a better share in feast situations. However, the common distributions of subsistence goods are explicitly geared towards levelling social differences and ensuring that everybody receives an equal share. This mechanism is stressed and strongly valued in Tokelau. In her analysis of Phonapei society, E. Keating writes about how unequal shares of food may be seen as associated with hierarchy and equal shares of food as typical of egalitarian structures (ibid.). As examples of hierarchical and egalitarian structures, she refers to Phonapei and Duna respectively. Typically, Tokelau may be said to express both hierarchy and egalitarianism. The dominant collective orientation and the egalitarian ethos serve to contain or place a ceiling on the existing social hierarchy, which is tolerated within certain limits.

A prominent trait of Tokelau social organisation is its complexity. This complexity provides a certain flexibility, which seems to be a prerequisite for swift and efficient organisation of people in relation to specific tasks. People constantly group and regroup for various work- and pleasure-oriented purposes, and an appreciation of the value which is placed on this capacity may be gleaned from the concept of *maopoopo*, meaning 'to be well organised', 'to go smoothly', 'well run', 'harmonious', but also quite simply 'to gather, to congregate' (Hooper 1982; Hooper and Huntsman 1996).

Life in the villages may be seen as a cycle fluctuating between ceremonial occasions of feasting with competitive presentations of lavish displays of food, speech making, dancing and clowning, and the lean periods in between such spectacular events, during which the events are prepared. Societies in this region have been described as culturally 'thin' (Marcus and Fisher 1986:45). However, as I have argued elsewhere (Hoëm 1995), rather than attributing this apparent 'thinness' to acculturation, this cultural pattern may be seen as an expression of the codes of behaviour that dominate everyday interaction, namely an avoidance of overtly competitive and expressive behaviour. This 'thin' pattern of behaviour may then be seen to alternate with the 'thick' behaviour at the ceremonial gatherings and competitive dances and games, where clowning and boisterous behaviour is expected. Thus, behaviour ranges from the 'thin' to the 'thick', just as village life fluctuates between lean periods of little activity and hectic, bustling times that are associated with abundance.[13]

The Emergence of New Forms and Means of Social Stratification

As has been thoroughly documented elsewhere,[14] Tokelau society has experienced major upheavals in the nineteenth and twentieth centuries, the historical period with which we are familiar. Since inclusion into the British Empire brought about the abolishment of the clan-based kingship system, major changes in social organisation have taken place. From a situation which seems to have been characterised by a limited number[15] of large kin-based estates (the clans being called *pui kaiga,* literally 'the walls or borders', 'the limits around', in other words what protected an extended family group), the society apparently went through a stage of fission which resulted in a proliferation of kin-groups (*kaiga*) and a splitting up of the larger land areas. In the early situation, occupational statuses, such as warriors, communal distributors and so on, seem to have followed the clan groups within a framework of totemism. This state of affairs changed rather fundamentally with the abolishment of chiefly leadership.

The subsequent historical period is characterised by what Hooper refers to as *the neo-traditional order* of Tokelau society, and carries in syncretistic fashion, traits from the old order along with other traits, many of which can be traced to the church institutions. A very strong communal or group orientation is evident throughout this period. Since the 1960s, a new state of affairs has been apparent, however. This new state has been brought about by a convergence of factors. Among the most important of these are the introduction of a market-sphere, the establishment of a Tokelau Public Service,[16] and an increase in migration from Tokelau to New Zealand, which had an incentive in the Tokelau Migration Scheme. The introduction of a scholarship-scheme and the establishment of education in Tokelau outside the churches have also played an important role in the last twenty to thirty years.

For a long time, the introduction of a monetary economy took the form of the establishment of a new economical sphere,[17] and Tokelau society was still essentially subsistence-based. The circulation of subsistence goods and tribute, gifts or *mea alofa* (lit. 'things of love') took place outside the monetary sphere, and in the main followed the principles of the *inati-* or communal share-system. For approximately twenty years, the subsistence sphere was dominant, but the monetary sphere steadily gained importance as the number of people who received TPS salaries increased. Hooper, in his 1982 working paper 'Aid and Dependency', describes how he observed what he calls a class awareness emerge on Fakaofo. The material changes he describes have been seen to bring about a difference in attitude. Where earlier ego-oriented attitudes towards material goods were severely condemned, now more and more people speak up for the legitimacy of 'looking out for one's interests' (*e kikila lava te tino kiate ia*) (Hooper 1982).

With the increase in wage labour, the importance of communal cooperation has diminished accordingly. The fact that individuals now receive salaries has supported a further step towards a social atomisation, in that wage earners are no longer solely dependent on their relatives for material support. The nuclear family is of growing importance, at the expense of the brother:sister relationship, and this trend is happily welcomed by many, as, among other things, it relieves the burden of work and obligations involved in the running of an extended family. The system of communal distribution and sharing, and its associated values of egalitarianism and caring for those with few resources, has persisted in the face of this development, however, as it is still unseemly to exchange fish for money for example. On the one hand, this points to the continued existence of sphere-barriers, with concomitant restrictions on the flow of goods and rules of exchange. On the other hand, it is undeniably the case that money-oriented activities account for an increasing proportion of the total amount of labour carried out.

For those who are concerned with the upholding of communal values, and who have the responsibility of making the villages run, this development has been the cause of many worries. The Councils of Elders (the *Taupulega*) have, for a long time, attempted to control this development, by placing a total ban on private enterprises for example. I believe that it is of telling significance that during the 1990s, this ban was partially lifted as a result of public demand.

To conclude, there has been a relatively recent growth in the importance of the principles of market economy, and following this, significant socio-economic differences between families have emerged. There are many new factors to cope with at present: along with the emerging socio-economic differences, great differences are apparent when it comes to mobility, for example, whether a family can afford to go to New Zealand, or to send for a family member to attend a wedding or a funeral. New tools of expression, such as videos that are sent between family members in New Zealand and in Tokelau, also serve to expand the possibilities and to demonstrate the limits of the knowable world.

Recent years have seen socio-economic divisions emerge that were previously non-existent. At the same time, new social institutions and networks have developed. Alongside the trend towards atomisation is a trend working in the opposite direction, which in a certain sense counters the effect of this atomisation. This second trend is manifest in the very high number of Tokelau organisations and institutions that have been established since the early 1960s, mainly in New Zealand, but also elsewhere.

Age, Gender and Kin: 'Sided' Relationships

Huntsman (1971) has pointed to the existence of what she sees as three structural principles informing social organisation in Tokelau. The first she calls 'sequential', the second 'complementary' and the third 'similar'.

In short, she describes the principle of seniority (the hierarchy of relative age) as 'sequential', and the roles relating to the dimension of gender as being of a 'complementary' nature. That is, in her analysis, the relationship between men and women is described as 'complementary', in that men and women occupy mutually dependent, but separate and different, domains over which they are in exclusive command.[18] The same relationship of complementarity exists between the two sides of the kingroup. The third structural principle she calls 'similar'. This relationship exists between any number of individuals or groups which occupy structurally 'similar' positions, such as the members of a particular age-cohort, or, brothers, sisters, mothers, fathers, sports-teams, dance groups and so on. These relationships are highly context-sensitive as parts of ongoing social interaction. That is, which one of them dominates a sequence of interaction depends on the definition of the situation (Goffmann 1959, 1974). For example, in a group of boys, the factor of relative age can easily enter into the situation and thus turn a 'similar' and competitive situation into one where the 'complementary' command/obedience pattern of interaction is dominant.

The principle of similarity, in Huntsman's definition, allows for relationships that are *competitive*. This is what really sets them apart from relationships defined by the principle of complementarity, at least if this concept is restricted, as in her analysis, to denote gender relations and the sided relations within the extended families. When describing other relationships of unequal status, such as between the political leadership and the villagers, that is, hierarchical relations, we may be satisfied to explain the existence of hierarchy by reference to the principle of seniority (what Huntsman calls 'sequential' relationships). However, to do so obscures the fact that fighting for ascendancy, which per definition is part of any interaction between similar groups, may also dominate interaction between groups of unequal status. Also, as I have described elsewhere, a seemingly non-political, non-serious situation, such as dancing at a feast, may be the occasion for people or groups to make claims for political status, precisely because this situation is outside of the formal political arena. However, this does not mean that such acts of identification, and such claims to ascendancy cannot and will not have consequences in the political arena proper at a later stage. In fact, and counter to Shore and Mageo's interpretations of the relationship between formal (political) and informal (entertainment) settings, based on material from Samoa, I would argue that it is most likely to have such consequences (Hoëm 1998a and b).

In short, I believe that we need to address the issue of how the dominant values of egalitarianism and the concomitant importance placed on communal cooperation and integration relate to the status rivalry that keep people preoccupied so much of the time. An illustration: not all elders possess or exercise leadership authority. To command respect in a most general sense is the prerogative of any older person, but if the position to command others has not been worked upon, that is, if the person in question has not achieved the support of a number of people, an elder may suffer the experience of being left to die on his or her own, with a dwindling food supply and with a steadily diminishing number of visitors and caretakers. If, on the other hand, the person has taken an active part in the establishment of his or her position as important, there will be supporters around to allow for the exercise of authority.

To fight for ascendancy, by making claims to positions of authority through public acts of identification (see Hoëm 1999), is an important part of village life, and no one escapes having to 'stage' oneself or one's group, to place oneself or the group one represents in a public position or *tulaga*. This fighting can be of a non-serious nature, for example, it can take the form of a mock fight, such as when two sides of a village compete to outdo each other in dancing. Alternatively, it can be serious, for example as part of political deliberation between two atolls. The sides that Huntsman describes as complementary (e.g., the two sides of a kin group, or the men and the women in the village) differ from the similar ones in that they do not usually engage in fights over ascendancy *with each other*. However, such complementary sides may easily turn into and function together as a similar side vis-à-vis structurally similar groups outside of, for example, the extended family. Thus, a kingroup (consisting of two different sides) is one of many (similar) kingroups and competes for ascendancy with these on an equal basis. In the same manner, the men and women of the village may combine as one dancing team, and thus being on one side, they can challenge an equal group from another village. Thus relationships between complementary (different) sides may easily be transformed into one collective, i.e., into one undifferentiated (similar) group facing a similar team. The dynamics of these transformations is ultimately controlled by the political leadership in the villages, that is, the Elders: they may, for example, decide that the competition between the two sides of the village has become much too serious, that it threatens village stability and therefore that the sides' activities should be abandoned for a while.

I believe that it was a variant of this mechanism that Robert Borofsky witnessed in Pukapuka (a society that closely resembles Tokelau), and that he profoundly missed the historical continuity that this mechanism of social transformation has in these societies (Borofsky 1987; Hoëm 2002). Through the creation of sides, a relationship is established. New sides may always be created, but the principle of 'sidedness' is not new. The control, regulation and orchestration of sides are the prerogative of the political leadership: in short *it is what they do*.

In other words, and to my reinterpretation of Huntsman's analysis: I find competition for respect, honour and status typical of what she describes as 'similar' relationships (which frequently turn into attempts at establishing a hierarchical relationship). The 'complementary' relationships between genders resemble the pattern described as common to so-called 'honour and shame' societies – that is, systems where a man's honour rests on the shame of the women of his family (their modest or shy behaviour, in Tokelau terms, *ma*). The 'sequential' relationships may be read on the one hand as expressions of an ideology of 'natural leadership', based on the principle of relative seniority, where everybody gets to be on top occasionally. On the other hand, it is also a social fact associated with the hierarchy of political leadership, of positions within the family, and of governing etiquette in village interactions.

In my analysis above, I have built on the structural analysis presented by Huntsman, but I have chosen to interpret the relationships in a dynamic perspective, as part of ongoing social processes. Furthermore, I ask whether the 'sidedness' of relationships found in Tokelau at present is a form of sociality that serves to keep both egalitarianism and hierarchy in check. I choose to describe the patterns of sociality as part of an ongoing social process, both because I believe that this gives a more true to life description of the dynamic workings of society, and also because new forms of social stratification are slowly emerging, and new media of expression are now available. How these factors may come to affect ways of life and representations of identities will be the subject of the following chapters.

Notes

1. A reworking of the field methods implied by the 'extended case method' developed by the Manchester School (P. Brown Glick 1984: 237–38.) See also E. Venbrux (1995) for an innovative application of this approach.
2. See F. Barth on fieldwork methodology (Barth 1993).
3. Mageo (1998) in her analysis of Samoan conceptions translates this term as 'secular power'. This sets the term in contrast to the 'spiritual power' exercised by women in their role as sisters. This opposition is also relevant for Tokelau (see Hooper and Huntsman 1975). However, as the secular and spiritual aspects of power have been intertwined historically (see Macgregor 1937 on the *vakataulaitu* or priest/chief), and as the 'spiritual power' (*mana*) today is only explicitly associated with the Church, in practice secular power has spiritual aspects and vice versa. There are still some differences according to gender, with respect to what kind of power(s) and control is attributed to men and women. See also Hoëm (1995).
4. See Huntsman and Hooper (1996), Friedman (1998).
5. See also Senft (1987).
6. See Hoëm (1998 a and b).
7. See Hoëm (1998 a and b).
8. Lit. 'sky-bursters', Europeans or Westerners. Now most commonly used to refer to Caucasians.
9. Ian Prior and John Stanhope (1980: 996).
10. For an overview of the Tokelau communities in New Zealand, see Sallen (1998).
11. On the 'days of war' see (Hooper and Huntsman 1985).
12. For a more thorough discussion of the concept of *kaukaiga*, see Huntsman, (1971: 327).

13. See Mageo 1998 for a description of the relationships between formal, political activities and informal entertainment in Samoa from a historical perspective.
14. See, in particular, Hooper and Huntsman 1972, and Hooper 1982.
15. Nine or ten 'houses' existed on Fakaofo, seven on Atafu and four on Nukunonu. For further information on this subject, see Hoëm 1992, Chapter two.
16. This particular institution can be dated to the 1950s. See Hooper and Huntsman in Wessen *et al.* 1992.
17. The use of this concept in economical anthropology is usually attributed to P. Bohannan. See also F. Barth 1967. For an application of this concept to economic developments in Tokelau, see Hooper and Huntsman 1972.
18. This last point may be contested on the basis of the fact that men as a group (outside of the family) can exercise the right, through the Village Councils, to direct and control women's work, but not the other way around (Hoëm 1995).

Chapter 1
Staging Identities

❧

'I will never say what I want in public' (Woman, 35 years, Tokelau)
'We want to tell the women of Tokelau to stop hiding' (Woman, 33 years,
New Zealand)

Negotiating Codes of Behaviour Through Performance

This chapter is mainly concerned with what may be called the socio-political aspect of cultural transmission in Tokelau. The aim of my exploration in this area is twofold. First, I wish to throw light on the intricacies of the interaction between what is conceived of as 'tradition' (*aganuku*), and performance or expressive culture. As Michael Jackson notes, this is a burning issue within public discourse in New Zealand, as it is related to questions of authenticity and minority rights (Jackson 2002: 114–18). Second, I wish to examine how the etiquette informing behaviour in everyday life relates to behaviour in situations specifically dedicated to various kinds of performances. In other words, I shall explore the dynamics between three elements: the focal events that per definition are occasions for the presentation of expressive culture, the formal political institutions, and everyday life. This discussion is also linked to the issue of cultural reflexivity and how it may relate to processes of identity-formation.

Expressive Culture and Political Life

History, or stories of the past (*tala anamua*), are frequently taken as synonymous with the period people call the 'days of war'. This was a period of inter-atoll rivalry and cultural heroes, which culminated in the dominance of one of the atolls, Fakaofo, over the two others until 1915, when its dominance was abolished by the British on the grounds that there should not be any colonies within a colony (Hooper and Huntsman 1992: 46). This historical period has been the object of extensive studies by Hooper and Huntsman, who have provided illuminating analyses of how the relationships forged between the three atolls during this period have had repercussions for the present day (Hooper and Huntsman 1985). Even today, and despite the end of the chiefdom represented by the rule of Fakaofo, these historical narratives, myths, chants and songs serve, in certain contexts, to inform the relationships between the atolls, providing a store-house from which one can draw to legitimise current positions (Hoëm 1992, 1999).

In the area of Austronesian-speaking cultures, Fox draws attention to the key role played by notions of origin when it comes to local representations of specific forms of social differentiation. He describes how he considers the notion of multiple origins as a prime means of social differentiation, and adds that 'such a notion may operate at many levels within a society' (Fox 1995: 21). Across the Oceanic region, indigenous knowledge about the past is cast in the form of genealogies, using imagery that includes features of landscape and the natural world. In descriptions of Polynesian societies, historical as well as contemporary, it is frequently stressed that such knowledge has one thing in common – the fact that it is not socially neutral. Genealogical knowledge, in the sense of knowledge of the pathways linking contemporary persons with the ancestral past, and associating them with particular land areas, fishing- and other occupational rights, is not information that is freely given. On the contrary, this kind of knowledge is a political asset. It has the character of a personal possession, and may be defined as a limited good, or as what Bourdieu describes as symbolic capital.

Therefore, to speak of the past, or rather, to speak 'the past in the present' is an act fraught with danger. To mention such pathways is to make claims to statuses and rights in the present, and this kind of talk is conceived of as highly instrumental in shaping contemporary social reality. Thus, Ton Otto, in an analysis of social change in Manus, writes:

> Many kinds of knowledge are restricted in some ways. Stories concerning a lineage's history and genealogy are closely guarded and are only fully told to selected individuals. Even first-born sons may miss out on this information if they do not respect and properly care for their fathers. More generally, knowledge is not something that is lightly disseminated. Apart from gossip, information of various kinds is mostly considered something of value that has to enter relations of reciprocity. (Otto 1992: 437)

He concludes by noting that 'the speech of particular leaders was seen to be especially powerful, they were masters of "strong talk". [… T]alking was seen as an action to influence reality and not just as a way of passing on information' (Otto 1992: 439–40). From this, we learn that knowledge of the past may be jealously guarded, and that displaying such knowledge is an act of high social significance. Furthermore, we may see this description of the agentive qualities attributed to particular ways of talking as an illustration of what has been described as 'the performative cast' of many societies in Oceania. As an illustration of the complex nature of this fact, I shall relate a story about a significant event in Tokelau history, which may on the face of it seem only to be an account of a song, but which also reveals something of the dynamic relationship that exists between expressive culture and political life. The following is my rendering of the local version of what happened, as it was related to me.

People say that in the mid-eighties, the Elders of Tokelau were made to sign a treaty with representatives of the United States, thereby signing away their claims to the fourth Tokelau island, Olohega. They explained that the Elders were informed that they had no real say in the matter, and that they should be happy that they had made such a good bargain, as thereafter the three other Tokelau atolls would be lawfully theirs (a fact which they had never doubted in the first place). Upon reading the documents of the transaction, one notes one or two curious details, for example, Tokelau tradition was brought forward as evidence of their rightful claims to the island, in the form of a Tokelau song about Olohega. This song was produced as proof that the island is truly theirs, along with the other three atolls. Furthermore, in the documents this treaty is called the treaty of Tokehega – seemingly a fusion of the two names Tokelau (Toke-) and Olohega (-hega).

When relating this case from an insider's perspective however, the significance of the name of the treaty changes. As one of the Elders who signed the treaty described it to representatives of the new political leadership in Tokelau: We were aware that we made a bad decision in signing that treaty, but we were weak. Therefore we took care to name the treaty Tokehega, which literally translated means 'subtract' or 'to take away'. We placed this hidden meaning inside the name of the treaty, so that the young generation would know the true meaning of what happened, and therefore be able to use this knowledge when they have the strength to do so.

We see here an example of what I previously referred to as 'the power of words'. We also see how two different interpretations of the same event may coexist, with the indigenous version hidden in a place where no outsider would ever think of looking for it – in full view of everyone. As noted in the prior example, certain songs contain knowledge about the past, and this knowledge may be used to legitimate claims to political status in the present. Some song-texts are explicitly focused on ties to the home atoll, and touch on the genealogical relations between the atolls. These themes are certainly not socially neutral, and they are not usually presented in situations where all three atolls are gathered.

In local arenas, that is, when only 'one's own are present', these texts serve as a reminder of the correct genealogical representation of the pathways that exist between one atoll and the others, and reinforce the social differentiation between them. An illustration of such songs is the Fakaofo song *Aue Pio e*, which uses the imagery of branches and growth to establish their genealogical precedence over Nukunonu. The song literally states that Fakaofo is the 'standing branch-post', *latupou*, whereas Nukunonu is said to be the 'leaning-branch-post', *lafalala*. To use this kind of imagery in situations where the involved parties are present is said to invoke an atmosphere of the 'days of war '(see also Hoëm 1992).

In other words, it is highly instructive to take into account the contemporary, pragmatic aspect related to the performance of such songs. In this perspective, to perform such a song is to make claims to genealogical precedence. That is, the contemporary balance of power between the atolls is still negotiated in terms of the pre-contact genealogical relationships between them, cast in terms of relations between 'standing' and 'leaning' branches. Hence, it carries a potential for shaping relations in the present.

In interpreting these genealogical representations, note also the long-term continuity that one can read from the idioms used. In this case, we find that they imply both a particular form of relationality and a conception of social change cast in terms of processes of growth and decay. However, and as noted above, we must also examine what kind of social effects the users of these idioms attempt to achieve through these performances. As one may learn from Otto's discussion of the agentive power associated with displays of genealogical knowledge (particularly as applied to the context of formal, public settings), these representations of relationships may not simply be seen as referential. They clearly represent claims to social statuses in the present, or processes of genealogical ascendancy, as Fox describes them, and may thus, by implication, have direct consequences for all persons or groups who participate in these networks of reciprocal relationships. With this in mind, I propose that we shift our focus from tradition, as connected with pre-contact authenticity, to the study of the dynamic relationship between expressive culture and identity politics in the contemporary Pacific. The following example serves as an illustration of how this might be done.

A Challenge to Dominant Practices

The formal political leadership in Tokelau has traditionally consisted of male Elders. During recent years, as a result of pressure from the UN to decolonise, which has been mediated by the New Zealand Administration, governmental powers have been delegated to an inter-atoll assembly, and an act of self-determination is awaited.[1] In this process, which entails the gradual establishment of an infrastructure with the purpose of serving the emerging atoll nation-state, the initiation of migration to New Zealand stands out, as it represents a clear conceptual break from the past generations. Lately, and as a result of people returning from overseas, the New Zealand experience has started to filter back into Tokelau society. The difference between life in New Zealand and in Tokelau, at least as it was in the early 1960's when the first wave of migrants left, can not be stressed too strongly.

In order to illustrate how this situation affected life as experienced 'on the ground', I shall describe how members of the song-group Tagi attempted to cope with such existential discontinuities through the introduction of a new genre to express their experiences, namely popular theatre, also called theatre for community development. Initially, this was done with the explicitly stated purpose of 'keeping the Tokelau culture alive' within the context of New Zealand society. At the same, time the members of the group added to the repertoire of expressive culture some new elements that they found important from their New Zealand experience. They did not think that borrowing freely from the non-indigenous tradition of popular theatre was detrimental to their project of defining new parametres for Tokelau living. However, the fact that the means of expression, and the issues they came to address, were most definitely not part of the dominant 'authorised and authorising' tradition (or *aganuku*), later caused the theatre-group some headaches.[2] (See also D. Spitulnik 1997, 1999). This last point is intimately connected to the question of how such performative activities are generally classified. In the introduction I described how entertainment and games, in their capacity as 'things of no account', (*mea tauanoa*), are opposed to the formal political structures, yet still carry a quasi-political potential. In this chapter, we shall probe further into the relationship between these spheres, which are structurally and conceptually separate in local perception.

In the early 1990s, some individuals from the Tokelau community living in the Hutt Valley area outside Wellington, in New Zealand, took advantage of the fact that a large proportion of all the Tokelau communities in New Zealand were gathered together for what is called the Easter Tournaments.[3] As V. Sallen vividly describes, this gathering has become a focus for the various Tokelau communities in New Zealand, in Auckland, Taupo, Rotorua, and the larger Hutt Valley area outside Wellington. In the twenty-first century. representatives of the Tokelau atoll communities have also participated in these gatherings. At the time, these individuals used the occasion of the Easter Tournaments as an opportunity to conduct extensive interviews with many of the participants, ensuring a wide coverage across gender, age groups and atoll-affiliations. The interviewees were invited to give their opinions about such gatherings, and they were asked whether they felt satisfied with the status quo of Tokelau cultural life in New Zealand. If they answered in the negative, they were asked what they would like to see instead.

The interviews were recorded on videotapes, together with the sports activities, the dancing, and the other happenings during the festival, and these tapes were widely distributed in the communities afterwards. Many of the interviewees responded that they were somewhat tired of what these gatherings had to offer. There was a widely shared feeling that the focus on competitive sports and *fatele* dancing[4] was too narrow. In general, however, people valued the opportunity to socialise with the wider community very highly. They said that they participated in order to stay in touch with the 'feelings of Tokelau' that these gatherings brought to the fore. Many added that this was particularly important so that their children wouldn't lose touch with their larger networks of kin and with Tokelau ways altogether. Younger people, and also quite a large number of women, said that they wanted something more than 'just the sports and the dancing', and added that they wished to learn more about other aspects of their culture. The youths also expressed a wish to be allowed to explore other forms of cultural expression. They were eager to utilise new media, and did not necessarily want to confine themselves to the repertoire of what is generally considered to be the Tokelau tradition.

Encouraged by this response, the interviewers then proceeded to create something new to fill this need. The result of this was what some years later came to be named *Tokelau Te Ata*. This name can be read as a play on the English word theatre, Tokelau Theatre, but it also carries a second, 'deeper' meaning[5] true to the canons of Tokelau poetry, 'Tokelau – the mirror/image', or 'Tokelau – the dawn' or, perhaps most poignantly, 'Tokelau – the reflection'. The initial members of the group then made a public announcement that they were going to produce a Tokelau drama, with the aim of exploring Tokelau history and culture. This information was presented at various gatherings in the Wellington region, along with an open invitation, stating that anybody who wished to participate was free to do so. The group finally stabilised at ten actors. Four of the actors were young, first generation New Zealand-born Tokelauans; five were middle-aged and members of the previously mentioned song-group; and the last member was a slightly more senior woman with strong links to the Women's Committee and the Tokelau pre-school movement in New Zealand.

One of the members of the song-group, who generally played an important role in community life and who was one of the main forces behind the project, had had some previous experience working with alternative theatre in New Zealand in the late seventies and early eighties. He approached a New Zealand community cultural worker with extensive knowledge of theatre production, who subsequently became an instructor for the group. One of the young cast members had also previously worked with this instructor at the Teachers' Training College, in a project concerned with unemployment among Pacific islanders in New Zealand.

The name of the first play, *Tagi* (cry or lament), was a reference to the devastating abduction of most of Tokelau's able-bodied men by slave raiders, and a tribute to the memory of those who were taken away. The production of the play was largely carried out as a collective effort. The bottom line was a general agreement that the play should be about Tokelau history. This choice was motivated by various factors, but most importantly by the cultural significance attached to the genre of history within Tokelau society. The *tala anamua* (stories about the past), a large proportion of which are about 'the days of war', concern the atolls and the relationships between them in pre-*papalagi*, pre-Western, and pre-Christian times. While set in the past and reflecting historical events and relations, the contents of these *tala*, and the songs and speeches which contain references to the same material, have a direct contemporary relevance and are highly politically charged when used today (See also Hoëm 1992, and Hoëm 1999). Another factor contributing to this choice of topic was the launching of the book *Matagi Tokelau* ('wind, news, memories, vigour, life' [from] Tokelau), a collection of various accounts of Tokelau history, moving from 'origin traditions [...] to descriptions of the contemporary scene'.[6] The material contained in this book was used by the group as a source of Tokelau history. Finally, another great motivating factor was the strong wish expressed by many of the interviewees to learn more about their cultural heritage.

The role of the instructor in the group, apart from being one of the actors, was to provide some guidelines on how to form the material so that it could easily convey a message to an audience. The material, in addition to what was drawn from *Matagi Tokelau*, was provided by the other cast members, and the language of the presentation was to be Tokelauan. This was quite a challenge to some of the younger cast members, who had only a passive knowledge of the language. The production process largely went as follows: the group decided on a theme, such as 'village life in pre-papalagi times', 'the slave traders', 'leaving for New Zealand', and so on. Everyone was asked to relate his or her associations to the theme. These associations were enacted and put together to form a scene. As the main frame was Tokelau history, and as this increasingly took the form of 'what has happened to our way of life during the last few centuries', the linking together of scenes became largely chronological. Songs were composed, among them the first *haumate*, 'lament' (about the slave-raids) to be composed in this century. A great deal of grief emerged in the process. This engendered soul-searching in some, and hard work and much practice for all. The script of the play as a whole was never written down, but notes with suggestions for dialogue, translations and ideas were circulated during the meetings.

The final product consists of three main parts: the pre-*papalagi* times, the coming of *papalagi*, and the migration experience. The scenes were as follows:

Tagi
Part One
Reciting of the individual actors' genealogical ties, linking them to each other and to their atolls
the individual actors' state their personal purpose with the play
enactment of the origin myths of the atolls
enactment of a scene from the days of war
enactment of typical scenes from village life in pre-*papalagi* times

Part Two
Enactment of 1) the first visit of the *papalagi*; 2) the coming of Christianity; and 3) the arrival of slave traders

Part Three
Reciting of the political developments concerning Tokelau during the last decades, cast in the form of a genealogy
reciting of individual accounts of their first journey to New Zealand
enactment of a party scene in New Zealand
enactment of the first Tokelau child being born in New Zealand
enactment of a school scene, where a ban is placed on using the Tokelau language
enactment of a scene with Tokelau street kids
enactment of a scene where a *kaiga* (extended family) comes in contact with the social services

Finale
Reciting of speeches and sayings about the extended family (*kaiga*), particularly as it relates to the role of women, ending with a song with this theme

The individual actors' personal opinions on the issues raised in the play were quite varied, as may be illustrated by their reactions to the scene of the arrival of Christianity. Some were rather uncomfortable with this scene, feeling that they didn't want to 'make fun of the Church', whereas others didn't think that what they did was taken far enough. Either way, the cast members unanimously agreed that it was a good thing to raise these issues, and that the time had come when it was necessary to bring out in the open the 'underside' or difficulties related to certain aspects of their way of life in New Zealand. In their opinion, such issues were usually denied within the community at large; it certainly was not considered fitting to bring up these things in public situations.

In short, regardless of how they themselves felt personally about the issues and how they were raised in the play, the members of the group were in agreement when stressing the importance of making these issues public. Furthermore, they were aware of the fact that to bring up social conflicts explicitly and to address problems, such as incest, for example, in a serious (i.e., not joking) manner, was definitely not considered seemly within the parameters of the *fakaTokelau*, or *aganuku* (the Tokelau way of life, or tradition). When they decided to do so anyway, this was out of a stated conviction that to continue to deny that these things happened only served to perpetuate the problem, and might in some cases even make things worse.

The presentation of the play *Tagi* to the larger Tokelau community in New Zealand took place as part of the 'cultural activities' of the subsequent Easter Tournament held in the Pahina Hall in Porirua.[7] The audience was entranced. They laughed, cried and joined in the singing of the songs. In all respects it was a great success.[8] Afterwards, however, the community was divided in how they responded to the event and the messages contained in the play. Some young women were prompted by the 'incest-scene' to contact members of the group, telling them how they had had similar experiences and now felt for the first time that it was acceptable to talk about them. Many identified with the migration experience, and many were happy to see, as they said, 'the culture come alive' as it was presented in the first part of the play dealing with the pre-*papalagi* times. A large number enjoyed the event more as a pure spectacle.

There were, however, others who objected to the play on various grounds. One objection was quite simply that the group's activities had not been sanctioned by the Elders. Another, which struck somewhat deeper, was an objection to the explicit mention of 'indecent' things in this manner in public. The reaction I heard mentioned most frequently, however, was a surprise to me, but since the play was about 'the history', and since history is commonly interpreted as synonymous with 'the days of war', it probably shouldn't have been. This objection was directed at the very opening scene of the play, where the individual actors come forth as their genealogical connections are called out. The genealogies were said to be wrong, or partly wrong, and the fact that the group had chosen to 'link' (*hohoko*) themselves through one of the possible 'paths' (*auala*) that they have in common, instead of through others, was a major source of contention. As one community leader put it to some members of the Nukunonu contingent, 'don't worry about that lot. They are from Atafu'. (The theatre-group were otherwise considered to be predominantly from Nukunonu.) In other words, this man, who can be said to belong to the traditionalist faction among the new leadership, tried to use the group's tools against them. His arguments drew legitimacy from the sphere of Tokelau tradition, and potentially could have set a large number of the community against the theatre-group and undermined its credibility. The group's way of linking themselves genealogically was, however, deliberately chosen to show the community that even such deeply rooted emotional identifications as the one with one's home atoll (which their adversaries played on) can, and in their opinion must, be transcended, if Tokelau is ever to develop a common national identity.

A Mirror 'Side' Emerges

These issues then, or variations on similar themes, became the talk of the community. The comments often took the familiar form of 'who are they to present these issues', referring to the role of the Elders as the custodians of tradition. In the meantime, the Pacific Islands Cultural Festival, an event that takes place every fourth year, was coming up, and it was to be held in Rarotonga in the Cook Islands. A team was to be sent from Tokelau, Nukunonu, and the drama group applied for funding and received the blessing of the village authorities in Nukunonu, who encouraged them to go. This caused much lobbying within the communities, and after a period dominated by trouble and conflicts, an alternative group arose within the New Zealand community. This side was headed by the leader of the traditionalist faction, one of those who had challenged the genealogical representation of the members of Tokelau te Ata in the play *Tagi*. This second side then started producing their own performance piece, this time with representatives of the Elders present, and with the backing of other members of the community. Finally, this group went to the festival, and the original drama group quickly withdrew their application so as to avoid an open confrontation. Instead, they decided to make a tour to Tokelau. In applications for funding to support Tokelau te Ata's alternative tour, the project was called 'the indigenous people's return to the homeland'.[9]

The advent of a second theatre-group, which challenged the goals of the first, is an excellent illustration of the character of symmetrical or, in my terminology, 'sided' relationships, as described in the introduction. The emergence of one such group almost automatically tends to produce a mirror image, or opposing 'side', which then stands in a position of clear competition with, and challenge to, the first side's performance. As a consequence of, and in response to this second group's challenge, the first group started the production of a new play. This play was to focus on the tension between individualism and the communal, extended family orientation in Tokelau. This play clearly illustrates the group's attempts to stage an alternative way of life, a goal integral to Tokelau te Ata's projects.

Whereas *Tagi* was produced with the New Zealand Tokelau audience in mind, to counter what they called the 'cultural erosion' they perceived to be taking place there, the second play was produced primarily for a 'Tokelau Tokelau' audience. This goal affected the production process in interesting ways, as it led to confrontations and reflections over the differences between life in Tokelau and in New Zealand, and also between the images held of Tokelau by cast members and the reality of contemporary life in Tokelau. By this time, some of the early cast members had moved on to other things, and new ones had joined. The theatre-group then consisted of the five original recruits from the song-group, Tagi, plus a middle-aged man also enlisted from Tagi, and a young woman who had spent some time in Tokelau and in Samoa working there as an adult, but who was now based in New Zealand. Furthermore, there was another young man who had some adult experience with Tokelau, but only from brief visits. Three of the members of the song-group had not been back to Tokelau since the early seventies.

The new play began with the present political issues facing Tokelau, but it shifted gradually to the situation of women, and particularly their role within the extended family. Eventually, it came to be called 'Woman' (*Mafine*). What follows is a rudimentary sketch of this second play. The main character, Tima, has been abroad to get an education, and she returns to Tokelau thinking that she is there for a holiday and only visiting. Her family, however, without her knowledge, has other plans for her. They want her to marry and settle down in Tokelau, to take up the responsibility of looking after her elderly parents. Tima becomes desperate and frightened when she realises what is happening. She feels trapped and appeals to her parents for help. When she tries to talk it over with her family, they only tell her to show respect and to do as she is told. She then attempts to enlist support from her father's sister (*matua ha*), a person of authority in a Tokelau extended family. The aunt is sympathetic to her pleas, but advises her that Tokelau needs people with her experience. The aunt tries to help Tima by defending her case at a family meeting, but this doesn't help either. Following this, Tima meets an old acquaintance who works as a teacher in the village. They talk, and he nearly manages to convince her to stay and work in the village. Unfortunately, they are discovered talking together by Tima's father, who then beats up the teacher. Thoroughly disgusted that this has happened on top of everything else, Tima really wants to leave. She rejects a potential suitor who has 'accidentally' turned up, but at this point, the village priest intervenes as the ultimate authority. He orders her to do as her parents say. The play ends with her marrying a suitor picked by her parents, not one of her own choice.

This genre of drama, called 'theatre for community development', has a narrative structure such that, at what in the technical terminology is called 'the situation of maximal oppression', the audience is invited to intervene and change whatever they think is wrong or should or could be different in the story. The scenes of the play are then enacted once more, according to the wishes of the audience, and if the audience agrees, the final scene is rerun, but this time with a song depicting women as powerful individuals in their own right.

Experiments with Masks

While working on this play, some of the female cast members experienced very strong emotional reactions when experimenting with possible scenarios. All of the women involved identified strongly with Tokelau culture and were active members of the community in New Zealand, even though the nature of their personal attachments differed. Why they had such strong reactions will hopefully become clearer in the light of the perspective offered throughout the remainder of this and the following Chapters. The starting point for this second drama was a strongly felt wish to, as it was put, 'tell the women of Tokelau to stop hiding'. During discussions, it emerged that they perceived the behaviour of Tokelau women in general (both in New Zealand and in Tokelau) in negative terms, as being hypocritical and dishonest. They described women as not showing their true emotions, as manipulative, as gossips and as conformists. These depictions reflect commonly held opinions, and are not views particular to members of this group.[10]

Various scenes were tried out, including the following: a group of women are sitting in a cooking house in Tokelau, when an outsider comes in and tries to learn and help with their work, but is only discouraged and ridiculed; a young woman tries on make-up, but her mother tells her off, giving the daughter no reason why such behaviour is unacceptable to her; family scenes, where the father rules and the mother always self-effacingly obeys him, even though he might be in the wrong, or the same scenario, but with religion entering into it. They also experimented with scenes where outsiders walk on the road, which is the public area in the village, and where, being outsiders, they don't observe what is considered to be proper etiquette in Tokelau when it comes to ways of walking, talking and dressing, and so on.[11]

At this point, two reactions became apparent. On the one hand, all of the cast members recognised that they had experienced such behaviour and felt victimised because of it. The fact that they were going to Tokelau only served to strengthen this feeling of intense discomfort. On the other hand, it seemed to me that everyone also recognised that he or she had occasionally played the role of oppressor and victimiser. Naturally this was deeply unsettling. Parallel to this, the cast members began to realise that it would not be a very good idea to go to Tokelau with only a negative image of Tokelau's way of life, an image based largely on their newly won freedom[12] in New Zealand society, and then tell the people there what the group, as outsiders, thought that people living in Tokelau should do about it. This way of behaving is, by the way, very common among people returning to Tokelau after having been abroad, but it usually results in alienation from the community, so the eventual message or potential for help is deflected.

There were some very heated discussions, where reactions and pro-posed solutions ranged from a defence of Tokelau etiquette to total rejec-tion of those codes of behaviour. These discussions, prompted by the experimental enacting of the scenes, were cast in terms of 'masks', in the sense of 'what is the mask of the woman who is in control', 'what is the religious mask', and even 'what is the Atafu, Nukunonu or Fakaofo mask'. An immediate reaction, true to the initial position of wanting to 'tell the women of Tokelau to stop hiding', was that the message should be 'for everybody to take off his or her mask' – thereby assuming that masks are purely negative, that they contain what oppress us. This led to the intriguing question of 'what is behind the mask?' At this point, opin-ions started to differ. Whereas one woman said that she saw behind the masks 'a very gentle Tokelauan', others stated that the masks are neces-sary for social life, that they are not only negative, but that they also con-tain and protect what is positive about life in Tokelau. The hermit crab was used as a metaphor, as it cannot survive without a shell.

Conceptions of Personhood, Emotions and Morality

Other common self-characterisations of Tokelauans, either as very 'deep' or as exhibiting a contrast between everyday appearances – characterised by an excessive 'shyness', (*ma*, often translated as 'shame') – and the forces hidden behind these appearances, speak of the same tension as these actors encountered and explored.[13] The contrasting 'facework' – alternating between what Levy describes as 'fragrantly presented sur-faces' and what Shore associates with the 'formal' or 'day-side' (*ao*) of things, and the exposure of the forces hidden behind these surfaces (or what Levy describes as 'private' and Shore describes as associated with the 'night-side' or *po*) – is also reflected in the difference between the 'thinness' of everyday life and the 'thickness' characteristic of certain cer-emonial occasions.

The observations of those who seemed to assume the existence of a hid-den side, obscured by the masks, are, in other words, supported by ethno-graphic observations from this region. In Shore's analysis of what he calls dual organisation in Samoa, a basic assumption is, as mentioned above, the existence of a division into a public(-ly acceptable), light side and an intimate, hidden side. The latter he mainly characterises as associated with darkness, animalistic impulses and as socially unacceptable.[14] In his analysis of Tahitian culture, R. I. Levy draws a similar distinction between what he labels public and private, interpreting 'private' as 'those aspects of an individual's experience which are related to his body, his feelings, his sense of self, his needs for personal definition and integration, his understanding of what is going on around him as involves himself'. By 'public' he means 'those aspects of his behaviour most related to, most influenced by, the systematic relationships and formal arenas of community life' (Levy 1973: xix).

N. Besnier's work is from the Tuvaluan atoll society, Nukulaelae. Of the ethnographies mentioned above, Tuvalu is the place that is perhaps ethnographically most similar to Tokelau. He is more cautious in applying such terms as public and private, or formal and intimate, as defining characteristics of situations and thus of relationships, and I will follow his example in my analysis. I prefer to analyse the dilemma experienced by members of the theatre-group by drawing on the insight reflected in various ways in much of the ethnography from this region that 'in these societies, emotions are defined in behavioural terms' (Besnier 1989: 89).[15]

To return to the case of the theatre-group, this particular orientation implied that when they started experimenting with enacting alternative ways of behaviour, they immediately came up against some fundamental principles that informed their sense of identity. Play is not 'just play'; in such a setting, it is a risky business. Whereas some of the members of the group were aware of this and had worked explicitly to bring about such a confrontation, many obviously were not and had not. Also, fundamental parameters such as those informing one's identity are, by definition, of a doxic, i.e., naturalised character, and so represent habitualised patterns of behaviour or 'how one goes about doing things'. This means that even for the experientially reflexive, there will always be potential for new confrontations and uncomfortable insights into the contingent character of social action. One woman put it this way: 'I entered the group because I wanted to be a mother, because I am proud of being a mother, and I asked for such a role. But I didn't know that it would be this deep'. By this she meant that she had wanted to play it safe and had not expected to have to confront the notions of motherhood; she had only wished to reflect the ideal back to the community.

In Tokelau, as I have touched upon in my discussion of 'sided' relationships, etiquette in ordinary mixed-gender situations can be said to be epitomised by the brother:sister relationship. This relationship is characterised by avoidance of conflict, by avoidance of expressions of self-interest, and by stressing a sharing, caring and compassionate behaviour (*alofa*). The competitive and boisterous aspects of behaviour enter only into relationships between 'similar' sides, between brothers and so on. Easy, joking relationships exist between cross-sex affines, and to some extent between members of 'similar groups'. For example age groups or 'mothers', and in some cases between grandparents and grandchildren.[16] This is not intended as a typology of relationships; the important thing for the purposes of our discussion here is to notice how behaviour and definitions of situations co-vary. General principles imply that in public, village situations, behaviour is, in most cases, informed by the brother:sister etiquette, meaning for example a taboo on everything of a sexual nature, and a quiet, self-effacing, shy (*ma*) demeanour, showing a *loto maualalo*, ('low or modest heart or inclination').

Clowning and Humorous Behaviour

On other occasions, in activities associated with entertainment and games, that is, non-serious matters (*mea tauanoa*), competitive and boisterous behaviour is encouraged. A main ingredient then is clowning, and a person who is considered to be beyond the 'dangerous' age, or who holds a respected position, may explicitly joke about sexual matters, and may thus put oneself forward without being censored.[17] If such behaviour is perceived as being *fai mea malie*, making sweet or nice things, for the enjoyment of everybody, it is accepted graciously. If, on the other hand, a person is seen to be too full of him- or herself, or to be self-serving, it does not go down very well. In most cases, a direct, confrontational style, for example, insisting on sticking closely to a subject, is likely to cause discomfort and alienate the audience, and will serve to isolate the speaker.[18]

Play-acting in Tokelau, defined as *fai mea malie*, is an integral part of many occasions, such as cricket games and feasts (*fiafia*), and may also occur spontaneously on other occasions as well. Skits (*faleaitu*) frequently depict well-known incidents, often picked from the Bible, but equally often parodying an event that has happened in Tokelau. The obvious humorous content of such skits lies most frequently in inversion, for example, by women acting as men, by acting counter to norms of respectability, by ordering individuals who are not married to act as if they were and so on (Hooper and Huntsman 1975). When parodying an incident, the fun is naturally at someone's expense, and a skilled clown or director of a *faleaitu* has to be careful not to lean too far towards the real. Once an incident has been immortalised in a story about 'the time that x did y', or has been turned into a successful skit, it may stick to that person's name or reputation in people's minds.

Humour is in many ways a naturally safe-guard, in that it allows one to turn things upside down and thus to modify or soften the norms and routines of everyday life, which as everybody knows have difficult sides and disadvantages. Equally obvious, however, is the cruel aspect of humour, with its potential for adding to or detracting from a person's name in the community. An 'upwardly mobile' person will be a likely target for community ridicule, and to take this in one's stride with a smiling face is not always easy. People have been known to die socially, but also on rare occasions to have committed suicide after going through such unpleasant experiences. This malign, 'cutting down to size' aspect of joking also enters very prominently into everyday interaction, mostly in the form of a constant verbal taunting. To stay on top of things, one must be able to answer such challenges in a funny, light-hearted way.[19]

Whereas some people are said to have inherited a talent for clowning and are active in instigating such activities, nearly everyone takes an active part in performing in skits and in making fun during, for example, the cricket games. Certainly everyone has been an unwilling victim of a village side's ritual humiliation of the other, for example, to be blackened with charcoal and be made to do silly things by the winning team after these games. All such occasions, spontaneous or otherwise, have one thing in common, and that is *that there is never an audience* in the strict sense of the term. No one can rest assured that he or she will not be made the topic of a skit, and certainly nobody can permanently avoid having to take part in one. At feasts, sides take turns in performing, and so they momentarily provide an audience for the other side, while plotting their own next challenge. Situations of spontaneous clowning often occur: as when an all-female group is away from the main village working together (Hooper and Huntsman 1975), or on other out-of-the-ordinary occasions, such as gatherings for farewells when the boat leaves for Samoa. Then, in a sense, everybody present constitutes an audience. Then again, what is enacted is about those present and what is happening there and then, so in that sense the performance is not detached from either situation or audience.

The following is an illustration of such a case: a large group of travellers had entered the boats, and was going out the channel to board the larger vessel going to Samoa. Many were crying, painfully aware that it would be a long time, if ever, before they would return to Tokelau or see their loved ones again. One woman, generally known and accepted as a great comedian, was standing on the wharf among the others, waving as the boats pulled away. She suddenly broke ranks, running and crying profusely, much more than anyone, however sad, could manage to do. Finally, upon reaching the end of the wharf at the mouth of the channel – in a final gesture of despair – she threw herself into the water. At this stage, most people in the boat laughed through their tears

Some people are funny in the sense that they are good comedians, but some are simply funny, i.e., fun to watch and parody. In Chapters three and five, I discuss further how people may end up more or less permanently in one role or the other. Here, we shall just look a little further at what may constitute the limits to what is *malie*, in its dual meaning of sweet/funny/agreeable and acceptable, and what is not.

At the end of several days of intensive workshops arranged by the Health Department/Ola Maloloina, to discuss the problem of Aids, the various community groups involved gathered in the meeting house for the closing ceremony. All of the groups were to present a skit which had something to do with the topic of the workshop. One group gave a skit highlighting the role of infidelity; another stressed the role of alcohol; and so on. All went well, and there was much merriment, until the following incident happened. One man, playing a doctor, ordered his 'patient' to open the zipper of his dungarees, and to the crowds' great amusement, he 'examined' the patient with a piece of copper wire, which he claimed was a medical instrument for detecting Aids. Everyone present found this hilarious, except the woman who in real life was married to the 'patient'. She felt her (and her husband's) dignity was threatened, and finally, when she couldn't take it any longer, she called out to the man playing the doctor, 'for everybody to hear' as it was recounted afterwards, 'if you want it so much, why don't you take it out?'

The skit was hurriedly ended, and everybody present behaved as if nothing had happened, except for some mumbling in the corners. Some days later, however, when the Women's Committee had their weekly meeting, the woman who had felt that moral standards were not being properly upheld in the skit was summoned and very severely chastised. The women told her that they had been disgusted by her behaviour; one said that she had wanted to slap her, another, that no proper woman from *this* atoll would ever behave like that (the woman was originally from one of the other atolls). The woman who had reacted against the skit was crying, and excused herself many times and said how sorry she was for what she had done, but even so she couldn't help mentioning again how horrified she had felt by seeing such indecent behaviour in the meeting house.

Afterwards, the women explained that that was precisely the point. As they put it, she took it seriously when after all it was just for fun. And anyway, it was clean (*mama*). It was clean because everything that happens when there is a festive occasion in the meeting-house, is dignified (*mamalu*). To shout like that, in front of everybody, for everybody to hear, is really bad. It sets a bad example for the children, and undermines the dignity, *mamalu*, of the village, as represented by the Elders. Some admitted that they could understand the woman's feelings on seeing the skit, but everyone agreed that she shouldn't have reacted the way she did, and they attributed her behaviour to her character: 'She is like that, she always wants to be different, to be better than others'.

This incident clearly illustrates how norms and etiquette guiding behaviour in various situations are not simply applied once and for all, but are constantly in the process of being defined and redefined through social practice. I would also like to point out the subtle differences we can perceive in this example between what is considered proper and acceptable and what is not. The woman who called out was quite in line with commonly held notions of morality, but, as she became bitterly aware of afterwards, this was not an ordinary situation. The situation was defined as fun, and, moreover, it was protected, set apart by its taking place in the meeting-house, which by definition is the most dignified public centre of the village.[20] The fact that the event was ceremonial only added to its dignity.

The Tour to the Homeland

This reference to some of the principles informing behaviour, in and outside of ritualised performances, may throw some light on what the theatre-group was up against. Their experiments with codes of behaviour, that were in earnest, not for 'making fun', can be seen as relating to a different frame of interpretation, one which allowed them to challenge the canons of tradition.[21] Also, it is apparent that they were used to different forms of interaction and communication than is the norm in Tokelau. This difference may be exemplified by common statements made by many of those who have been overseas, such as, 'the people over here (i.e., in Tokelau) are never themselves, they are their family', or, 'they don't have any emotions', 'they never say what they mean', 'they seem to treat everything as one big joke', and so on.[22]

Following the first performance of the second play in New Zealand, and during the actual tour to Tokelau, group members came up against these issues many times, and again their reactions varied. One immediate response to the women's issue play, among some people both in New Zealand and in Tokelau, was that 'this is not the truth'. In Tokelau, the notion of truth (*moni*) is closely connected to notions of beauty and quantity, of fullness of detail, and of abundance (*katoa*, or what I have described earlier as 'thickness') but, in this case, people's comments took slightly different directions. As was the case with the earlier play, people's conceptions varied. Some referred to the fact that arranged marriages as such do not exist anymore in Tokelau. Others seemed rather to mean that the play did not truthfully depict the real story of a particular girl that they knew. As it was only a made-up story, many didn't quite know what to make of it, and were uncertain whether they liked it.

Others saw the play as true, in the sense that they thought the individual actors were expressing their own personal beliefs and lifestyles in the characters they played. The following incident is an illustration of this. One morning, after the play had been presented the evening before on one of the atolls, an old woman walked up to a man who played what he himself considered to be a role representing everything he hated about his culture – that is, he played an authoritarian patriarch legitimising his self-seeking actions by reference to the Bible. She said, 'I was so happy to see that you have turned out to be such a good person. Your mother would have been proud of you'. He related this afterwards, saying that he didn't have the heart to tell her how he really felt about the role that he had played. Other members of the group experienced increasing difficulties with separating themselves from the role they were playing in the eyes of the community, so much so that when the woman who played 'Tima' reached her home atoll, she found it necessary to make a public statement saying that she was not Tima.

But in general, the plays were graciously received. People enjoyed being entertained, and some people were deeply moved by seeing the history of Tokelau, as depicted in the first play, 'come alive'. The controversies surrounding the 'genealogies' part were avoided this time. Upon coming to each of the atolls, the oldest man of the group went to consult with an elder known for his proficiency in genealogies. Thus, the first scene represented different 'paths' (*auala*) linking the cast members to Atafu, Nukunonu and Fakaofo on the respective atolls. This relativistic and detached attitude towards atoll affiliation is highly unusual. As far as I know, it went unnoticed by the very few spectators who travelled to all three atolls during the tour.

The group held workshops on each of the atolls, teaching the methods of popular theatre to those who were interested, mainly teachers. During these workshops, and also as a result of presenting these plays to a 'Tokelau Tokelau' audience, some members of the group came to question what they were doing in yet another manner. Conflicting views on Tokelau skits and forms of communication in general arose. For example, during the workshops the instructor dismissed the genre of skits, claiming that it allowed people to be 'stuck in the clown', that is in the status quo of Tokelau performances and etiquette of behaviour, whereas others increasingly defended the indigenous forms. More precisely, some of the performers actually began to wonder whether the form of the plays, developed expressly 'for the third world' from a branch of western radical, action theatre, wasn't in fact antithetical to Tokelau forms of performance and styles of communication. What in New Zealand had seemed a culturally neutral tool for allowing the messages to get across to an audience suddenly didn't seem neutral at all.

Vilsoni Hereniko, discussing clowning as political commentary in Polynesia, makes an explicit comparison between skits (or *faleaitu*) and popular theatre (Hereniko 1994). He describes how the popular theatre form is 'popular in many third-world countries and now has counterparts in Vanuatu and Solomon Islands', and he points to the potential use of the 'indigenous form to disseminate developmental and educational information' in Polynesia. There is, however, a not insignificant difference between the genre of *faleaitu* (or skits) and popular theatre, in that the skits are not really for 'dissemination of information'. They have their roots in the sacred (as Hereniko discusses in his works about the 'sacred clown' in Rotuma, and as is indicated by the name of skits, *faleaitu*, lit. 'house of spirits'), and they always stay within the boundary of the humorous. Clowns or skit-makers may address delicate topics that they could not address in their ordinary capacities, under the protection of the set-apart nature of the performance. This may have socio-political consequences if someone in the audience later on decides to modify his or her behaviour or instigate a certain course of action because of what he or she saw caricatured in the performance. However, the inversions of ordinary roles that are the main topic of skits in Tokelau are only acceptable because they are not for real, as the performance takes place within a joking context.

The actors' doubts were linked to a realisation that the seriousness of their performance could be interpreted as attacking the traditionally humorous cast of such performances. Following Hereniko's discussion of the historical links between clowning and politics in this region, it seems generally to be the case that it is precisely this characteristic, – humour – which safeguards the expression of subversive statements. In other words, some of the members of the group began to worry that they were perhaps applying too strong a medicine, undermining the arena that allowed them to present their alternative vision in the first place.

Shifting Interpretative Frames – From 'Taking a Message' to 'Presenting a Gift'

To allow us to gain a better understanding of the interpretations and reception of these plays, I would like to refer once more to the changes in social organisation that have taken place within the Tokelau society during the last thirty years (approximately). As I have already mentioned, recreational activities are defined as 'things of no account' (*mea tauanoa*). –*Noa* can, in this context, be interpreted as opposed to *tapu* or *ha*, which is used to characterise 'restricted' or important events. This situational definition, i.e., a '*noa*' activity, embedded in a '*tapu*' context, allows for a certain amount of flexibility when it comes to what people may actually present during public events. The theatre performances fitted neatly into the category of 'things of no account', and this meant that those who had serious objections to the plays being performed, or to any of the messages in the plays, didn't really have to confront the issue, as they could make their opinion known by their absence. It was in fact striking during the performances in Tokelau how many of the Elders, i.e., the old men holding formal political power, were absent or were seated in the dark outside the meeting house. In this way, they avoided giving the event a definite blessing by their presence. That they did this may indicate that they realised that a popular theatre performance was a different kind of performance to the ordinary skits, and that they recognised the group as communicating something more serious than just a playful challenge to their authority.

After their arrival in Tokelau, and before presenting the plays, the the-atre-group was invited to come to a meeting of the Council of Elders to explain the purpose of the tour. The members of the group decided to con-tinue to put their principles into practice, and so one of the women was chosen to give the opening speech on behalf of the group. She gracefully stuck to the canons of Tokelau speech-making, and named and placed the members of the group so that the Elders would know who they were in terms of local affiliations, and, most importantly, she and subsequent speakers stressed that they had come to Tokelau to present a *gift* as a token of their gratitude and love for Tokelau.

This way of framing what they were doing seemed to arise sponta-neously out of their previous familiarity with, and present exposure to, ceremonial exchanges in Tokelau. The fact that they were there as a group on a *malaga* – a term signifying the journey of a travelling party, certain of the customary hospitable reception and at the receiving end of food, gifts and other produce, served to make this a natural choice. The intention of presenting a return gift, as a celebration of the *malaga*, was very well received by the Elders, and many of them seemed genuinely to look for-ward to seeing the plays. As I said, when the night came, quite a few of them were there, but very few actually entered the meeting house. Instead, they chose to sit outside in the darkness. It is common when there is to be a gathering in the meeting house for people to avoid being the first to arrive, and generally to avoid entering the house before 'everybody else' is there. This means, for one, that such gatherings often take an extraordinarily long time to really get going.[23] There are, however, always certain public figures (who they are will vary somewhat according to the nature of the occasion) who are responsible for the particular event. They will come first, a few others will stand around and gradually, the house will fill up. That these houses are open[24] means that it is easy for people to wait outside in the shadows, to see who is there, and to merge with the crowd so as to avoid sitting conspicuously inside, 'as if he or she consid-ers him or herself to be an important person'.[25]

At the first performance in Tokelau, the house filled slowly, led by some teachers, lots of children (which is unusual – in most other gatherings in that house, children would normally have the 'lowest' place if any, i.e., in the outskirts of the group), some relatives and friends of players, and grad-ually quite a few older women and some of the men.[26] The Elders' absence, and that of several of the village leaders, was noted and commented upon, and it lent the occasion a feeling of something 'extra', something unim-portant and apart from ordinary village activities. It must be said that this was in a certain sense the case, as the performance took place at Christmas time when the island was full of visitors: scholarship students were home for Christmas holidays; there were many weddings being held; and every-one was extremely busy. The Elders, being responsible for organising the weekly schedule of activities, had the power to make priorities regarding what counted as an important event and what didn't.

I interpret the absence, or in any case, not full 'in house' presence of the Elders, as symptomatic of a certain insecurity and ambivalence among the Elders that is also expressed in many other situations. In situations where they traditionally and unambiguously rule, such as in running the weekly work schedule, the Elders are present and take an active part. In situations where the emergent, younger leadership is most competent, and which happen on their initiative, the Elders tend to withdraw so as to avoid being compromised, either by being transparently un-knowledgeable or (because of lack of familiarity with whatever is happening) by appearing to give their blessing to something they wouldn't have wanted to support had they known what it was.

During the Tokelau sojourn then, the members of the group actually moved closer in their definitions of what they were doing to local notions of festivity and prestation-exchanges.[27] This shift was encouraged by the local communities reception of the touring group, the *malaga*. It was also reinforced by the uniform local production of counter-plays: whenever the theatre-group presented their performance, the local communities answered with one of their own – thus turning the political challenge into a competitive exchange between equal sides.

Thus the theatre-group's interpretative frames gradually shifted. From a framework where their perception of what they were doing was defined as 'taking a message to an audience', i.e., to disseminate information in Hereniko's terms, they were led step by step towards an altogether different definition of situation (Goffman 1959). This new definition of what they were doing, clearly more fitting in the context of Tokelau, was expressed as 'we are coming to Tokelau with a gift, to celebrate our homecoming'.

The difference between what is done in ordinary performances (skit making or clowning) and what the group attempted to do with the plays can be described as a difference between a temporary inversion of codes informing identity (as is the case with ordinary performances) and negotiating codes of behaviour with the explicit goal of transforming commonly held conceptions of identity (as was the case with the plays). To challenge people's conceptions of their way of life, and to do so in a serious and direct manner, is unusual in Tokelau, and the group clearly felt that to enter the meeting house at the centre of the village in order to present this anomaly in front of everybody was a grave undertaking. To enter the ritualised space of performance with the goal of redefining the parameters of the culture through theatre was indeed 'deep play', with implications beyond the actual event, in the sense that what happened had the power to affect the actors' individual standing and credibility within the communities (Geertz 1973: 412–53).

Effects and Arenas

Events such as the ones staged by the theatre-group may eventually have a cumulative effect on basic patterns of orientation, in such a way that conceptions of selfhood and life horizons change, but before proposing such an analysis as a fitting description of the empirical situation depicted here, there are some important factors to be considered.

First, there is the important matter of how such activities are classified. In this case, the gift presented by the actors seems to be defined (by Tokelauans) within a special framework. This framework acts a barrier against the messages the performance contains having any 'spillover effect' into everyday life. Whereas this representation is true on one level, things are more complex than apparently implied. If turned into a theoretical model, it conceptualises the existence of separate spheres, for political and expressive culture respectively, and allows for no interaction or feedback effects between these spheres.[28]

However, given the fact that these spheres, which are certainly locally conceived as being conceptually separate, are mostly constituted by the same actors, who frequently pursue identical goals in both spheres, it is clear that interaction and 'spillover effects' must occur. This is what I have called the quasi-political potential of the activities classified as entertainment (Spitulnik 1997, 1999). It can be illustrated, for example, by my analysis of how songs sung at inter-atoll gatherings may have political repercussions (Hoëm 1992). It is also, of course, possible to see influence going the other way, for example, when art-forms such as speech-making or songs enter into political contexts, or quite simply shape the reputation of a person, who earns a certain standing in the community because of the flow of information across such 'spheres'.

To keep the 'spheres' conceptually separate allows for the creation of certain situations as set-apart, as out of the ordinary and as subject to different rules; this is illustrated in the case of the womens' committee's interpretation of what happened during the skit in the meeting house. This mechanism allows for a temporary objectification of various aspects of the flow of everyday life, such as making genealogical relations the object of dispute in relation to landclaims during a political meeting, or turning the same topic into a song and displaying it at a village feast, or turning the experiences of Tokelau people during the last 300 years into a play and offering it back to the communities as a gift.

On the other hand, the infrastructural changes which I have described serve to set a precedent for certain messages; these changes, which I will describe in more detail in the subsequent chapter, may constitute a certain resonant ground, facilitating the perception of the messages contained in the plays.

Creative approaches to the Tokelau tradition, such as that represented by the plays, and alternative visions of 'the Tokelau way' are gradually becoming conventionalised through various events over time. This also implies that we cannot assume that we know once and for all the empirical meaning of terms such as fiction, myth or even performance. To learn to 'read' unfamiliar cultural products is always a difficult task, as every Polynesian migrant (and every anthropologist?) surely knows.

Notes

1. See e.g., IWGIA document No. 104, 2001: 177.
2. Earlier versions of parts of this section of Chapter one have been published previously. See Hoëm 1998a and 1998b for further descriptions of the activities of this group and of the role of humorous performances within Tokelau society.
3. See Wessen et al., 1992, pp. 133–6, 138–9 and 143, for a detailed historical description of the development of this institution.
4. For an account of the dance form, *fatele*, see Thomas 1986.
5. On local conceptions of levels of meaning, see Thomas 1986.
6. This book was produced by the Elders in Tokelau in cooperation with Hooper and Huntsman.
7. This is the meeting hall of the Fakaofo community. The name means literally 'white pearl shell lure', and this is one of the treasures in Tokelau, the gift or *kahoa* which is given to a bride by the groom's parents as part of the wedding ceremony.
8. For example, D. Long, from the New Zealand Ministry of Education, subsequently described the event the following way: 'Something happened at the 1992 Tokelau Festival of Sport and Culture. Something deeply moving and special. Pahina hall in Porirua was packed this Easter for the premiere of the first ever Tokelau play. […] Theatre has become such a part of the modern entertainment scene – it has become almost impossible to move audiences anymore. […] Imagine then a packed hall, hundreds and hundreds of people. All of them weeping, tears running down their faces. So many people, from children to grandparents, laughing and holding on to each other. Nodding and gripping each other's hands. Singing parts of the songs along with the actors. For this was an audience witnessing a play that mattered to them. That spoke to their lives. A play – the first play – about them. Have you any idea how rare an experience that is in the world of contemporary theatre?' He concluded by saying that 'I doubt if I ever will see again a group of actors reach an audience quite so powerfully again'.
9. This is a relevant way of defining oneself as an ethnic group within the New Zealand context. Thus one simultaneously establishes oneself as indigenous and therefore of equal status with the Maori (but as different from all the other Pacific islanders in New Zealand, who don't have the dual citizenship that people from Tokelau do), while establishing the Tokelau people as different (and better) than the Maori because they have their own homeland where no one can contest their ties and their rights to the land. To enter into this kind of discourse, and to establish one's claims in this kind of inter-ethnic landscape and hierarchy, is a necessary part of surviving in a minority situation, such as that faced by 'Pacific Islanders' in New Zealand. The Maori situation can

obviously also be described as a minority situation, but in addition it carries the particular traits which have caused it to be likened to a case of internal colonialism.

10. Cf., Chapter four (Hoëm 1995) on 'women's talk and men's talk'.
11. For an analysis of similar behaviour in Samoa, see Mageo (1998) on *faipona*, 'smoothing out', i.e., eliminating undesirable behaviour through ridicule.
12. See also the discussion of the term *haoloto* in Chapter five.
13. Cf., R. Simona quoted in Thomas 1986: 'Tokelauans are the shyest people in the Pacific (but) in the first part of the *fatele*, that is not him yet, the true Tokelauan is shown right at the end'.
14. Shore 1982, see especially Chapter twelve; see also Mageo 1998, on the concept of *loto*.
15. The full paragraph reads: 'Recently, much work has been devoted in anthropological circles to the cross-cultural study of emotions and affect. Central to much of this work is the warning that Western views about the relative 'genuineness' of affect displays in non-western societies are at best suspect (Irvine 1982; Levy 1984; Rosaldo 1980, 1983, 1984). This warning is particularly relevant to Western Polynesian societies, where the boundary between emotion, affect, and social action is extremely tenuous. [...] In these societies, emotions are *defined* in behavioural terms'.
16. For a full analysis of various relationships within 'the family' and 'the village' as she calls it, see Huntsman 1971.
17. For a description and analysis of clowning in Tokelau, see Hooper and Huntsman 1975. For a description of the Samoan concepts *faipona* and *ula*, see Mageo 1998.
18. For a detailed illustration of this phenomenon in Samoa, see also Duranti 1994: 116–121.
19. For a similar description from Samoa, see Mageo 1998 (in particular, her analysis of the concept and practice of *faipona*).
20. The church may of course also be described as a 'centre institution', but the pattern of communication is differently ordered there. Cf., Besnier (1991) on the role of the church in the Tuvaluan atoll Nukulaelae, which has striking similarities to the role of the church in Tokelau. In Chapter five, the cultural significance of different *places*, areas in and outside the village are described.
21. For a fuller discussion of different attitudes towards knowledge, see Hoëm 1995.
22. For an analysis of different styles of communication in Tokelau, see Hoëm 1995.
23. See also S. Philips' 1974 article 'Warm Springs "Indian Time": How the Regulation of Participation Affects the Progress of Events', for a very interesting analysis of a similar phenomenon.
24. But see Chapter five, which discusses how the meeting-house on Atafu, the Lotala, is no longer open.
25. See also Duranti 1994, Chapter three, for a discussion of correlations between seating arrangements (places) and positions (status).
26. In this case, there was some disagreement between the *papalagi* instructor (who wanted the children placed up front) and some of the cast members who didn't want them to be there at all.
27. The term 'prestation' is M. Mauss' (Mauss 1954, see e.g., page xi.).
28. For an example of an analysis that seems to be based on this premise, see Shore 1982.

Chapter 2

Political Activism: New Media and Arenas of Leadership

As we can see from the ethnographic background presented in the Introduction, there is a proliferation of groups in the atoll communities, and these groups are constituted with varying degrees of formality and institutionalisation. When Tokelauans became established in New Zealand, the same phenomenon emerged there (Sallen, 1998). In the larger Wellington region, where approximately two-thirds of the Tokelauan population in New Zealand live, a rather close association between area of residence and atoll affiliation emerged quite early on. These localised communities – Nukunonu centred on the Hutt Valley, Atafu and Fakaofo in the Porirua region – met for church activities, but more importantly in this connection, they gathered for sports tournaments.[1]

A pan-Tokelauan, national sports association was established, and regular gatherings that included the various communities in New Zealand began to take place. These institutions have always had a socio-political function, but their importance definitely seems to have been growing during the last ten to fifteen years. The formal political institutions governing Tokelau in Tokelau, that is, the Councils of Elders, and since the 1970s, the Assembly of Representatives of the Three Atolls, called the General Fono, were not transferred to New Zealand soil for obvious reasons. The position of the Elders as formal political leaders and decision-makers in New Zealand, was not challenged, however. The difficulty faced by the various Tokelau communities in New Zealand would thus seem to be *how to perpetuate this authority structure when the institutional backing was lacking.*

The immediate response to this difficulty – still a current attitude – seems to have been to refuse to see it as a problem. This has been achieved by constantly referring back to the institutions in Tokelau as the ultimate source of authority; the Elders in New Zealand are presented as the decision-makers and there are institutions alive in Tokelau to prove it. While this has served to secure the New Zealand Elders' authority and to ensure a continued deference to the Elders' position, it does not mean that their position has continued to be the same as it was in Tokelau. Leaving aside the effects of the New Zealand Government both in Tokelau and in New Zealand for the moment, we may note that a new political leadership rooted in these sports and cultural organisations has gradually emerged within the Tokelau communities in New Zealand. These leaders were from the beginning young, far too young by Tokelau standards to be eligible for any positions of political importance. Most were male, but the number of females involved was very high compared to what used to be the case in Tokelau itself. A high proportion of this group consisted of former scholarship students, and many held jobs that were only accessible for those with higher education.

The individuals who fall into this category have tended to provide a bridge between the old leadership, with whom they are in constant contact, and the larger New Zealand society. Recently, they have also assumed the position of mediators between the younger generation of New Zealand-born Tokelauans, whose familiarity with *papalagi* lifestyles is often greater than their familiarity with things Tokelauan and the Tokelau community as a whole. These individuals have gradually taken on an enormous workload. In most cases, they hold ordinary jobs and at the same time assume most of the administrative responsibilities pertinent to the running of the Tokelau institutions. The Elders are present, at meetings and gatherings, as arbiters of disputes and as speakers, in general filling the main ritual functions, such as reciting the opening and closing prayers, sharing their vast knowledge of Tokelau songs and so on. They provide the framework that allows any meeting to take place within the aesthetics of Tokelau etiquette. Even so, although this is not explicitly or formally recognised, the practical leadership seems largely to have moved into younger hands.

In the atolls, the picture is somewhat different. This is due to two factors: first, the Elders still hold formal power; and second, the group of individuals who are comparable to the new leadership in New Zealand, and who often overlap with them, usually work in the Tokelau Public Service, and are thus at one remove from the formal political structures of Tokelau (in that they are not members of the Taupulega or the General Fono). Within these limitations, however, the tendency for younger people with a greater familiarity with the outside world and with international politics to take over positions of responsibility is also present in Tokelau.

As mentioned earlier, new forms of social stratification have emerged. Most importantly, these social differences relate to highly varied life-trajectories, which did not exist before the 1960s, at least not to any comparable degree. Seen from Tokelau, a significant difference is between those who have been outside Tokelau and those who have not. Another important difference, which coincides with having been outside, is between those who work in the Tokelau Public Service and those who do not. A previously non-existent local categorisation of people into (using the English terms) 'unskilled', 'semi-skilled', and 'skilled', underlines the importance of this division. The 'unskilled' are of course those who are only skilled in the subsistence activities which a short time ago were the only skills recognised in Tokelau. The 'semi-skilled' are usually manual labourers with some basic training in carpentry, plumbing and so on. The 'skilled' are those with a higher level of education than is provided in Tokelau, which at the present is up to Form Five (i.e., around the age of 16).

There is, however, no easily detectable conflation of these categories and attitudes toward traditional Tokelau values and the values associated with the *papalagi* lifestyle (such as consumerism and individualism). In real life, all sorts of combinations exist. One may find staunch traditionalists who are avid consumers of karate videos, or other goods associated with capitalist societies, in their free time.[2] In short, the influence of the outside world has increasingly made itself felt, and nobody has been left unaffected. However, there are several discernible trends, some of which are associated with the emergence of the dimension of ethnicity.

Organisations within the Tokelau communities in New Zealand that had their origin and rationale in culture and sports organisations seem to have undergone a transformation, as yet covert, i.e., not formally recognised, towards taking on a more political role. That is, a role which was traditionally reserved for Elders in the *Fono*. Positions within the organisations have changed accordingly. The structural precondition for this development is the lack of institutional recognition of the Elders' political power within the New Zealand society. The group of people who, in practice, assume most of the leadership functions at present still constitute a new and undefined element within the Tokelau organisations. To move into a position giving some kind of formal recognition of the political nature of this leadership would have constituted an open challenge to the older authority structure. This has, so far, not been seen as desirable. It has not been deemed necessary, partly out of a recognition of the important function the Elders perform as arbiters of dispute, and also out of a deference to older people's authority in general. Even so, the process of turning this emergent form of leadership into a conscious model is ongoing, and in this work, legitimacy is drawn from a variety of sources, from Tokelauan notions of egalitarianism to political theories of democracy. In the following, I shall describe in more detail what visions these people adhere to, and how they go about bringing them to life in the Tokelau communities. In the context of the present discussion, the important question is whether what we observe can fruitfully be seen as the development of a new form of political leadership and a new arena for political expression, or whether it is more fitting to see these developments as just a new generation of Elders in the making.

When individuals who occupy such positions of leadership, which emerged during the last period, are asked what they think, many say that they feel a need for other forms of leadership than that which is represented by the older model, and many work with the explicit goal of bringing about a change in this area. How they conceptualise the alternatives, and how far they judge the alternatives to be antithetical to the older model, varies quite significantly from person to person. Empirically, at present, the social form may be described as exhibiting a precarious balance, as illustrated in the above description of how the role of the Elders has moved towards an increasingly ritual function, while the role of the younger leaders has taken on more substance in processes of decision-making. There is, as I have pointed out, a change in the function of the leaders of the sports associations and cultural groups, and this also affects the status of the traditional leadership structure and gender relations. This shift in leadership structure and what it might entail socio-politically will be discussed further in the remainder of this Chapter.

Cultural Identity and Ethnicity

The emergence of a pan-Tokelauan national sense of identity has been running parallel to societal expansion since the establishment of the Tokelau Migration Scheme in the early 1960s. An automatic consequence of facing the outside world seems to have been a certain transformation of relationships. In Tokelau, an intimate familiarity with personal biographies can be assumed, and a classification of individuals according to their cultural identity, such as, 'he is part Samoan', or, 'that family is from Tuvalu', or, 'her Grandfather was a Portuguese', occurs in situations where such an ascription may be used to explain some characteristic trait (*uiga*) of that individual's behaviour. Having a part-Samoan side would often be used as shorthand for a person being considered too aggressive, or too pushy. Being from Tuvalu would often imply a certain familiarity with healing crafts, and having Portuguese ancestry may be used in various ways, either as a sign of being 'Western', or business-minded, or as a reminder that 'those from Portugal' were really 'Negroes from the Cape Verde', and thus lower on the hierarchy of race than Polynesians. Which interpretation to choose is also part of the communicative job of the person who is referred to, and whether one is able to take such commentaries in a light-hearted way or not is really the measure of whether or not one is able to survive happily in such a tightly knit community.

Given these variations, I suggest that we make an analytical distinction between internal classifications of individuals according to cultural background on one hand and according to ethnicity on the other. These internal, specific, classifications may better be seen as belonging to the ongoing process of defining and negotiating identities, which relate to the larger picture of individuals' life-careers and their quest for position and influence within the community. From what I have called the 'internal classifications' of cultural identity, there is a qualitative step into ethnicity, in that the internal classifications are characterised by the form of sociality I have described as 'sided', and thus reciprocal, relations. Ethnic relationships, on the other hand, are characterised by cross-cultural relations of incorporation and asymmetry. Comaroff and Comaroff, for example, describe ethnicity as related to 'the asymmetric incorporation of structurally dissimilar groupings into a single political economy' (Comaroff and Comaroff 1992: 54).

People who leave Tokelau describe how they experience categories converging with increasing distance, so that in Samoa, one is suddenly translated into a Tokelauan, rather than being a person from, for example, Atafu. Among the *papalagi* population in New Zealand, one becomes a Pacific Islander, and so on. In other words, the experience of leaving Tokelau tends to give people a consciousness of Tokelau as a whole and of the Pacific as an area, in a way that is not felt when living in Tokelau. This emergence of a national consciousness, and of a consciousness of being an ethnic group among many others in the Pacific and in the world, is qualitatively different from what I have described as internal classifications of cultural identity, in that it is produced by relationships which are, so to speak, between Tokelau and the rest of the world, not by relationships that are multiplex and small-scale.

So far, ethnic relations have carried a different weight and assumed another importance outside of Tokelau, mainly in New Zealand, but also in Samoa. In as much as Tokelau has increasingly had to deal with the world of international politics, as demonstrated by the relationships between Tokelau, New Zealand and the UN, it is also possible to see a qualitative change taking place within Tokelau itself. One can even interpret the moves towards establishing an infrastructure, which would allow a greater measure of self-government, as an ethnic process. However, it seems more in line with actual historical development to attribute the emergence of ethnicity, as an aspect of Tokelau political relations, to the situation faced by Tokelau immigrants to New Zealand. In a very telling description, V. G. Sallen writes:

> Tokelauans generally took little interest in New Zealand politics, perhaps because they were so absorbed in their own community politics. [...] What concern they had was focused on issues that affected them directly – for example welfare and state housing policies – or those affecting their homeland. Wary

of governmental initiatives involving all Pacific islanders as a group, *they argued that they were truly New Zealand citizens* and did not want to compromise that status by joining with others whose status was less certain. They also contended that they would have nothing to gain by joining forces with other Pacific island groups, since any such organisation would be dominated by the voices and interests of these larger ethnic groups. (Sallen, in Wessen *et al.* 1992: 125)

In other words, the Tokelauan immigrants found themselves in an uncertain position within a hierarchy of various ethnic groups within the New Zealand society. This was a completely new situation. In Samoa, the Tokelau community lived in a 'mini-Tokelau', in a situation where they had their own land, and where there were no uncertainties in terms of their cultural identity. Samoans and Tokelauans were in general equally vehement in distancing one group from the other, but as the group of Tokelauans was small, and they were not in competition over local resources, no real difficulties resulted from this.

As it became more difficult for Samoans to migrate to New Zealand, while Tokelauans experienced no such difficulties because of their New Zealand citizenship, the relationships between them became somewhat more strained. It is also possible to see traces of this in the quote from Sallen. Note how the communities stress their status as true New Zealanders vis-à-vis the other groups of Pacific Islanders with which they continually run the risk of being grouped. From an outsider's point of view, and in this case it could equally well be a member of another group of Pacific Islanders as a *papalagi*, Tokelauans were not visible as a group. Samoans were, and so Tokelauans and Samoans were often lumped together, in spite of their mutual attempts at distancing.

The various ethnic groups in New Zealand occupy different niches, for example, the Indians are shop-keepers, and the Samoans and Cambodians are taxi-drivers. The first groups of Tokelauans were forestry and carpentry workers, and later on, large numbers worked in companies such as General Motors. The success of an increasing number of East Asians, in particular Japanese, has caused the public evaluation of other ethnic groups, including the indigenous people of New Zealand, the Maori, to change somewhat, at least in public opinion as represented by the media. The fact that East Asian groups have markedly better educational scores than Maori and so-called Pacific Islanders, has led some New Zealanders to conclude that the measures taken (after a long process of winning public support for them) to support the less-privileged groups within New Zealand society have been a mistake. The conclusion is that if these immigrants can do it, then other immigrants can; those who do not succeed fail because they do not work hard enough.

However, a markedly greater proportion of the Tokelau population in New Zealand has succeeded in getting a higher level education and in finding employment in the New Zealand Public Service than, for example, Samoans. It is interesting to link this fact to the size of the group and to the development of the Tokelau Public Service (TPS). The Tokelau Public Service has created both positions and scholarships for Tokelauans, giving the recipients a strong sense of obligation towards serving the Tokelau community. For many, it is the knowledge that 'if I don't, there is nobody else to do it' that finally motivates them to following through on a career choice.

During the years in which the Tokelau communities have been in New Zealand, there has been a gradual rise in the level of participation in Pan-Pacific gatherings, such as Pacifica (The Pacific Islanders Women's Organisation) and the Pacific Islands Cultural Festivals. To conclude, the Tokelau communities taken as a whole seem to have pursued two different strategies in dealing with the hierarchies within New Zealand society. One has been to distance themselves from the other ethnic groups from the Pacific and the Maori, on the grounds of their special relationship with *papalagi* society. They were an 'indigenous people' on the same basis as the Maori, in that they were automatically New Zealand citizens, and they were also a minority group in New Zealand (as with all the other 'Islanders'). They differed from the Maori in that their attachment to land areas in Tokelau was not contested. Their small number also made them highly conscious of the ease with which they could be swallowed up by any larger group. These factors, plus the occupational policies pursued by the New Zealand Government, worked together to keep them separate, and in relative isolation as a group. The other strategy, however, has been to present themselves as one ethnic group among many. On the multicultural stage of so-called cultural gatherings, Tokelauans have, with increasing strength, presented themselves as a people with a distinct history, culture, language and so on. Taken together, it seems at present as if these two strategies have worked to keep the group distinct from others. At the same time, it is obvious that, due to ever increasing contact with 'others', of which the papalagi lifestyle is so far in many ways the dominant influence, aspects of that lifestyle have been adopted.

The Activist Role and the Community

The following poem was written in relation to the changes in the political infrastructure of Tokelau described above. The writer is a young woman, who worked closely with the communities in Tokelau from within the framework of a TPS position. Obviously, she would not have been in a position to make such a public statement about cultural or political developments if she had been operating within the previously established institutions, at least up until very recently. She writes about the role of the activist, and the rise of a new political vision in Tokelau. The poem is rendered as it was written, in English.

The vision in your eyes

It's been a long Sunday
full of dreams
discoveries ...
sharing of gems
colours entwine
melody from afar.
Rekindle of a new race
to be revived into a new dawn.
I hear your cry
saw the vision in your eyes
felt it in your voice.
It is just the beginning
the mapping of a nation
'in failure or success'
turned inside out
You made it!
Created from the vision
of your soul.
Eyes for the blind
Ears for the deaf
Voice for the dumb.
A warrior for the multitudes
True son of the nation!
Where are the rest?

T.M. Pasilio

What is it that such a person 'has made', in the line 'you made it?' And why does she chose the image of a 'warrior' to describe the role of an activist? And finally, what is the answer to her poignant question 'where are the rest?' To answer the first question, which I interpret as addressing the distances such a person has covered, and what obstacles he or she has overcome, we again need to direct our glance backward in time. In the subsequent Chapters, I shall do this in more detail, following the life-trajectories of a few individuals whom I believe exemplify certain typical adaptations and common migration experiences. Through the medium of these histories and the two dramas described in the previous Chapter, I seek to illustrate the span which exists within the Tokelau communities between different possible life-careers, thus demonstrating the variety of possible experiences existing within what is Tokelauan today.

In the following, however, I shall dwell on more general, common aspects of the changes and discontinuities that people from Tokelau have experienced during the last decennia. In the post-war period, as mentioned earlier, things Tokelauan did not have a place within the educational system or in anything 'official', that is, for example, political dealings with the outside authorities. The use of the Tokelauan language was restricted to informal, everyday contexts, and everything having to do with the pre-Christian world-view was stigmatised by the church as belonging to the period of 'darkness' (*pouliuli*), to the shamefully heathen past. In response to this stigmatisation, the older generation of Tokelauans seem mainly to have adopted a strategy of adaptation. By becoming good Christians, morally pure and 'civilised' in every way, they earned the right to (self)respect. In the different political climate of New Zealand in the late 1960s and early 1970s, however, a shift took place amongst members of the younger generation from such meek attitudes towards more rebellious ones. It took the form of the establishment of relationships and groups on another basis. A shift began to take place in the premises for group formation. Instead of being based on atoll affiliation, groups were formed on the basis of place of residence in New Zealand, as well as on common interests. This may seem a harmless change, but in fact it constituted a major challenge to the existing authority structure and to the position of the Elders, as I have argued earlier.

Among the young and middle-aged people who find themselves in positions of leadership, it is possible to detect at least two commonly held attitudes and strategies. These individuals share upward mobility, in that they are better educated than most members of the communities. They differ mainly in their attitudes towards their cultural past. To simplify, while the majority glorify the past and want to maintain what Hooper calls the 'neo-traditional order', as epitomised by the (in their view) unquestionable authority of the Elders, the others want to pick the best from both worlds and develop new models of leadership. It is for the latter group that I reserve the term 'activist'. There are people who are cultural formulators in the first group as well, and I shall deal with differences in their forms of cultural expression in the remainder of this Chapter and also in subsequent Chapters.

The role of the 'warrior', as used in the poem, refers to a conscious breech with traditional norms and conceptions, the uncomfortable role of having to bridge two cultures in the way that people who are in the activists' position do. The term warrior, however, also gives this difficult position legitimacy in that it reaches back to what I have referred to earlier as 'the days of war', i.e., the days of open inter-atoll rivalry. The *toa* or warrior is a cultural hero of a semi-divine nature, and he is capable of dividing or uniting the three atolls. In terms of the present situation, the political battles he has to fight are still the old ones of handling the relationships between the three atolls, but he must also deal with the outside world, of which he has intimate knowledge, as he has been there and returned successfully – as a *true* son of the nation.

The last question, of 'where are the rest', can be answered in a simplistic way: somewhere along the continuum uniting these two positions of 'traditionalist' and 'activist'. As I have already mentioned, I shall go into greater detail when it comes to describing where different people 'are' with respect to the current political developments in the following Chapters. In the remainder of this Chapter, I shall concentrate on the development of new forms of cultural expression in relation to what some have called cultural activists' development of a 'master paradigm for selfhood'.

New Forms of Cultural Expression

I have described the social mechanism of making sides, with the resulting proliferation of structurally similar groupings. It is also possible to observe this phenomenon in the case of the emerging leadership in the Tokelau communities in New Zealand. This is particularly interesting in as much as this actually occurs between groups who hold diametrically opposed views on what kind of leadership structure it is that they seek. Earlier in this Chapter, I related the change in leadership structure to the fact that, in New Zealand, the necessary institutional backing for the Elders' political power was lacking, thus creating room for an increase in the importance of educated members among the younger generation. At the same time, the group as a whole, and individuals as middlemen between the communities and the *papalagi* society, entered into previously non-existent inter-ethnic relations. A similar shift has also taken place in Tokelau, although to a slightly less dramatic extent, given that there was institutional backing for the Elders and that inter-ethnic relations are activised in fewer situations than in New Zealand.

However one chooses to interpret the changes in leadership structure, it is impossible to ignore the quasi-political role played by the Tokelau cultural organisations in New Zealand. Whether we think about sports associations, song-groups, dance teams or theatre groups, women's organisations or pre-schools, they have in common a focus on the 'Tokelau culture' or the 'Tokelau language' and so on. In Tokelau, as I have described elsewhere (e.g., Hoëm 1992b), the quasi-political potential of the sphere of entertainment or expressive culture has always existed, as exemplified in the institution of clowning, which sometimes takes the form of rather explicit political criticism and commentary. What is new, however, is the feedback into the Tokelau institutions of the New Zealand experience, as expressed by the introduction of Tokelau language, history and culture into the national curriculum in Tokelau; the establishment of a forum for debate, such as newsletters, on all three atolls; and the writing of poetry, songs and drama, some of which carry highly critical messages and analyses of Tokelau's predicament, navigating through these times of globalisation.

The change within the Tokelau communities can easily be described in terms of the different models of knowledge that people hold. The traditionalists claim that to grow older is to grow wiser, and that old age is synonymous with the possession of knowledge. This was a cornerstone of the subsistence-based Tokelau, where knowledge was vital for survival, for example, knowledge of the seasons, the stars, navigation techniques and, perhaps most importantly, of genealogies, which could give legitimacy to land claims. This knowledge is treated as esoteric, but it is simultaneously taught in the schools and written about in the newsletters. In other words, there is an ongoing negotiation about what should be shared, and it is often the case that despite part of 'the culture' being circulated in newsletters or in speeches or songs, those who are not supposed to have that kind of knowledge quite simply don't pick it up (see also Hoëm 1995). Hence, the reference to the deaf ears in the poem in the previous section.

It is possible to say that the activities of the 'cultural formulators' create what has been described as a new context for the development of self-hood 'seen as a directional historical trend', through various politically significant events over time (Eidheim 1992). There are, however, equally strong forces that pull in other directions. As we saw in the case of the theatre group, it is not sufficient to present a new model of self-hood, nor is it sufficient that the structural conditions for developing one are present – people also have to accept this new vision.

Whether one chooses to interpret the emergence of such new cultural forms, including both the new means of social stratification that I have described and the vision emerging through the expressive culture, as the development of a new 'master paradigm' for Tokelau self-hood, is an open question. The distance between the vision held by the activists and 'the rest' is sometimes great. In other contexts, however, there is considerable sharing of vision.

The emergence of new forms of social differentiation and new forms of cultural expression has also been followed by changes in attitudes towards 'tradition', 'knowledge' and 'the culture'. Differences in these attitudes create a major barrier between people.

Eidheim's analysis of what he calls 'a cultural process of revitalisation' among an indigenous group in the Circumpolar region, the Saami, is based on the premise that this process is brought about as a result of 'participation in global culture', particularly through contact with representatives of other Fourth World populations. My reservations with respect to Eidheim's model concern the fact that, although I do accept his analysis of the political actions of Saami activists as having consequences for all Saami, regardless of their attitudes towards such action, I contend that it is of utmost importance to specify how such actions attain political significance. This may be achieved by accounting for how they relate to local conceptions of *events and relationships* (See Mageo 1998, for an analysis that does this). In other words, while such actions may be deemed as having consequences for all, it is equally important to note how attitudes towards such actions may differ. When analysing inter-ethnic relationships, processes of dichotomisation between 'us' and 'them' are apparent (T. Hylland Eriksen 1993). This does not, however, absolve us from accounting for a greater degree of conceptual and social differentiation, both in the inter-ethnic and the intra-cultural field. If the material and conceptual distance between activists and 'the rest' is great, for example, if people are opposed to the activists' actions on the grounds that the activists do not interact with them as they do among themselves, then these discrepancies should be noted. This is not to say that Eidheim does not note such discrepancies, but rather that they are not taken into account when it comes to the question of 'the rest's' eventual adoption of a new 'master paradigm' for self-hood. I would argue that the significant factor in the question of whether political events that aim at redefining cultural parameters may affect people 'at home' on a deeper level, that is, apart from the macro-political arena, is to be found precisely in local conceptions of events and relationships.

In my description of how the introduction by Tokelau activists' of a new media of communication relates to Tokelauan conceptions of performances as politically insignificant but ritually significant spaces, my point about the analytical significance of local conceptualisations of events has been discussed in detail. In the following Chapter, we will also learn more about Tokelau conceptualisations of relationships.

Notes

1. V. Sallen has described these communities and their congregations in detail. Cf., Chapter seven, Wessen *et al.* 1992.
2. For a detailed analysis of the situation in Tokelau, with a focus on variation with regards to attitudes towards knowledge, see Hoëm 1995.

Chapter 3

Learning a Sense of Place

❦

'Te fia hili – kae maulalo!' ([You] want to be high – but [you are] low)
Common taunt.

In the previous Chapters, I discussed the cultural role of performance within the context of the communicative practices in Tokelau/New Zealand. I have examined this through a focus on the creation and presentation of two dramas made by the group *Tagi*, which at the time of their performances was based in the Wellington area in New Zealand. The plays addressed questions related to social change and the experience of discontinuity. The actors, who also were the authors of the plays, sought to articulate such experiences to provide an opportunity for reflection, in the hope of engendering a new sense of direction for the people of Tokelau, both in the atolls and in New Zealand.

In this Chapter, we shall look at some individual experiences of issues similar to those addressed in the plays. My aim is to develop a perspective on how events, such as those represented by the theatre-performances, can fruitfully be seen simultaneously as the result of multiple actors and their individual goals *and* as the result of a common definition of a situation achieved in interaction. I believe that such a perspective will lend greater credibility to our analyses of events, in that it allows for more precise descriptions of the interplay between individual motivations and structural factors than would be the case if we were to limit ourselves to a purely structural description or a typology of relationships.

As described in the previous Chapters, the vision sought by the members of the drama group is articulated in relation to, and in partial opposition to, a pervasive cultural orientation. In this and the following Chapter, we shall focus on some aspects of the various practices that together tend to produce this underlying orientation that I describe as '*a sense of place*'.

In this Chapter, I present two narratives that two women told about themselves and their lives. The first narrative tells the story of leaving from Tokelau to New Zealand, and the second tells of the return to Tokelau from New Zealand. Both stories clearly express the trauma or 'culture shock' connected with the migration experience. This narrative plot, although important and interesting in itself, is however, not the sole focus of my reading of the two stories. I also want to point out how the experience of displacement seems to *activate fundamental orientations*. In my analysis of the two narratives, therefore, I will concentrate on how prevalent conceptualisations of *place* and *position* serve to inform, shape and make sense of subjective experiences of displacement and readjustment.

The conceptualisations of place and position are related to what I have described earlier as 'sided' relationships, producing interactional patterns of command and responsibility (see also Chapter four for a further description of these relationship patterns). In this Chapter, I wish to give the reader a chance to observe more closely how such patterns come to be expressed in individual lives, and to learn more about how these relationships, and conceptualisations of such relationships, may be experienced and negotiated in real life events.

Changing Horizons of Expectation

As has been described elsewhere[1] the New Zealand-instigated scholarship scheme was started with the explicit intention of facilitating the transition for Tokelauans to a life in New Zealand society. As the scheme went hand in hand with a so-called Resettlement Scheme, the plan, as it was originally conceived from the New Zealand Administration's side, was to move the whole Tokelau population from Tokelau and resettle them in New Zealand. This plan was seen to have the advantage of easing New Zealand's burden in providing for the Tokelau population. The atolls were prospected for use as coconut plantations. Hooper (1982) has commented dryly that, not surprisingly, the scheme did not prove a great success among the Tokelau population, but that it acted as a certain incentive for private migration. He also comments that the scholarship-scheme facilitated the breaking away from the, until then, overwhelming dominance of the church within the field of education. Hooper and Huntsman describe how

> by the early 1970s, as the number of families applying for 'assisted' resettlement was dwindling, relatively larger proportions of migrating Tokelauans were using channels of chain migration; they preferred to be assisted by kin already in New Zealand. By agreement between the Administration and the people of the atolls, the emphasis was changed from 'assisted' migration to

an expanded scholarship scheme. During the years from 1973 to 1980 more than 100 children were sent to school in New Zealand. By *1976 the Scholarship Scheme had totally replaced the Resettlement Scheme.* (Hooper and Huntsman: 1992: 84. Emphasis mine)

The government-sponsored migration, which started in the early 1960s, thus underwent a transformation, ending up as a scholarship scheme. The plans for resettlement were abandoned. Such ideas resurface occasionally, however, and more recently in connection with the threat of global warming. The Education Department in Tokelau has, since the 1980s, put greater stress on providing education, which also has relevance for life in Tokelau, and the relocation of the main part of the Tokelau Public Service from Apia in Samoa to the atolls provides more jobs for Tokelauans with higher education in Tokelau itself. The current situation is such that there is practically no family which does not have one or more family members living overseas. However, it is also the case that most families have one or more 'representatives' living in Tokelau, to hold the family land.[2]

The first narrative presented in this Chapter begins with extracts from a life history recounted by a woman who grew up in Tokelau and went to New Zealand as one of the first sponsored migrants. As a contrast to this, the subsequent narrative illustrates a journey in the opposite direction, i.e., of a person leaving the, for her, familiar environment of New Zealand to go to live in Tokelau. As mentioned above, these stories have not simply been chosen because they vividly depict the migration process, but also because they clearly show the habitual patterns of interaction that produce a sense of social and geographical *place*.

Narrative One: Leaving

The following narrative is told by a middle-aged woman, married and with grown children, who has lived in New Zealand since she migrated at the age of 18. She has returned to Tokelau for short visits, one of them in her capacity as a central figure in the development of Tokelauan pre-schools in New Zealand. She is also active in one of the Tokelau women's organisations, instigated by a larger organisation for women in the Pacific region, and she was one of the members of the theatre group up until the time of the tour to Tokelau, which she was unable to attend.

Her life history is actually much longer, and I have cut some parts out of the section presented here. The omissions are marked in parentheses. While I have other accounts of the first journey to New Zealand in my material, some recounted by men, I chose this account not only because it is representative, but also for the humorous qualities with which she relates what must have been a terrifying and, in some respects, rather sad and disappointing experience.[3]

1. In 1963, I finished school in Tokelau, and my thoughts were that I wanted to go to study teaching when the boys and girls were shipped to Samoa. But then, in 1964, we were given explanations and clarifications that New Zealand had a new scheme, so that unmarried boys and girls could be shipped here. At that time I was 18 years old, and my thoughts that I wanted to go to teacher's training college were gone at once, and I wanted to go to New Zealand, to see what New Zealand was to me, to my view. I had seen it on photos, and in the accounts of New Zealand at school, but that did not stop my wish to know what New Zealand was.

2. I then went and said to the priest that I wanted to go to New Zealand, and it was quiet for a while, and then it became known that we were going to New Zealand. As for me at that time, I was very happy, I thought to myself that in New Zealand everything is obtained easily. You sleep, sleep, sleep, sleep for the whole day and don't do anything else. And I thought that in New Zealand, the people, who are called *papalagi*, work in offices and that is their whole life. All working people are office people and there are no other jobs.

3. When we were leaving I remember well that I was happy that I was going to New Zealand and that I was becoming like a *papalagi*. I thought that when I got to New Zealand I would be a *papalagi*. I would also know how to speak English like a *papalagi*.

4. We were trained in how to eat with spoons and forks by another priest, Father Michael Goldfinch, who came from Hastings. He lived in Nukunonu for a while and we had a class in how to drink tea! People drink tea and eat cakes. That same priest had an English class for us. Well, I know well that I was ashamed [*ma*] to face [*fakafeagai*] the priest when he was teaching us about spoons and forks, because I was laughing, laughing and laughing, and the priest scolded me and then it was finished and I came home. I was scolded many times for always laughing.

5. We were also taken to be admonished by the Elders; how we were going to go [*pe ka omai vehea, ke fai fakalelei matou amioga*] so that our behaviour was good, so that we were to be called good girls, that we should feel that Tokelau was well talked about where we were going.

6. We went to Samoa by boat, and then I felt for the first time some sadness when I saw that I had left my parents and my relatives – I had gone on board the boat. I didn't realise what I was getting into, for I was seasick. […] Luckily my brother was going with us […] and it was like I didn't feel too sad for I saw that another person from my family was going with me to Samoa. […]

7. As the boat was going towards Samoa there were thoughts about what kind of place Samoa was, for [I] had never been to Samoa either. At last the boat reached Samoa on that first morning, and I remember well that I saw the … I thought they were dogs. They ran to and fro, and only then I realised they were cars! […]

8. Well, [we] arrived. I remember well how we went ashore and a priest came […]. He said that we were to be taken to meet the nuns. So then we went into the car. Father showed us how to sit in the car. So we sat there and he told us that we were to be taken to the nuns at Savalalo. As for me I had heard that name before, Savalalo, but I didn't know at all where Savalalo was or what Savalalo was to me.

9. So we went on the road, and Father had not explained to us that when we go in a car there will come another car in the other direction! I can well remember when I was sitting inside that car, how afraid I was! because as

the car was going, when another car was coming from the other side, I looked at it. When it was about to arrive at us, I just thought that the cars were about to crash! Sometimes it was probably big cars such as lorries and pickups. I only later realised the names of those cars. Now when the car we were going in met a car like that, I [...] bent my head down, just like I was hiding, because I was afraid, because I just thought that the cars would crash, and then I just thought that I was going to die just there.

10. So we were taken to meet the nuns, and when I was walking up – how large the house was. We were walking on the steps, and … it was like a high house, and at that time I was walking on, but it was like my mind wasn't with me because I didn't know the people! Father [...] had been to Tokelau before, that was why he knew us, but he came to take us to the nuns at Savalalo. As for me, I was laughing, but I didn't know why I was laughing, because I didn't understand. My mind was just going around like … like it was gone. It was like it was circling around: 'Hey! Where am I? Hey! Why have I come to Samoa? Is this the place called Samoa?' It was like the mind was astray.

11. Well, when we had said hello to the nuns, we went down and did our bags. We took them up, relatives came, but at the time [the bags] were opened, Tokelau vapoured away. [I] couldn't see the features of the relatives anymore, couldn't see the faces of [my] parents. What [I] felt at that moment was very unusual. It was like [I] was about to start longing for Tokelau. The people I saw were different, [I] wasn't used to the people. [...T]he first night I didn't sleep, but I know well that I cried, cried under my bed sheet, and I thought, 'oh, if only I had stayed in Tokelau, [if] I hadn't come to Samoa it would be better.'[...]

12. [W]e commuted to Apia [the capital of Western Samoa] every morning. That was another difficult moment, because [I] wasn't used to walking in shoes. [I] entered shops. How big the shops were, and [I] looked at what I saw in Apia, and then I just stood looking for a long time. Only when my eyes were satisfied did I walk away, when I had understood. It wasn't an [intended] action, for the time just passed, but when I just stopped to look at a Samoan who looked different or acted differently, then I just stopped and … 'Hey! Wow! Hey! Look at that person, he is doing something strange, his face is strange, his way of walking is strange, his …' But [I] went on for I seemed to be always frightened of Opeta [a person working for the Office of Tokelau Affairs], that I shouldn't stare, as if I had understood. 'Hey! Yes! This is indeed Samoa and not Tokelau!'

13. Another habit of mine when [I] went to Apia was that I just wished that I would see some Tokelauans that I knew. Another habit of mine I was continually scolded [for] was this one: [If] I was standing inside a shop and I just saw a Tokelauan child outside in the street I just shouted to him! I just jumped out from the shop and crossed to the other side of the street. When I saw the child I would shout to him or her by name, and Opeta said to me: 'Hey! Don't you understand this is not Tokelau? How shameful to shout in the middle of the street!' But when I shouted the name of a child it was as if I remembered, you know, I was very happy, I was like being in Tokelau at that moment. And I shouted at him or her in Tokelauan, 'Hey! Where are you coming from'.[4] So when I was laughing and shouting like that, I saw very well that Opeta was angry! It was as if he was ashamed because of those ways of ours. And especially me because [I] laughed all the time. [...]

14. So now we had prepared and were about to go to New Zealand. Another thing that was very problematic for me was that we went to try

shoes in the shops in Apia. I was so angry when we were trying those shoes, because [when] I walked in the shoes I felt, 'Hey, the shoes are so heavy!' But I still did it because … What was said was that [we] would go like that in the planes to New Zealand, go in shoes, but now I thought, 'now why does one wear shoes? What are shoes for? And so tiring!' Well, but [I] still did it, because [I] obeyed what those people did who went to New Zealand, travelled to these places. These islands, New Zealand.

15. Well, we came in May [...] 1964. And I had no idea at that time New Zealand was so cold. We came to Auckland, we came all the way down to Wellington, we arrived in the evening, and we stood outside the airport. [When we] spoke to each other there came smoke out from the lips, and we felt like laughing, 'Wow! Now why are [our] mouths smoky?'

16. [When] we got there, there were Tokelauans meeting us. [We] immediately looked at the Tokelauans, but the mind, at that moment the mind was far away, eh! [I] thought, 'Hey! Now why have I come to New Zealand? If only I had known that it was something like this. It is cold, [I] walk in shoes, when [I] walk there are clothes that are heavy. [...] Why have I come? If only I had stayed in Tokelau, the Tokelauan things are better. Going to the sea, learning to make mats. Women's things. Playing cricket.' Those were the thoughts that came. [...]

17. [M]y eyes were looking at how high the shops were, and the place were we were, as I saw the different faces, [...] and I was astonished, 'Hey! The *papalagi* don't know us!' I had thought it was just like Tokelau, people know every person. Now I thought, 'Hey! The *papalagi* just walk like that [and] don't speak at all to us standing here!' [...] My eyes were again running everywhere, how I was missing the things, when I was looking. [...] So this is New Zealand? How high the houses were, and the cars were never quiet, the cars were just trafficking around. And in my view, so many *papalagi*, white people, eh? [I] saw almost nobody with my colour … Since it was just so new, 'Hey! Is New Zealand really all *papalagi* people!'

18. That was one of my feelings, the new things that I had come to. [...] Well, so now we went to stay with the family where we were staying. I saw well how that couple were trying to let us become used to New Zealand matters. And I looked at the group that had come to New Zealand before us. It looked like they had understood living in … going to work, they were able to go outside. It looked like they had mastered that behaviour.

19. But as for me, one morning I went to sit behind the home where I was staying, and I looked at the mountains. No wish to stay in New Zealand was coming in on me at that moment. I wanted to go all the way to Tokelau! Now I thought, 'Hey! If only I had known something like this, I wouldn't have come to New Zealand.' As I was looking, there were many thoughts coming. Missing the relatives, the food, about the climate I had come to, no Tokelauan houses … 'Hey, it's a *papalagi* house I live in!' Everything [I] had come to was just new, sleeping at night in blankets, [you] seem to go inside [them], but the sheets just feel cold. How I didn't want to live in New Zealand at that moment. [I] looked at the mountains, the tears were flowing, I wanted to go all the way to Tokelau. But on the other hand [I] realised that nothing could be done because [I] had arrived in New Zealand, [I] saw it. [I] thought deeply, imagined Tokelau being close by, [I] would probably have gone right to Tokelau at that very moment. But [I] saw that it wasn't an easy thing [to do].

20. [...] And then we got jobs, a sewing factory, that was the factory where we started working. [...] That was another difficulty which made me not

want to live in New Zealand, waking up in the morning [and] going to work. [When I] woke up in the morning, it was cold, [I] didn't want to sit up in bed, [I] just wanted to sleep, [I] still prepared [and] went off [and] chased time. I was told it started at eight, oh! [I] woke up at around half past six. [When] I was walking on the street [I] just cried with anger! Why had I come to New Zealand!

21. So we walked, we went to chase the time of the bus, so that we caught it, and [you might think] the bus was waiting outside the house, [but] no. The bus stop was rather far away, and [I] couldn't walk straight either on the street that I walked to it, but in zigzag. It went down like that, up like that on the street where [I] went to catch the bus. Those things where why [it] came [to me] 'Oh! No wish to live in New Zealand!' And so packed inside the bus! When I got there [and] there were many people, it was as if [I] got ashamed without reason because it was so packed inside the bus. But [I] still did it, it seems that in my thoughts I forced myself at that moment to get where I was going, because I faintly realised that that was the necessary thing to do. I had thought in Tokelau that [people] didn't go to … money, I had thought, is received for free! But [when] I came to New Zealand, 'Hey! Only when a person works, only then does [s/he] get money. One works and is paid. That's where [one] gets money.'

22. And another thing, [when] I arrived at the factory, I was looking forward … something I liked about going to the factory was the English. For I knew there that I very much wanted to speak English, and I wanted to know how to speak English. It seems I had realised that there, from the English, I would know what the person who was teaching me my work was saying, [she] wasn't speaking Tokelauan to me, but English. And it seems that, for me, it was the only thing I liked about the job … I didn't want to go to work. Catching the bus, the cold, but I wanted to go to the factory, so that someone would speak English to me, so that I could know what I was doing.

In the first paragraphs, the narrator describes the circumstances leading up to her going to New Zealand, and tells of her expectations of what life over there would be like. These expectations might be summed up in her telling of how she thought that in New Zealand 'everything is obtained easily', that there is only office work, and by implication, no heavy manual labour. She relates how she assumed that she 'would become like a *papalagi*' and that this included knowledge of how to speak English fluently. She doesn't present herself as having harboured any misgivings as to the ease with which this could be achieved, and in fact much of the narrative's liveliness and humour comes about precisely as a result of her skilful rendering of the great discrepancies between her expectations and her actual experiences abroad.

In paragraph 4, there are two different topics to note. First, the training they were given in European eating practices, which many first-time travellers abroad from Tokelau have been through. Second, she describes how she knew that she was *ma* (usually translated as 'shame' or 'shyness'), to face (*fakafeagai*) the priest, as she was laughing all the time. In other words, she says that she knew that she was ashamed because she was laughing, not the other way around, and moreover, that this shyness had to do with having to 'face' the priest. This is interesting in that it speaks of a confrontation with a foreign etiquette which demands a different bodily hexis, and which attaches a different significance to the act of 'facing somebody'. Further on in the narrative, she gives more examples of how, upon her arrival in Samoa and in New Zealand she has to adopt another bodily hexis, as her habitual ways of greeting people (phatic talk), of sitting (on the floor), and so on are clearly not acceptable in the new contexts she encounters.[5]

Based on observations of similar training sessions, I would compare the etiquette the priest attempted to inculcate here to the bodily hexis encouraged by the New Zealand-oriented education system. As in many schools throughout the world, the Tokelau pupils use chairs and tables, they sit individually separated, and they are encouraged to ask and answer questions, again individually. Evaluations are made on the basis of individual, not group performance, and last but not least, the pupils have to speak up clearly, preferably meeting the eyes of the teacher while responding – i.e., facing the authority figure directly.[6]

In contrast, in Tokelau, as in many other Pacific Island societies, such behaviour would be considered completely unacceptable. In everyday situations characterised by authority differences, the person who is lowest on the scale of hierarchy would lower his or her gaze, lower his or her voice, sit in a lower (physically or by classification) position, often bowing his or her head, and the prerogative of command, of direct gaze and of speech, belongs solely to the highest-ranking person.[7] To 'face one another' and to answer another's gaze either implies equality or assumes authority and, outside of such relations of command and responsibility, is fitting in situations where similar groups, such as the sides, meet and compete. Such behaviour is absolutely not suitable or acceptable, however, in situations where 'brother:sister etiquette' is dominant, as in the phatic-talk exchanges when meeting someone 'on the path'.

Apart from relations where a person in authority 'faces the people',[8] and is faced by them 'bowing to this authority', the expression 'to face one another' would most commonly signify a sexual relationship. In Tokelau, this could be legitimately expressed by individual persons only if married to one another, or tempered, controlled and sanctioned by being within the confines of a group, as in dance contests. The shyness she speaks of expresses the restraint which is adopted in hierarchical relationships, and which is upheld as the ideal of cross-sex relationships outside of marriage. Observed breeches in the etiquette informing these relationships are experienced as 'shame' (*ma*). The point that something (intimate) is experienced as shameful when seen, i.e., when it is made public, is clearly illustrated in the play *Mafine*, in the scene where Tima meets up with her teacher friend on the beach, and he tells her that he has heard that she is getting married. She responds by describing how hurt she is by the fact that her family has 'ganged up against her *and made it public'*. At the time the narrator speaks of, that is the early Sixties, the school and the Church were the main, perhaps only, institutions with markedly different seating arrangements and speech patterns from the etiquette dominating every-day life, and only in those contexts would one, individually, be expected to comply with other standards of behaviour (see also Besnier 1991). These situations were highly structured and regulated, however, and the behavioural expectations were strictly limited to those institutions. The codes of behaviour favoured in those contexts can even be said to have been (and still are, but not to the same extent) actively discouraged and disapproved of in almost all other contexts in everyday life (Hoëm 1995, Sallen 1983).

The training given by the priest was intended as a guideline for every-day life however, and, as such, it and similar instructions communicated, in a fundamental way, a message that both runs counter to Tokelau expec-tations and is experienced as highly embarrassing. So what does one do when caught in this uncomfortable double bind? One obvious way out of the dilemma is to do as the narrator does, to stay true to another largely unspoken principle that informs proper behaviour in Tokelau. Do not confront it, do not address the pain or discomfort directly, but make it go away by turning it into something funny, something sweet and accept-able, something *malie* – that is, do as she does, and laugh.

She then moves on to describe how the group that was to leave was taken to a meeting of the Council of Elders, where they were 'spoken to' (*tautalagia*) and told how they were 'going to go' if they came somewhere (*pe ka omai vehea, ke fai fakalelei matou amioga*) to ensure that they would behave in such a way that they would be called good (*lelei*) and that Tokelau would be well spoken of. To be 'spoken to', 'instructed' or 'admonished' by the Council of Elders, is in most people's mind a fright-ful experience which is best avoided. In Tokelau this only happens if one is summoned for having broken a village law and is to be punished, or if, as in this case, one is to be told something that is of grave importance (Hoëm 1995). The formulation used, i.e., 'how we were going to go', is sig-nificant, as it points to an association between morally proper behaviour and 'ways of going', both in the sense of a specific bodily hexis, i.e., a par-ticular balance between freedom and restraint of movement, and of life-trajectories in general. These points will be further elaborated in Chapter five.

The first indication of a transition in her story comes in paragraph 6, where a momentary realisation of actually having left her parents and rel-atives behind is dulled by her seasickness and the fact that she still has the company of her brother. In other words, she anticipates a state, never before experienced, of being on her own, which hasn't quite happened yet. In the next paragraph we get her first impressions of a place other than the one she grew up in. No features of landscape are mentioned; it seems as if the 'dogs'[9] that subsequently turned out to be cars are chosen to stand for the whole experience in a metonymic fashion.[10] This narrative twist certainly serves to convey the feeling of strangeness that unfamiliarity engenders.

In paragraph 8, I would like to draw attention to a phrasing in the last sentence, where, in her description of her first experience of going somewhere she hasn't been before, the narrator chooses to reflect on the name of the place, when she says: 'As for me I had heard that name before, Savalalo, but I didn't know at all where Savalalo was or what Savalalo was to me'. (*E ... ko he ... ia te au, e ko lag... na ko lagona lava te igoa muamua ko Havalalo kae he ko il ... e he ko iloa lele, pe ... pe ko fea ia Havalalo pe he a t ... pe he a ia Havalalo ite au.*) I shall return to the practice of naming, and to the relationship between places and names, in the final Chapter.

In paragraph 10, there are two topics I would like to draw attention to. The first is her observations about the difference between the scale of architecture in Samoa and Tokelau, in her mention of the stairs and the height of the buildings. (At the time, the only large, elevated building in Nukunonu was the Church.) The other is her statement that 'it was like my mind wasn't with me', and her explanation of this as a result of her not knowing the people. Again (cf., paragraph 4) she reacts by laughing, but this time she doesn't seem to know why.

The liminality of this stage of the experience is evident in her description of losing her bearings. She doesn't understand, 'the mind is going around like ... it was gone', and she tries to orient herself, expressed in her asking 'where am I', 'why am I here', and 'is this the place called Samoa'. She concludes laconically: 'It was like the mind was astray'. In addition to the sense of liminality this conveys, I would also like to draw attention to the phrasing, such as in the following: 'the mind is going around', 'it was gone', 'it was away' (*[T]e he ko haofia ko toku mafafau e ... e tamilo lele, e ve ... e a nei? E ve e ... ve e galo. Ve e fakatamilomilo. E! Ko au kua i fea? E! He a ko kua pa mai ai au ki Hamoa? E... Pe ko te la te mea e igoa ko Hamoa? E ve e he te mafaufau.*)

This curiously impersonal way of referring to what in Western models of folk-psychology would be a matter of 'personal ownership', is common. It is noted by E. Ochs and Duranti in their Samoan material (e.g., Duranti, 1988, and Duranti and Ochs 1986, 1990) and it is paralleled in Levy's discussion of Tahitian psychological makeup. The way she describes her behaviour in paragraph 12 is another example of the same tendency to downplay agency.

In paragraph 11, the feeling of liminality is further strengthened, in the more definite (as compared to paragraph 6) realisation that the faces of relatives and parents are not there, are not present. As she opens the *ato* or bags, to present the gifts to those who have come to welcome them, Tokelau 'vapours away', she says. At this precise moment she feels something unusual. It is as if she is 'about to start longing for Tokelau', as she puts it. It is as if she recalls how this unfamiliar feeling of having to long for people who are elsewhere demanded an interpretation as well as an expression (which it gets in the last part of this passage, as she cries at night and regrets her decision to leave Tokelau).

The following paragraphs describe some incidents and experiences during her first encounters with the capital of Western Samoa, Apia. Paragraph 12 speaks in a condensed way of her responses to sensory overload. She stops and stares, and only walks away when her 'eyes are satisfied', when she has absorbed the fact of what she is contemplating. In her own words, when she has understood. Being made aware that it is considered rude and unsophisticated to stare like that,[11] she learns to be scared of doing so, but still she can't help herself. 'It wasn't an [intended] action, for the time just passed', she explains. The skill of observing other people's characteristics, their way of walking, their looks and so on, and of memorising these observations for future use, a practice that is so highly developed in Tokelau, is obviously something of an embarrassment in this new environment, and indeed she is told to behave '… as if I had understood'.

To ask everybody one meets where he or she is coming from, where s/he is going, what s/he is going to do there, and eventually to tell them to come back again, or variants of this, is part of everyday communicative practice in Tokelau. These phatic-talk exchanges, which are such a prominent part of everyday village life (a matter which is stressed in the second narrative. See also Hoëm 1993) are clearly not common currency in Samoa. Again she is being shamed, and again she makes references to laughing 'all the time' (*kata ho*).

Paragraphs 14 and 15 contain two common experiences which are emblematic of 'the New Zealand experience', namely having to wear shoes and the coldness of the weather. She doesn't like it but obeys, because even if she doesn't understand why one has to wear shoes, if that is what one has to do to go to New Zealand, so be it. Note how she, by classifying New Zealand as 'islands', manages to place New Zealand on an equal level with Samoa and ultimately with Tokelau, stressing the one factor they *do* have in common in the face of all the differences she increasingly experiences between them.

In paragraph 16, she arrives in Wellington and is met by a group of Tokelauans. She describes how she immediately turns to them, but that again 'the mind was far away'. As she questioned coming to Samoa, she questions coming to New Zealand, and this time the questioning is accompanied by a dawning realisation of what it will be like to be there, to daily experience a harsher climate, new ways of dressing and behaving, strange faces and a foreign language. This time, however, she is not prompted to reflect on relatives' faces, but on what she calls the 'Tokelauan things' (*na mea faka Tokelau*), i.e., in her account 'going to the sea, learning how to weave, the women's activities, playing cricket'. Again, as I commented above, the phrasing downplays agency: 'It was like ... these were the thoughts that came' (*E ve kua ... na mafafauga iena kua hau*).

The remaining paragraphs are quoted only to give a few samples of her descriptions of life in New Zealand, as this is not the focus of my discussion here. I have included some extracts, however, as they demonstrate her gradual integration into a new environment after the experience of temporal suspension. She again speaks of the height of the buildings compared to those in Tokelau and of the noise and busy-ness of city life. Her main observation is that, to her astonishment, people don't know them (i.e., the group of Tokelauans she came to New Zealand with). This is, of course, something that she had observed in Samoa, too (cf., paragraphs 10–13); what is different here seems to be how the *papalagi* in the particular situation she describes (that of a TV interview) seem to find it natural to go about their business without taking any notice of them, without even addressing them. She also describes how she notices that there were mainly *papalagi* people in New Zealand: '[I] saw almost nobody with my colour'.

In paragraph 18, it is important to note the implicit distinction she makes between 'inside' (*loto*) and 'outside' (*fafo*), when she points out that those who had 'understood living in [New Zealand]' were also 'able to go outside'. This distinction is highly relevant as a principle of orientation regulating village life in Tokelau, of which we shall learn more in the final chapters.

The last parts of her narrative speak of a gradual transition to life in this unusual environment, with mountains and cold weather, as in her resigned comments towards the end. Paragraphs 20 and 21 describe her traversing unknown territory, and getting used to 'going by time', as she puts it elsewhere. Again (in paragraph 21) she describes her feelings as 'coming to her', finding it very difficult to accept the hard facts of the working-class life she previously didn't know existed, but forcing herself to go through with it, as it dawns on her that this is probably necessary. Based on this she revises her notions of New Zealand as a place where one receives money 'for free' as she phrases it. Finally, in paragraph 22 we leave her as she persists in her project of finding someone to speak English with 'so that I could know what I was doing'. I might add that her efforts were rewarded in this respect, but that her concerns now have shifted to how to amend the loss of competence in Tokelauan in the second-generation Tokelauans growing up in New Zealand.

Moving Between Social Spaces

The contrast between an 'easy life', as represented by her image of white-collar jobs in New Zealand, and a 'hard life', as represented by the manual labour in Tokelau, is common (Hoëm 1994). Since the first contacts between the various groups of people occupying the South Pacific region and the 'sky bursters' (or *papalagi*) depicted in the first sequence of the play *Tagi*, a lot of things have happened. The accounts we have of the first encounters speak strongly of mutual incomprehension, and a profound ambivalence on both sides. The explorers saw the natives as god-like creatures inhabiting a paradisical state known only to (European) man before the Fall, but also described them as 'savages', as bearers of culture without culture (Hoëm 1996). The natives were reported by some to have seen their visitors as 'white gods', but since these gods behaved in 'uncultured' and asocial ways, their lofty status became at best suspicious. This profound ambivalence, albeit expressed in a different fashion, figures in the intercultural relationships of today as strongly as ever.[12]

In Tokelau, as in most other areas of the region, a profound shift in the nature of the contact with the so-called 'modern' world took place in the early sixties. As Western Samoa gained independence in 1962, with many other nations following suit, this development was paradoxically connected with a rapid increase in the scale and intensity of the integration into world wide (and region-wide) networks of both economical, technological and social importance. The anthropologist Epeli Hau'ofa, discussing the situation in the South Pacific today,[13] points to the emergence of a 'global' or rather, a pan-Pacific network, which integrates people on a much larger scale than only a few decades ago. On the other hand, the people of the Pacific region have always travelled. They are world famous for their navigatory skills, and it is widely accepted that to view pre-contact society as consisting of largely sedentary, isolated, self-contained units is highly misleading (E. Hviding 1994). Even so, the speed with which travel is carried out today, the pace of life, is very different from the world which we all inhabited, as it were, only yesterday.

To go abroad, for instance from Tokelau or Samoa to New Zealand, means coming to a country with another language, and a very different culture – a highly literate one – with all the difficulties this entails. Most, if not all, of the migrants will live in a native community within the 'modern mainstream culture' of their host country, and – if the host country is New Zealand – in a country where the indigenous people occupy a position which has been likened to internal colonialism. These difficulties are clearly not part of the expectations of the woman telling the story of her first journey abroad. Her assumptions of instant assimilation, culturally as well as linguistically, hark back to a time with a different political discourse, a time when the experience of racial discrimination and socio-cultural differences were not common awareness in Tokelau.[14]

Leaving home means increased opportunities for wage labour, for tasting the supposed freedoms of modern life and so on. With an income in New Zealand, it is possible to send money back home, often to support more people than if one stays on in Tokelau. By 'taking care of relationships', as it is called, the migrant can earn the respect and gratitude of his or her extended family in a way that might be difficult for another family member staying at home to match. In other words, there is a lot to be gained, both outside of and *within* the sphere of the close network of the kin group, by going overseas. The other side of the coin, so to speak, is that the 'islanders', as the people from the island territories or independent nations of the Pacific are referred to in New Zealand, in most cases occupy the very lowest rungs of the job hierarchy. Their level of unemployment is also quite high at present, and many people depend on social security for a living.[15] The historian Malama Meleisea points to the paradox of how urban, middle-class Samoans living in the capital of Western Samoa, Apia, look up to and frequently envy those who have gone 'overseas', despite the fact that they often occupy the lower working-class rungs in the host country (Meleisea 1987). There is, as I have mentioned, an inherent ambivalence in the picture of 'modern' society as seen from home. On the one hand, *papalagi* are notoriously uncultured, immoral and godless. On the other hand, they are rich in material goods and need not engage in menial labour, and, after all, they were the 'bringers of the light of the gospel' to the 'heathens living in darkness'. The *papalagi* are weak and effeminate vis-à-vis the strong Tokelauans, but they lead what is called an 'easy life', which may for some look seductively nice and clean (Shore 1982). We find a similar image or stereotype reflected in the first paragraphs of the first narrative.

Some individuals attempt to resolve the dilemma of these discrepant scales of evaluation by making a definite crossover, by being assimilated, often by marriage, into the white, *papalagi* life-world. These people are condemned and castigated by the native community as *fia papalagi*, wanting to be *papalagi*, and they often experience a highly stressful life-career, scoring higher on tests of lifestyle diseases, such as hypertension, than the people who choose to live within the community (Huntsman, 1975: 191). Given the high value placed on a communal lifestyle, it is not strange that the stakes against these ties and against the choice of a more socially isolated, individualistically oriented way of life are very high. Such a break is fraught with emotional difficulties and anxieties.

One factor which complicates the smooth transition between home and host country is that many young people do not enter into an already established network when they leave home. This is true in particular of the scholarship students and those going for further university training abroad.[16] They go to boarding schools or to stay with *papalagi* host families, etc., and many of these individuals have the very unusual experience, for any person coming from a close-knit Pacific community, of being totally alone, i.e., without any familiar faces around. Significantly, this experience is what most debut poems accepted in scholarship magazines, etc., are about. Again, we find this experience of being without familiar faces reflected in the first story of leaving Tokelau.

For this reason, among others, schooling is seen as perhaps the most important factor when it comes to changing people's outlook on life in general. It is a high priority task for many Pacific communities to create their own educational institutions to counteract this effect. The establishment of a University of the South Pacific (the USP) can be seen as an example of the many attempts in this direction. People from Samoa and Tokelau, for example, in the main consider it better to send their students to such an institution, preferably as close as possible to the home country, than to risk 'that their children turn into *papalagi*' in an attempt to get a degree. The development of the concept of 'a pan-Pacific way of life'(Williksen–Bakker 1994) and the frequently voiced wish to 'keep our own culture', are answers to the pressures from a 'modern', white, *papalagi* way of life.

What factors, then, are considered to be the main threats to the 'Pacific Way of Life?' A central problem is linked to the modern educational system, which is seen as a threat to local communicative practices. A frequently voiced complaint is that schooling causes children to 'behave out of their station', that they begin to 'say things' and to 'ask questions'. Indigenous ideals of communication link verbal activity closely to the principle of seniority, in a pattern where the elder commands and the younger complies, as we have seen illustrated in this narrative, and as I and others have described elsewhere (Sallen 1983; Huntsman 1980; Hoëm 1995).

Finally, I wish to draw attention to the way in which the experiences related in the last narrative may be interpreted in the light of the differences between what is often called multiplex and uniplex relationships (Gluckman 1955; B. Kapferer 1969; T. Hylland Eriksen 1993). The storyteller describes how she, in Tokelau, knows everybody, and moreover, how everybody's presence is constantly recognised. She tells of how the Elders as a group have a collective responsibility for instilling in her the purpose of her going abroad, and how she is supposed to behave on her journey. She has to 'face' the priest who instructs them in the mysteries of European table manners, and she laughs all the time, *because* she is ashamed or shy. In Samoa and in New Zealand, on the other hand, there are many people with whom she has to interact, even though they don't know each other and don't seem to acknowledge her presence. She is told to adjust her behaviour, acting 'as if I understood'. In the narrative of leaving, we are told of the experience of having to 'unlearn', as it were, one sense of orientation, and of the process of adjusting to another one.

How the Drama Tagi ('Lament') Reflects the Narrative of Leaving

Whereas the first drama, *Tagi*, directly reflects the migration experience as described in the first narrative (in the third part of the play), in its depiction of leaving the atolls and attempting to come to terms with life in New Zealand, the second drama, *Mafine* ('Woman'), is about the return to Tokelau. If we turn to the enactment of the migration experience in the first play, *Tagi*, we find a similar structural division as in the first narrative: (1) the leaving of family, relatives and Tokelau; (2) accounts of the journey to New Zealand; and (3) life in New Zealand. The farewell scene (scene 2 in part 3) depicts a public leave-taking on the beach before the migrants are to enter the boats which will take them away. Those who are to leave say good-bye to those who will stay behind. Most of them cry, and all of this takes place to the accompaniment of songs, the words of which can be summed up in the lines: *Aue te Faigata. Ko te Mavaega* (Alas, how difficult. The farewell).

The next scene, which contains the individual accounts of the journey to New Zealand, is kept in a minimalistic style. Again, and as I referred to in my discussion of the first narrative, the accounts of the experience select one or two elements to 'stand for' the whole transition. The first actor recalls going in a boat all the way to Auckland, and seeing the lights in the harbour upon arriving there. The second account fixes on the coldness of New Zealand, and asks 'where is this that I have arrived at? A new life. For what?' She answers her questions by referring to the decision that her family made on her behalf, i.e., that she is to leave Tokelau to get a job and donate money to support them. She tells of being excited by the thought of coming to see a 'different life', and wonders how her dreams can be reconciled with those of her family.

The third actor states that he didn't want to go, but that he had to because his family decided (*kua fakatonu*) that he should go and work so that he could support the family financially. He adds that he found that he was the oldest child in his class, and that it was very difficult to speak English. The other children in his class laughed at him because of this. The next actor is happy with her school years, because she made a lot of friends from other Pacific islands. She mentions how one boy from Tonga was 'like a boy from Tokelau'.

The fifth actor tells of her realisation of the differences between life in Tokelau and in New Zealand. Whereas the people in New Zealand are good (she says), if she doesn't work she cannot live there. It is not like in Tokelau, where there are lots of fish and coconuts which don't have to be bought. The third actor enters again, reflecting on the pace of life, and the unfamiliar character of the environment: 'The sunset is so slow, [and] the people [are] here, [go] there, [go] to there, to there'. 'Where are they going?' he asks. The first actor adds, 'alas for Tokelau. [In] Tokelau, love goes to the family, the people are compassionate, aren't they? But here, you are only looking after yourself'. The second actor thinks back to life in Tokelau and wonders what her family members are doing. She repeats that it is cold, and asks herself whether the life here (in New Zealand) is a difficult or a happy one. She is still looking for the answer, she says. The last actor says that it is painful for her: on the one hand there are many things that are good in New Zealand, but on the other hand it is better for her to live in Tokelau. She ends by sending her love to her parents over there.

I would like to draw attention to the contrasts that are made between a life in Tokelau which is ruled by family concerns, by sharing and by *alofa* (that is, 'love' in the sense of compassionate behaviour), and the life in New Zealand where 'money and time rules', and where everyone has to 'look out for him- or herself'. The tensions and difficulties inherent in the situation of belonging to both worlds are stressed openly and not in a humorous way, and this serves to distance this play from other ordinary performances. Some of the actors speak of their family's *fakatonu*, that is, the taking a collective decision at a meeting of the extended family that their child should go abroad, and refer to their role in supporting their family financially. In these cases, the individuals have little say in the matter; the family council rules, and the person picked obeys (*uhitaki*).

Finally, the contrast drawn in the first narrative between an 'easy life' (in New Zealand) and a 'hard life' (in the atolls) seems to have become reversed in the play. Tokelau is here represented as a land of leisure where one can obtain food for free, whereas in New Zealand 'if you don't work you cannot live there'. This, in fact, reflects images held in Tokelau and in New Zealand respectively, and whereas these conceptions may allow some a 'happy life' in both places, for others they may serve as a perpetual source of disappointment and dissatisfaction, as both places fail to live up to the paradisical visions entertained of the other place. It is important to note here how the atoll environment provides a model informing life in New Zealand. See also Pacific Studies (2002), for a similar observation of the relationship between what they there call 'atoll' as a model for community life in 'urban' settings.

In the next scene in *Tagi*, some of the older actors enact their first experiences in a foreign country, i.e., they actually depict what happened to them. This is done in the form of skits (*faleaitu*) or funny stories (*faitala*). In my opinion, it is significant that this form is chosen, and this observation is underlined by the fact that this is the only scene which uses this form.[17] This scene (i.e., the party scene) is a beautiful illustration of the 'one-upmanship' characteristic of relationships of equality, and the joking, taunting, competitive, but usually friendly spirit which is dominant on such partying occasions (Hooper and Huntsman, 1975).

To turn embarrassing episodes, which when experienced may have been quite traumatic or unsettling, into the subject of 'funny stories' is a skill in which many are adept. In *Tagi*, in the party scene, the first story, which is turned into a skit, is told and instructed (as part of the play) by one of the men. The skit (story) is about a man from the same age-group in Tokelau, *tupulaga*, as himself, and with whom the instructor of the skit went to school in New Zealand (i.e., the 'swimming competition story'). The next story however, is a 'challenge' from one of the other men present, who proceeds to tell a story about the instructor of the first skit (i.e., the 'diving story'). In this part of the play (and also in the opening scene), the actors use their real names,[18] and as I mentioned above, the stories they refer to are stories that did indeed happen to them.

The person who made this challenge is then again challenged by one of the women, who this time does not make a skit, but tells a story (*faitala*) of how this man, when he had first arrived in New Zealand as a child and stayed at their home, had fallen off the bed during the night and made such a big noise that everybody woke up as he rolled across the floor, because he had never slept on a bed before. This is typical of this genre of stories about 'first time abroad', to make fun of the lack of familiarity with the new environment.

To summarise the main points I have extracted from the first narrative: a prominent trait, and a key to my interpretation of her story is the humorous rendering the narrator gives of her experiences of conflicts, confusion and discontinuity. The tendency to smooth over difficulties by joking, to keep a smiling face, seems to prevail in spite of the tears she admits to having shed in the process of transition.[19] The spatial orientations that I wish to highlight, and that become activated by the experience of displacement, are expressed in terms of 'face' (see paragraph 4) and the breech of proper ways of 'facing' (*fakafeagai*), i.e., in her having to 'face directly' within the context of a hierarchical, and hence vertical, relationship are described in terms of 'shame' (*ma*), and in terms of her response in such situations, i.e., by laughing. She discusses her behaviour generally as 'ways of going', and she provides many illustrations of how difficult it is 'to go properly' in unfamiliar terrain, where people don't even greet her as they should (e.g., paragraphs 5, 12, 13 and 17). Finally, she discusses 'ways of going' in terms of an implicit spatial distinction between 'inside' and (explicitly mentioned) 'outside' (paragraph 18).

The Return

The experience of going overseas also has another aspect, which first appears on the return to Tokelau. As A. Wendt has vividly described in *Sons for a Return Home*, his novel set within the context of Samoa, the transition to village life is often hard and fraught with practical and emotional difficulties. 'Do you know this fellow', a Tokelau man asked about another in jest. 'He has been abroad to have his brain drained'. This was said in a discussion among TPS employees about a conference on the problem of 'brain-drain' in the Pacific, but it points to a real difficulty experienced by those returning home – that of being totally inept at the survival skills, such as fishing techniques, climbing coconut trees, weaving, and so on, that people still depend on in Tokelau, even if not to the same extent as before.[20] Another aspect of this problem is the loss of able-bodied men and skilled persons to New Zealand. As one middle-aged woman living in Tokelau put it:

> I don't like to say this, but, you know, all our best have gone to New Zealand. In my family for example, it is really difficult for me to keep my temper with our *matai*, our family head. He is so stupid. And he is the one to speak our case in the *fono a toeaina*, the Council of Elders! But this is the case in so many of the families over here. The knowledgeable ones have left, and we are stuck with the ones who didn't make it. And so we suffer. [And she added with a sigh] I really hope that some of the group that went overseas to get an education will come back and put some time into Tokelau.

Sallen, in her analysis of the experience of Tokelau scholarship students in New Zealand, quotes the following statement made by one of them, describing the experience of going overseas (see also Hoëm 1994).

> It is a journey, like the first really alone sail across the lagoon ... You have seen others going ... you are exited ... You [drag] the canoe down ... The scraping is like a apprehension, a just beginning apprehension, a shivering ... Then you are away, away from [the village] ... Then you are out, out into that indigo. Then it is not what you thought ... The wind is all the which ways ... The way is not straight ... You try to remember all the things they have said ... You try to do them. It is confusion ... You try a different perching, a different sail pull ... You are frightened. The *vaka* [canoe] goes around ... like it is a hurricane. But it is not a hurricane of the weather. It is inside of you ... Then it is a feeling of the *vaka* ... You stop remembering all the things they have said ... You FEEL what you must do now ... [The islet] does not seem so far ... slowly it is closer ... It is good now. You can choose a landing ... you can choose a place. Then you can stay. Or you can return. Both are possible. Both are comfortable. You can choose ... It is like that, like the learning on the lagoon ... You may not use the learning a lot ... to make the journey often ... Of course it is a different journey then because you have the experience, you have the learning to use. (Sallen 1983: 89)

On the basis of this and similar statements, Sallen proposes that the scholarship experience may be seen as a 'sequence of phases' (Sallen 1983: 89). She labels them 'the launching', 'the indigo', and 'the landing', respectively. As I believe that the process of 'crossing the lagoon' can be used as a metaphor for the process of going overseas generally, we shall now look at how Tokelauans, in Sallen's description, envision a successful crossing. It is apparent in the above statement that a happy outcome involves the achievement of the freedom to *choose*. In the concrete example of crossing the lagoon, to choose to stay on the outer islets is no permanent alternative. No one is ordinarily allowed to settle on other islets than the village islet, and so the freedom of choice is limited. When going overseas, in contrast, the option of permanently staying in New Zealand is a real one. The ideal of an ultimate 'successful state' for most scholarship students thus, according to what Sallen's interviewees express, consists in becoming a 'trans-cultural person'. Another of her interviewees puts it this way:

> When you do not feel trapped between them [Tokelau and New Zealand] when they are both a part of you ... that is the success space. Then you are a trans-cultural person, that is a good place to be. You may decide to live in one place because you marry, or because your parents are old ... but you know inside of yourself that it will be all right ... But most students are still on the way to being that person ... it is a long way ... a lot of years ... . (Sallen 1983: 132)

Many migrants are a long way from attaining this ideal state of occupying such a trans-cultural space. The process of moving back and forth between discrepant social spaces such as the home, *papalagi*-influenced institutions (e.g., school and church) and the world of the host country, is to a greater or lesser extent a part of everyday life for all Pacific Islanders. (Hoëm 1994). The possibility of having a choice in these matters, however, the experience of not feeling trapped in one place, neither in the village nor in New Zealand, is a not-as-yet obtained goal for many, if not all, Tokelauans.

The following is a narrative presented by a Tokelau-born woman who moved to New Zealand as a child, grew up in New Zealand, and was ordered by her family to move to Tokelau as an adult. In other parts of her narrative, not presented here for the sake of maintaining her privacy, she expresses some bitterness, pain and frustration, much in the same fashion as 'Tima' does in the play *Mafine*, over having had so little say in important decisions made by her family on her behalf.[21]

Narrative Two: Returning

1. I was born 1966 in Nukunonu, Tokelau, and in 1969 we migrated to New Zealand. And I was brought up in New Zealand and my first time back to Nukunonu was in 1989, and after twenty years in New Zealand and coming back to Tokelau in 1989 it is not what I expected, and after about the first week here I really wanted to go back, and from then and even up until now I don't feel, I don't know; I don't feel I belong here I suppose. I can't really explain it, but I sort of feel like an outcast. Even the people here to me are different from ... Oh, I don't know how to explain it. They are different any-

way. I suppose it is because, *he ilo*, [(I) don't know] probably because it is only a small community. Like I say, the people are different. *Vehea nei*? [How then?] I mix with the people but I don't... how would you put it? I feel out of place. They are different. They are different from the people I grew up with, *i Niu Hila* [in New Zealand].

2. Coming back I was sort of expecting, like, white sand all over the place, like. And the houses. When we got here my auntie took me to our place and my first question was, we stood outside this house, *ko te tatou fale tenei* [is this our house]? And she goes, *Io* [Yes]! And in my heart I was, within myself I thought oh my God! I just stood there, to me it looked like an old shack sort of thing to me, *ke iloa* [(you) know]? *E kino* [it is bad], it is you know, coming from the outside, it is not what I am used to. And then when I walked inside I thought oh my goodness, I didn't expect the open housing, *ke iloa* [(you) know]. I didn't know what to expect, coming here. Because I had only just heard stories, and, Tokelau people who had been here, and who had gone back to New Zealand and they said, oh you know you should go back to Tokelau, it is really nice.

3. And then I said to her, because I was really starving because I was really seasick on the boat, this was the first day when we came here, can I have a bath, and she says yeah, and I say where's the bathroom, and she goes, just outside, and I said where! I looked at the door, and she goes, oh, it is just there, outside the door, there is no bathrooms here, this isn't New Zealand, it is just the water tank. And I said, isn't there anywhere I can hide? And she says, no, you just go and sit out there and ... And I thought oh my God, and I felt really embarrassed. So I went outside, and I got the bucket, put it under the tap, let the water on, and I was sort of standing there with my *lavalava* [wrap-around cloth], and I looked around to see if anybody was looking. That's something I really miss is privacy, *ke iloa* [(you) know], it is the open housing. And also, because, being married and living with a lot of other people in the house. It is, it is, I've gotten used to it now, but it is still, I really miss my privacy.

4. Where we are staying now, my husband and I are sleeping in the umu [cooking-house]. Because, *ko na tino i kinei* [the people over here] they don't really show their true emotions, even the married couples *ni* [politeness particle, equiv. in this context to 'you know']. You don't really see them walking around together very often, or even at all in some cases, just letting people know, for people to see that they are married, and that they love each other. My husband and I, when we go somewhere together, we can hold hands. We don't care about the people, but I know that there are reactions, because sometimes I hear, *kila, kila, kila...* [look, look, look...].

5. I was used to all things being clean, and when I walked into the house, it wasn't my impression of a home. Anyway, it took me blimmin ages to get used to living in a house like the one that we were living in. Cause everything, it just looked like one great big mess. And if it is one thing that I hate, it is a bloody mess. I just can't stand looking at things just lying around, *ke iloa* [(you) know]? In New Zealand they've got wardrobes, they've got drawers, they've got cupboards and things to put everything in. Here they have suitcases and boxes, like glory boxes and that sort of thing and ... it was just, it was really hard for me to get used to, and ... *he ilo* [(I) don't know] ... I still see it like that, but I try to live the way I used to live, I mean, I try to make my home feel as comfortable as possible because... I hate living in the house that we are living in now, [a Tokelauan, open house], because we are still waiting for our proper house to be built. This house, *e*

he manaia [it is not nice], it is just like, when you've got no room to put things in and you go, oh I'll just put this in the corner, I'll just hang this up on... you see what I mean? I don't mind having it as an open house, only as long as it would look more like a home. I don't know, we just have to make do with what I have got here. I don't feel at home. Probably just because it is not what I am used to. *Tena* [(it is) that]. I am used to lots of housecleaning, *ke iloa* [(you) know]. I am used to doing the Hoover and cleaning the windows and things like that, dusting the shelves... I hate cleaning the dishes here because there is no sink.

6. Coming here, the place is small. It *is* small. It is small. Anyway, the place itself, *kiate au* [to me], is really beautiful, *te manaia o te fenua* [the beauty of the land]. It is really nice, but, *e manaia* [it is beautiful]. After the first week here, I used to go alone out by myself, I felt I needed to be alone. I hadn't mixed with anybody. Every time I walked past somebody they'd always say something, because when you walk past somebody's house or just anybody they'll say *Ko koe ka fano. Fano ni. Olo la mai i ai.* [You are about to go. Go then. Go then and come back.]

7. When I first arrived and someone would say, *Ko koe ka fano. Fano hau ai* [You are about to go. Go (and) return here], or whatever, and I would say what, what the hell would they say that for? Because I didn't know *ko he mea lava* [it is just one of those things], it is just how it is here. And then I used to go home, and I'll ask my mum, mum what do they say 'are you going now' for, 'go and come back?' *Ke iloa, faka Tokelau* [you know, the Tokelau way], but I'd be talking to her in English. And she'll say *ko he mea lava e mahani ai* [it is one of those things that is common (to do)]. And I thought oh, why do they say it all the time. I get sick of the people saying *Ko koe ka fano. Fano hau ai.* [You are about to go. Go and come back], and I don't even know who the people are. Well I didn't at the time.

8. And then, the first week here, I used to go out alone, by myself. *E kino* [it is bad], I hadn't mixed with the people and I, I didn't feel right. Anyway, I used to go out and sit by myself, in the evenings. Late in the evenings, I used to go out by myself and just find a quiet spot where there wasn't anyone around and I used to just cry and cry. I used to get real homesick. – I call New Zealand my home because that's where I was brought up. Even though I know I am Tokelau, but ... *he ilo* [(I) don't know] ... I am proud of being Tokelau, but I just don't feel, *he ilo* [(I) don't know]... And I think, if I hadn't been brought up here, gone outside and come back, I don't think it would have been so bad, *ke iloa* [(you) know], my coming back. But my coming, but my being born here, going out and coming back for the first time in twenty years, that's a long time. And it is just, it takes a hell of a long time to get used to the big change, *ke iloa* [(you) know]? *Ke iloa he tino kehe* [(you) know, a stranger], that I don't belong here?

9. Like, *vena*, if I am going somewhere, because I keep to myself, I keep my business to myself *lava* [only], if I am going somewhere and they'll ask you, where you are going. And sometimes I feel like saying, mind your own bloody business, *ke iloa* [(you) know]? But, being here, being Tokelau and my being a Tokelau, a respectable answer would be, *ke iloa* [(you) know], to just tell them where you are going. When I first came here I would go straight out and tell them where I am going, and in my mind I would think, why are you being so bloody nosy, but now I just say 'over there', *ko fano fai fekau*, I am just going to do something, I am just going to take a message. But to me, I would prefer for me to just be going on my way and for nobody to

say anything, *ke iloa*. Not that I am a snob or anything. But, like I said before, you can run but you can't hide. Cause everybody is watching you. You may think that there is nobody watching you, but ...

10. When we came here I met people because I am a friendly sort of person and like socialising, meeting people, and I met a lot of people and I became friends with them and I thought they were my friends. Then as time passed there were rumours about myself and they told me who told them this and so I approached them and they said, oh no it wasn't me, somebody else told me and I only told such and such, and I approached and approached and I got down to number one. She was about my best friend when I came, a really good friend of mine, and I approached her and she lied to me and then I talked to her like a friend and said, I thought you were a friend, I thought that I could trust you. And she beat around the bush, but then she finally said it was true, that's what she said. And I told her that I didn't want to know her because, like ... I don't know how to explain it.

11. I made friends with other people, and I would say what happened between myself and her, and [they would say] you shouldn't stick with her, she is such and such and she is such and such. And I would make another friend, and that friend would say: Oh such and such is like this and such and such is like that, and it just went around in circles. And I thought, My God, what the hell are these people ... they must be sick in their heads or something, because I am not used to the gossip way. I am not used to hearing rumours. In New Zealand friends will confide, we will talk to each other and it would just be kept, it wouldn't be put to anybody else. And that is something I can't really stand, the gossip. [...]

12. I don't, I haven't, *e he ko iloa he tino* [(I) don't know anybody] for me to really confide in. In the three, going on to four years that we've been here, sure I mix with the people. The only time I will go out, is *kafai* [if], because they have a lot of customarily things *i kinei* [over here], *ke iloa* [(you) know], *na faiga mea* [the way of doing things], when they have cooking for whatever is coming on. That will be the only time I go *eva ki ni mea* [going to the things] is when they have got something like that on, or if I feel like it, the women's meeting, plus coming to work and just meeting people there, but I never go to anyone's place for a chat or *ke iloa* [(you) know] cause I haven't, not that I don't want to, but only because, it is only that I don't feel, there is no one here that I feel that suits me?

13. I've been to drinking parties, but I keep quiet. I keep quiet until I feel in the party mood, or maybe until I am a little bit tiddly and then I will, *ke iloa* [(you) know], gossip. But it will only be party gossip, nothing ... I can't say that I haven't had any fun here, cause I've been to a couple of good parties, but there's, I find the men here aggressive. Because, there's a, the men are into their booze, *ke iloa* [(you) know]. And I've been in a couple of situations where you have guys, married men make passes, which really disgusts me. And I've been in a couple of situations where my husband has taken it the wrong way, and he has been like ... a punch up. And I don't [like it when], the men drink and they become aggressive. But the booze! I wish they'd bloody stop importing it here. It is something that I see, *ko na pia na olo mai i fafo, e vevehi ai na kaiga* [the beer that comes from abroad, it disturbs the families]. Husband and wife, and then the husband abuses the wife and the children, *e he fakaalofa* [it is not compassionate behaviour]. There is a lot of that, that I've seen *i kinei* [over here]. And I really wish that I could do something. But what can I do? It is a small place, but it can get ...

The first part of this story tells of thwarted expectations, of the place and the people being different from what the narrator had become used to in New Zealand. Her first reaction was wanting to go back (a parallel to the story of leaving), and she says that, after an approximately four-year stay, she still feels as if she doesn't belong there. She feels 'out of place', like an outcast.[22] She attributes this to the size of the place, that is, that it is such a small community. We are told of how she expected Tokelau to be some kind of tropical paradise, 'white sand all over the place, like', and elsewhere she tells jokingly of how she had imagined the *fala* (or pandanus-fruit) to be some kind of pineapple.[23] The stories she had heard among Tokelau people in New Zealand had all stressed the beauty and attractions of the place, and nothing she had heard had prepared her for the realities of life there. In this we can see almost an inversion of images, in the vision of the other place as something akin to paradise on earth. The image of Tokelau which is upheld and cherished in New Zealand is, as illustrated in many Tokelau songs, one that highlights and depicts in great detail the natural beauty of the landscape and the social gracefulness with which one moves across it.[24]

When she speaks of her initial experience of the open housing and what she calls a lack of privacy, she clearly comes from an opposite life-world than the one from which the first narrator started. She is constantly in the presence of others, and she finds it hard to accept that there are no ways to escape this social fact. Her story describes her encounters with unfamiliar standards of formality and intimacy, such as those concerning how couples behave in public. Interestingly, she interprets the lack of public displays of affection as a sign that, as she puts it, 'people over here don't really show their true emotions' (cf., Besnier 1989). She explains how, to counter this, she and her husband deliberately 'show their emotions', for example, by holding hands when they are 'walking on the road'. She thinks this is good; she is aware that people notice, but, upon further questioning, doesn't seem aware of why people would tend to take offence at such behaviour.

She then goes on to describe her images of what a home should be like, again based on what she is used to from New Zealand, and she vividly describes the adjustments she has had to make to the different conditions in Tokelau. She comments on the smallness of the place, the beauty of the place and the isolation she felt upon first arriving. In this and in the following paragraph, the habitual phatic-talk exchanges are described, and the social pressure that is an integral part of this communicative practice is strongly conveyed.[25] She gradually learns to accept this as being 'one of the things that is common to do over here', but she sees it as a way for other people to control what you are doing and says that if it were up to her, she would rather tell them to mind their own business and be on her way without having to be accountable all the time. She adds that she has learned not to give too precise or too truthful answers; rather she answers 'I am going over there', 'I am going to do an errand' and so on, and avoids mentioning the specific nature of her task.

She experiences a strong longing for solitude, and tells of her dreams of escape and her homesickness. She pauses to consider whether it is right for her to talk about New Zealand as home, since, as she says, she 'is a Tokelauan'. She hastens to add that she is proud of her ancestry, and excuses herself for harbouring these feelings by saying that it probably would not have been so difficult to live in Tokelau if she hadn't been away for so long. As she says, 'it just takes a hell of a long time to get used to the big change, you know'. Despite just having mentioned her pride in being a Tokelauan, she concludes by describing herself as a *tino kehe*, that is, a stranger, and says that she doesn't belong there.

In subsequent paragraphs she explains what she means by this, and tells of why she has come to feel as if she doesn't belong. I have touched upon most of what is contained in paragraph nine above in the reference to phatic talk in the discussion of paragraphs six and seven. There is one more small point that I would like to draw attention to in this paragraph, however. In her last comments on how she prefers to go on her way and for 'nobody to say anything', she quickly adds, 'not that I am a snob (*fia hili*) or anything'. She ends by commenting on the fact that one is always seen, always observed, and that even if one may trick oneself into believing that one has escaped the public gaze for a moment, there is really no place to hide or run away to. The expression 'being a snob', *fia hili or fia palagi* (literally wanting to be high or wanting to be (like a) *palagi*), is used in the taunt I quoted in the introduction to this Chapter. Note how, in her narrative, the accusation of 'wanting to be high', or rather, her defending herself against such an accusation, is related to her way of walking on the road through the village.

The informal mechanisms of disseminating information throughout the village which she encounters and describes here obviously run counter to her expectations of what intimacy and friendship entail. She is disgusted and horrified to find that what she has told someone in strict confidence, not expecting it to go any further, is soon all over the village.[26] This form of communication, which is very common, and which is particularly attributed to women as a group, is a powerful mechanism of social control. It is telling that in response to her encounter with yet another level of communality, represented by the lack of 'discretion' and individual ownership and control even over 'intimate details' of one's personal history, she retreats.

As mentioned in paragraph twelve, she now goes out only if there is a communal task involving the women of her age group. *Eva ki na mea* ('going to the things') is conceptually opposed to *eva tauanoa* (that is, going without a purpose, roaming around for no reason) and only the former way of going out earns common public approval.[27] I included the last paragraph as it clearly shows that the norms and etiquette informing behaviour are sometimes broken, and points to the disruptive influence of alcohol, which is an increasing problem. It also demonstrates her feelings of powerlessness against this development, which is one of the issues which the first drama attempts to address.

When the narrator of this story came to Tokelau, she was in for a big surprise. The place was different to how she remembered, as it was smaller, and the houses had no walls. First she talks of going out, of going 'on the road', and of finding it hard to be held accountable for her actions all the time. She is aware that by acting in the wrong way, that is, by not responding politely and telling people where she is going and what she is doing, she will earn a reputation for acting 'high', i.e., above her station. She also walks 'on the road' with her husband, showing affection ('intimacy') in public and, while she realises that people consider this funny, show-offy or embarrassing, she feels that she is within her rights in doing it, and that she maybe can teach them to 'show their true emotions' as she does. One of the other interesting things about this part of the story is her attempt to confide ('intimately') in a friend (not her cousins, i.e., not in someone it would be natural to choose as a *hoa*, or companion).[28] She learns to her disgust that the information that she gave in confidence, expecting privacy, is all over the village. After several confrontations like this, she gradually gives up and, checked by subtle (and not so subtle) social pressure, she ends up staying in her proper place, namely, inside the house.[29]

How the Drama *Mafine* ('Woman') Reflects the Narrative of Return

Whereas the story depicted in the third sequence of the first play, *Tagi*, is the story of leaving Tokelau, the story of the second play, *Tima*, is about returning to the atolls. The feeling of 'being stuck', expressed by the narrator of the second story, is echoed in the story of *Tima*, where no room is left for the female character to make a choice. Everything that argues against attaining the trans-cultural ideal expressed by one of the persons interviewed by Sallen is stressed. This, of course, is what turns it into the particular form of action theatre it is. As mentioned in Chapter one, after this scenario has been presented, the audience is invited to intervene and to change what they would like to see happen differently. When this play was performed in Tokelau, the audiences' responses covered the whole spectrum of possibilities, ranging from lecturing the actors on proper behaviour in terms of kinship and age to a radical feminist view. The first response frequently came from parts of the younger population, many of whom didn't want to change the contents of the play at all, except for a strongly expressed wish that 'Tima' would stop complaining and behave herself.[30] The majority of the remaining audiences would try to mediate and to stress the need for all of the family members to be more aware of each others' needs, particularly as these needs may change under the pressure of recent developments.

There were many incidents of humorous squabbling, and these most frequently took the form of confrontation between the men and the women in their capacity as representatives of their respective groups in the village. The men addressed the issue of modesty, as depicted in the first scene where 'Tima' is told to cover herself up, and the women retorted that if the men didn't have such dirty minds, the women wouldn't need to obey these inconvenient rules, stressing how hot it is to be dressed like that.

Even when pressed, the audience never came down unanimously on the side of Tima's not getting married, maybe because the suitor chosen by her parents in the play seemed much more attractive, in terms of local ideals, than the teacher Tima herself might have chosen. After some coaxing and questioning from the group's speaker, however, most people agreed that they were in favour of her making the choice herself.

In the second narrative, some aspects of the processes through which one learns to balance the demands of village (or community life) with family and individual concerns are described. In the final Chapter, I shall discuss further the particular orientations which make some individuals feel trapped in a particular place and position, but which provide others with the mores that make life possible.

In summing up the points I wish to highlight in the second narrative, I will first discuss the conflict expressed by the narrator in paragraph 4. I interpret this as conflict between the etiquette of 'masks' (to use the terms adopted by the members of the theatre-group), as related to relationships of command and responsibility and to etiquette related to gender, and what for want of a better term we may call 'individualism' (where the dictum seems to be, as expressed by the theatre-group, show your true self, under the mask). Interestingly, she interprets Tokelauan behaviour as indicating that they 'don't show their true emotions'. The narrative speaks of a gradual learning of a proper 'sense of place' in Tokelauan terms. There is a development from paragraphs 6 and 7, where she is bewildered by the constant phatic-talk exchanges, to her descriptions in the latter parts of the narrative (as in the first narrative) where she expresses her experiences in terms of 'ways of going' and in terms of the opposition between 'inside' and 'outside'. She is gradually pushed into a sense of her place within the community. One result of this can be found in the distinction she makes between staying inside, going out 'socialising', 'going to anyone's house for a chat', and 'going to the customary things' (*eva ki ni mea*). Finally, she makes the distinction between 'being high', and by implication 'being low', echoing the moral implied by the taunt quoted in the introduction to this Chapter (paragraph 9). Through various experiences, such as when she is confronted with the 'talk' in the village, she gradually learns to orient herself in the, for her, unfamiliar landscape of Tokelau atoll life. Her tone in rendering these experiences is also humorous, but it cannot be said to be explicitly clowning or comical in style, in the manner of the first narrative. She also comes across as accustomed to addressing conflict in a more direct fashion.

Before we turn in the following Chapters to a more detailed description of space as a social construct in Tokelau, I shall sum up some of the characteristics of the specific balance – at once aesthetic, moral, social and political – that is sought in the organisation of experience, according to concepts such as 'high' and 'low', 'inside' and 'outside', and in terms of 'face' and 'shame'.

Conceptions of Personhood and Forms of Sociality

As attested by A. Wiersbicka, on the basis of her comparative studies of linguistic semantics, the individual 'I' is universally linguistically recognised, cross-culturally (Wiersbicka 1992). In Tokelau discourse, the existence of an individual, separate self, character or personality is recognised most generally by reference to *tino* (or person), or through the use of the first person pronoun, *au*. However, the innate character (or 'meaning', *uiga* and dispositions, *loto*) of a person is intimately connected with a conception of light and dark sides, which is akin to, but not identical with, Western ethnopsychological notions about internal processes over which the individual is assigned personal responsibility (Levy 1973, 1984; Shore 1982; Mageo 1998). These light and dark sides may be seen as forces, and the individual is not granted the capacity to control certain aspects of the dark side, hence the stress on the light side of sociality, through which control (*pule*) is exerted. Local conceptions of personhood show, as Mageo found in her analysis of Samoan models of selfhood, *a foregrounding of the social personae*. In other words, the performative aspects of selfhood are seen as innate, in contrast to European ethnopsychological notions, which see them as constructed.

In terms of self-reference, the first person pronoun may be used, that is *au* or I. When expressing the equivalent of the term 'myself', this becomes *ko au tau tahi*, (literally, me by myself – a pitiful state indeed). In most verbal interaction, however, direct reference to oneself is avoided, and a directional such as 'hither' is employed instead, for reasons linked to the stress on relationality (or 'sidedness') that I noted prominent when discussing identity in its genealogical or kinship-related aspect. For further illustrations of language as a resource in the representation of relationships, see the following Chapter.

The play *Tima* allows us to examine how these patterns of communication and of 'sided' relationships are represented in the new media of expression. Exceptionally, in this performance, the 'I' that is most commonly backgrounded in Tokelau discourse is explicitly and deliberately brought to the fore. This may be interpreted both as an expression of social change and as an expression of the actors' desire to bring about social change. Here we see how the introduction of a new medium of expression, in this case, theatre, can allow for the establishment of novel acts of identification. However, as we shall see in subsequent Chapters, we must not forget that the theatre group's presentation of their project of self-empowerment changed quite significantly in accordance with their relationship to their audiences, both in New Zealand and in Tokelau. In other words, we must examine how a common definition of situation is reached in the presentation of a new medium of expression, in order to establish how its message is interpreted and received. To allow us to do this, however, we need to take into consideration how the conception of relationships, and not least, the situational constellation of relationships, affects the definition of a situation and thus which frame of interpretation is made relevant.

Notes

1. See Hooper 1982, also Sallen 1983.
2. The statistics of this are presented in Wessen *et al.* 1992.
3. Extracts from a recording in Tokelauan, made by A. M. Vonen, in Hutt Valley, New Zealand. The translation is mine, and is made on the basis of the Tokelau transkription by Vonen.
4. Cf., Chapter one about phatic-talk exchanges. Also Hoëm (1993) and (1995).
5. The concept of bodily hexis is taken from Bourdieu (1977: 93) who states: 'Bodily hexis is political mythology realised, *em-bodied*, turned into a permanent disposition, a durable manner of standing, speaking, and thereby of *feeling and thinking*'.
6. For a description of bodily practices and spatial arrangements in various contexts in Tuvalu which shows some interesting parallels to the Tokelau situation (church, cook-house, formal gathering and so on), see Besnier (1991).
7. See also Hoëm (1995), Toren (1990, Fiji), Morton (1996, Tonga), Ochs (1988, Samoa).
8. This form of speech is used, and I have it documented, for example, in a case of a pulenuku (village mayor) describing what he finds hard with his work, i.e., to 'face', *fakafeagai*, the people. For a discussion of the concept *fakafeagai*, 'to face', and in connection with relations of authority in Nukulaelae, see Besnier (Besnier 1996).
9. There are no dogs in Tokelau. Cats, chickens and rats are the only non-native animals present on Tokelau.
10. There are a few other such metonyms for 'the Samoan experience' in her full

story, but they come later on in her stay there. (I.e., having to cut prickly bush-es, crying and hating it, and not knowing how to make a Samoan *umu* or earth oven.)

11. Contrary to the situations where she has been taught that it is proper to look, e.g., where she was taught to 'face', e.g., the priest. The distinction between, e.g., 'stare', 'look', and 'gaze', is interesting in how it is made, evaluated morally and varies situationally, e.g., the area of eye-contact, exemplified in beliefs such as that of the 'evil eye' varies cross-culturally and has a lot to do with the perception of gestalts encoding a specific bodily hexis. Accordingly, to learn to see differently implies experiencing things differently. This is one of the reasons why visual behaviour is hedged cross-culturally with strong sanc-tions. Cf., Duranti (1994: 78), for an illustration from Samoa.

12. See, for example, the description given of the stereotypical self-image of Samoans vis-à-vis *papalagi* given by Shore, (1982: 277).

13. In the book *Class and Culture in the South Pacific*, published by the University of the South Pacific, in cooperation with the University of Auckland, 1987.

14. Her father, interestingly enough (P. Harper, personal communication), subse-quently moved to New Zealand, and in his old age still claimed never to have experienced or have any knowledge of anything akin to racism. The inter-viewer attributed this to his strong belief in 'everybody being equal before God'.

15. This was not the case in the mid to late sixties when the first migrants went from Tokelau to New Zealand.

16. Cf., V. Sallen (1983) on the experience of Tokelau scholarship students in New Zealand.

17. In comparison, the plays created by the 'mirror' group that emerged in response to the drama performances (see Chapter one), had this skit-like, humorous form. The same was the case with the plays created in Tokelau, as a response to the performances there. Those 'counter-plays' were also 'funny'.

18. They do this in the introductory part, i.e., when the genealogies are called out, as well, but not in any other part of the play except for this one. In the second play, Tima, the characters have fictional names.

19. See Hoëm (1995) on the value placed on keeping a 'smiling face' in Tokelau. See also Chapters one and five this work.

20. The same point was made into a joke when a group of New Zealand-educat-ed Tokelauans came to Tokelau as a support group for the newly founded Council of Faipule. This team's sojourn was named *te malaga o na kafaga*, 'the journey or travel-group of supporters'. As the word for supporters generally refers to the rope that men tie around their feet for support when they climb a coconut tree (usually done by younger men on behalf of older men), and as the members of this support group were not adept in this skill anymore, this was the cause of much joking and merriment during their stay in Tokelau.

21. This story was recorded in Tokelau, and the language was English with some Tokelauan. I have rendered the language here as it was spoken, but edited the story mainly in the sense that I have left out some interruptions and some of my questions, plus a large proportion of the story that follows the introducto-ry part presented here

22. However, she is not, by any standard, not even in public opinion, regarded as among the more maladapted, but perhaps as a *fia palagi*.

23. The joke is the lack of fruits in Tokelau, and her foolishness in expecting such goods.

24. The shock many experience upon returning (having nothing to do with the beauty of the place, but rather of a social/scalar nature), is particularly clear-

ly illustrated by some of the interviews made by New Zealand TV, on the occasion of the opening of the *Lotala*, the new meeting house on Atafu.

25. See Hoëm (1993), and Senft (1987), (1991).
26. For a discussion of the social role played by gossip, as opposed to the formal, political institutions of the Council of Elders, and of the women's committee, see Hoëm (1995). See also Besnier (Besnier 1994), (1996).
27. Or a felicitous balance between the two. It is not good either if one is too aloof, as this can be read from her cautioning that she is not staying away because she is a snob.
28. Cf., Levy (1973: 190, 199–201).
29. The ultimate sanction, except for withholding of food (which is not a village rule, this is only done privately, signalling a withdrawal of social support, and very quickly gets people to cooperate), is what is called *tu noa*, lit. stand alone (or unrestricted), i.e., without support. This is a house arrest, where the person who has not 'gone the right way' has to stay in the house and is only allowed to go to the toilet and to the Church. In other words, the ultimate punishment is social isolation, to have to 'stand alone'.
30. This is not as surprising as it may seem. It is not the role of the young to question things. The more critical individuals are more frequently found among those who are middle-aged, but who have not yet attained a fixed position of authority within the community. See also Hoëm (1995).

Chapter 4

A Sense of Place in Narrative

This work addresses the changes in social organisation in Tokelau: changes related to developments within the Tokelau communities in New Zealand, and changes related to developments within the field of international politics. As I referred to in the introductory Chapter, people experience a tension between what in the song 'O my child' (Taku tama e) is spoken of as 'the different colours of this life' and the 'sweetness' that may be said to be 'inscribed' in the words or sayings of the Tokelau language. As I have already discussed, some people attempt to address and resolve those tensions, so deeply felt in their daily lives, through the establishment of new forms of expressive culture. This search for new ways and means of identification occurs, as we have seen, in active relation to existing norms of interaction and communicative practices – sometimes in accordance with them, and sometimes in clear opposition. The existential nature of this quest, propelled by the enormous force of the changes of recent decades, combined with the existence of rather clear and deeply ingrained moral orientations, makes the Tokelau/New Zealand situation a particularly fruitful arena when it comes to examining the political aspects of representation. I propose that we see what I call the 'politics of representation' as consisting of the strategic use of various resources. In this perspective, conceptions of language and language use can be seen as such resources, which are employed as important aspects of the politics of representation.

As described towards the end of Chapter two, cultural formulators seek to establish channels of communication that were previously non-existent in Tokelau. They do this mainly through the utilisation of new media, such as video, popular music, theatre and newsletters, and use these media to develop new forms of cultural expression (Spitulnik 1997, 1999). The establishment of local newsletters in the late 1980's, written in the Tokelauan language, and distributed on the three atolls, is but one example of such an effort. In that case, the main motivation behind the project was to keep people informed about the proceedings of the Councils of Elders. To appreciate the enormous change in communicative practices this potentially represents, it is necessary to know that such dissemination of information generally was, and still is, actively discouraged by the councils' representatives, and that prevalent patterns of leadership and authority effectively advocate against it.[1]

When I use the phrasing 'potentially represents' I do so to underline the fact that the attempt to establish new channels of communication cannot be counted as having succeeded until the product is actually consumed by members of the intended audience. We need also to have some knowledge of how the product is eventually consumed, i.e., how it is interpreted or 'read' by the consumers, to ascertain its impact. Furthermore, it is important to know how the relations between producers or performers and audience or consumers are constituted in Tokelau society. This is perhaps the most significant factor for a researcher to take into account when 'reading' new cultural products. On this basis, in this Chapter, a focus on linguistic representation is chosen, because it provides us with a key to local interpretative practice, expressed most clearly through what I call 'relations of command and responsibility'.

Narratives and Frames

In his analysis of communicative practices in Samoa, Duranti describes the politics of representation as consisting of, and constituting, resources. To recapitulate parts of this argument, such resources may be seen as part of the local 'technology of power' (Foucault 1980, 1989), and, as such, they serve to constitute 'local authority and local hierarchies' (Duranti 1990). An advantage of this perspective is that it allows us to see what is often referred to as expressive culture, or discourse as an indication of deeply rooted orientations, which are not only embodied and largely naturalised practices, but also potentially accessible to consciousness. An externalisation into narrative is a primary way to realise this potential (M. Jackson 2002). Narrative may be defined generally as 'verbalised, visualised, and/or embodied framings of actual or possible events' (Ochs and Capps 1996: 19). Ochs and Capps describe how narrative activity occurs at the interface between the self and the larger field of sociality, and add that narrative plays a central role in bringing 'experiences to conscious awareness' (Ibid.: 21). I use narrative in this broad sense, but in my presentation of narratives in this Chapter, I also draw on the more technical definition in relation to linguistic representations, where narrative is taken to be 'two or more temporally conjoined clauses that represent a sequence of temporally ordered events' (Labov and Waletsky 1968).

In examining what we may call the representation of agency, agency can be defined as the 'causal relationship between participants' actions and certain states of affairs or processes' (Duranti 1990: 646). Duranti explores the possibility that there is a connection between the occurrence of certain grammatical forms, and the more general processes of the constitution of social agents and political process in a community.

He suggests that:

> [T]he particular ways in which agency is grammatically expressed in Samoan political discourse are connected not only to different points of view or frames, [...] but, more fundamentally, to local political praxis. (Duranti 1990: 646–47)

Duranti examines his hypothesis about connections between the linguistic and the social through the use of the twin concepts of 'moral flow' and 'information flow'. The moral flow is, according to his definition, 'a progressive and cooperative framing of characters and events in terms of their positive or negative value vis-à-vis community standards as defined in the ongoing interaction' (Duranti 1994: 121). In my discussion, I shall refer to 'moral concerns' and the 'moral universe' in place of Duranti's concept of 'moral flow'. The term 'information flow of discourse' (Chafe 1979) refers to 'the way in which an argument of the verb is grammatically expressed (e.g., by a pronoun or a full noun) or left implicit (by a 'zero' form) [which] depends on whether or not it represents a 'concept' that is currently 'active' or in a person's focus of consciousness' (Duranti 1994: 172). He adds that '[i]n this approach to the organisation of information in discourse, a concept that has been active is called "given" and one that has been inactive is called "new" ' (Duranti 1994: 173).

However, and as Duranti also comments, this perspective does not tell us why such a difference between grammatically expressed arguments and zero-marked arguments exists, and what this difference may communicate. Consequently, Duranti addresses the question of a possible connection between the grammatical and the social. The particular connection that he explores is between the speakers' choice of specific grammatical forms and their (political) concerns in the ongoing interaction. He states that:

> [G]rammatical framings [...] have pragmatic and metapragmatic functions, in that *they do not only tell us about the events, they also say something about what the events mean to the speaker and what they should mean to the audience.* The differences in the ways in which different social actors choose to tell or describe the facts are relevant for our understanding of the relation between discourse and social structure on the one hand and discourse and political process on the other. (Duranti 1994: 121. Emphasis mine)

Given the fact that the material on which my analysis is based is presented in the form of longer, and presumably more self-contained, narratives than verbal exchanges such as dialogues, and that they are rendered in the written medium, there are some difficulties connected with a direct application of Duranti's model. This is because he formulates his project as a study of the speakers' '*progressive and cooperative framing* of characters and events in terms of their positive or negative value vis-à-vis community standards *as defined in the ongoing interaction*' (Duranti 1994: 121. Emphasis mine). On the face of it, narratives, not to mention written texts, may not seem to represent such 'progressive and cooperative' enterprises, nor do they seem to occur in, or to reflect, an 'ongoing interaction'.

However, it is possible to apply C. Geertz' method of 'thick description', that is, to interpret a text (or a sequence of interaction) by locating this sequence of interaction (or in this case a text) descriptively within the setting of the larger context of which it is a part (Geertz 1993). I would also argue that it is possible to find what are often called contextualising keys in the actual structure of narrative: e.g., in the anchoring of the plot and in the subsequent deictic (i.e., spatio-temporal reference) representation of relationships between characters and places. According to my approach, then, 'framing' in Duranti's sense may also be seen to occur in narratives and in written texts, and grammatical framings chosen by the author(s) similarly 'not only tell us about the events, they also say something about what the events mean to the speaker [or author] and what they should mean to the audience' (Duranti 1994: 212). In other words, I propose that there is a connection between the information flow of the text and the social context for which it is produced. I shall explore this hypothesis in this chapter through an analysis of three narratives of different genres and, on this basis, offer a further interpretation of the two life histories presented in the previous Chapter.

E. Goffman has defined the term 'frame' so as to refer to the interactional cues that 'mark the boundary of a social event and that provides guidelines for the interpretation of the event' (Goffman 1974). Duranti, in his analysis, shows how grammatical structures may serve as what he calls 'framing devices' (Duranti 1994: 121). In the following, I shall use the term 'framing' in a general sense, to refer to the metacommunicative message about how an action is to be interpreted, that is, actions defined as including grammatical choices. However, in Chapter five I will focus on the marking of boundaries of events as a quality distinct from these general processes of 'framing'. When I do this, I shall refer to the 'setting apart', the boundary-creating aspect, by the term 'bracketing' also used by Goffman (Goffman 1974: 251–52).

Intertextuality and Instrumentality

Elsewhere, I have discussed the variety of genres within Tokelau expressive culture, and have described the structural aspects of these genres, as well as the interpretative practices and related beliefs about instrumentality (Hoëm 1992, 1995). I have chosen to include narratives as material for the study of representation of agency, because a large proportion of new cultural forms in Tokelau are represented through the medium of writing, and I wish to examine what effects this choice of medium may have on communicative practices and patterns of identification.

In the introduction to the book *Songs and Stories of Tokelau*, Huntsman and Allan Thomas quote a remark made by Tokelau elders who explain that *'ko te pehe ko te pepa a Tokelau'* – 'the song is the paper of Tokelau'. Huntsman and Thomas stress the particular significance of songs as repositories of 'things from the past' *(mea mai anamua)*. They describe song-texts as preserving and validating such 'things from the past'. This mnemotechnic and legitimising effect is achieved, not through the recounting of particular stories, but in a metonymic fashion. That is, the words of a song 'stand for' a particular story and, as Huntsman and Thomas says, the text evokes this story for those who are 'in the know' (Thomas, Tuia and Huntsman 1990: 11). For a further illustration, see the story about the treaty of Tokehega in the Introduction to this book.

The authors discuss how songs and stories are integral parts of performances. Songs are also important parts of folktales. In public gatherings, various genres such as formal speeches, skits, songs and song-dances serve to constitute the totality of the event. However, and as the remark referred to above suggests by indicating the prominence given to *songs* as the main medium through which inscription of 'things' of cultural importance takes place, not all of these genres are perceived as having the same reality-status.

There is a high degree of inter-textuality within the universe of discourse constituted by Tokelau expressive culture.[2] This implies that no genre can truly be said to exist in isolation; that is to say, no genre comes close to resembling the ideal 'detached' or 'autonomous' text that is frequently associated with so-called high literacy. The existing norms of exegesis or composition in Tokelau do not demand that one stay only within the boundaries of one genre or a specific area of knowledge. The differentiating criteria are in most cases rather to be found in how the information is represented, i.e., in the form, and in how the information is to be interpreted. Thus formal speeches may draw upon song-texts to lend authority to a certain argument, and song-texts may be drawn from folk tales or from the Bible. Skits may also be based on a biblical theme, and so on. The forms of these genres differ, however, and most importantly, the genres differ with regards to how they are to be interpreted.

Duranti, in a discussion on intertextuality in relation to speech genres in Samoa, draws the conclusion that Samoan political oratory may be described as parasitic on the genre of ceremonial speeches (Duranti 1994). Given the prevalent intertextuality of the Tokelau material, I choose not to operate with a typology of more or less pure or hybrid genres as Duranti seems, at least implicitly, to do. Among New Zealand Tokelauans, certain phrases are described as *na kupuga Tokelau*, or in Tokelau, as expressive of the 'things of the past'. I propose that such occurrences of 'phrases', that is, Tokelau words (*kupu*) or sayings (*alagakupu or muagagana*), be seen as expressive of strategies of legitimation.[3]

So, to draw on 'traditional sayings' may serve to lend more authority to one's words. In Tokelauan, at least, such phrases or sayings are to be found distributed across *genres*, but occurrences tend to cluster around *situations* where hierarchy is an issue, thus serving as markers of authority (Hoëm *et al*. 1992). The frequency of these occurrences is admittedly higher in genres most closely connected with political relations, such as formal speeches, than in everyday speech. However, the occurrence of such phrases is also high in folk tales, for example, and it is indeed the case that much formal speech making draws its analogies precisely from folk tales (*kakai*).

On the one hand, the reality status of genres is connected with the criterion of 'truth', *mea moni* (literally 'real things'). Thus according to Huntsman (1977: viii), people distinguish between stories that are 'neither true nor false', as is the case of *kakai* (or folk tales) where the criterion of truth is not relevant, and those that fall into the category of 'true things from the past', such as *tala anamua* (stories of the past), and *pehe mai mua* (songs from the past). On the other hand, and as I have described elsewhere (Hoëm 1995), local theories about the relationship between words and the world imply a strong belief in the potential for creating reality through the use of words. This is perhaps most strongly expressed in the no longer common practice of uttering spells or invocations (*fakanau*), in an instrumental fashion, to ensure a good catch of fish, a favourable wind and so on.

Generally, as Duranti also observes for Samoa, concern with a speaker's individual intentions is downplayed, and the utterance is awarded far more significance *as a speech event*. A statement made in a public situation carries the potential of bringing about a new state of affairs. For example, a story 'about somebody', i.e., gossip, is likely to have consequences for the person talked about, regardless of the gossiper's intentions and also regardless of whether the story that is 'going around the village' is true or false (*pepelo*).[4] Similarly, speeches made during political gatherings may bring about a new reality by the very fact of their being made, rather than by being 'symbolic of' something else. For example, a speech is ritually necessary to bring about a reconciliation between estranged parts within a family, rather than the other way around, i.e., that a reconciliation is considered necessary to allow a meeting to be held in which speeches can be made about it.[5]

This is a subtle difference, bespeaking an accentuation and ritualisation of social interaction that produces a pattern where, as Duranti says, it becomes meaningless to negate responsibility for one's words by saying 'I didn't mean it'. The ability to create reality by words, or in other words, to achieve ritual/political efficacy (*mana* or most commonly, *pule*) is differently distributed socially and is an aspect of the life-long quest for what I have described as 'excellence in performance'(Hoëm 1995). The authority and/or status of the speaker, the genre(s) employed, and the audience's reception of the performance thus work together to constitute, on the one hand, a common definition of situation, allowing for the interaction to take place, and, on the other hand, to produce a text or a performance that is more than the words uttered – that comprises the multiplicity of interpretations given to the speech act.

Information Flow and Social Face

In Tokelau narratives, we find a great deal of variation with regards to the degree of implicitness and explicitness with which information is represented. Moreover, this variation seems linked to factors such as 'topic', 'genre', and 'situation', including participants and the relationships between them. In many cases, the deictic (spatio-temporal) anchoring of a particular narrative is provided by gestures and glances, and to deduce the references of spatial clues to the relationships between characters and arguments, outside of the context of production of the narrative, is difficult and sometimes impossible. Sequences like 'Went there. Walked on and on', (*Fanatu. Fano, fano, fano*) are common, and in itself, taken in isolation, such a passage gives no clues to 'who went where', if one weren't there to witness the act. (For another illustration of this, see Duranti 1994: 30–32.)

Syntactically, Tokelauan is a verb-initial language. This implies that sentences beginning with a verb and/or in combination with a tense/aspect marker, such as in the sentence above – *fanatu* (went there), or *kua fano* (has gone) – represent the typical, unmarked category. Sentences that place the topic of discussion first, as in '*Ko au*, ko Kula Fiaola (first sentence of narrative 2, this chapter), 'I, am Kula Fiaola', while syntactically possible, are less common and occur, as we shall see, mainly within particular genres and speech situations. Verb-initial syntax is a feature Tokelauan share with many Polynesian languages (V. Krupa 1982: 122–23).

In Tokelau formal speeches and public story-telling however, a certain kind of information pattern is common. It occurs in everyday speech as well, but it is much more noticeable in formal speech acts. This narrative structure is what Robin Hooper calls 'informative presupposition', based on Chafe's distinction between 'given' and 'known' information. This speech type contains 'a focused constituent which is largely anaphoric in its relation to the preceding discourse. The presupposition contains *new* information which is *presented as known*' (Hooper 1987: 20). She comments that this construction obviously lends itself to a variety of rhetorical purposes[6] (see also Hoëm 1995).

This phenomenon could be taken as an illustration of what is frequently labelled 'context-orientation'. That is, an interpretation of this and other narrative structures that share this trait seems to depend on extra-linguistic information, or so-called 'knowledge of the world'. However, having made this observation, we then need to examine to what degree such context-orientation occurs across genres and speech situations, and to explore what factors govern its appearance. To answer these questions, it may be helpful to make an analytical distinction between the amount of communicative 'work' falling on the addressee(s)[7] when it comes to identifying linguistic referents, and the question of how the information is encoded.

In the case of our example of 'informative presupposition', the value of such a distinction is clear in that it makes it possible to point out a connection between a linguistic trait and characteristics that have to do with the communicative *situation*. To put it simply, in some situations, such as at a political meeting or when discussing certain *topics* – as when speaking about a morally sensitive issue – it might be of crucial importance for the speaker to control the addressee's access to information. In such speech situations, accordingly, the linguistic material is often highly obscure. In other situations the need for control is not marked in the same way, and information is represented more explicitly.

What is interesting in this connection is that concerns related to the social distribution of knowledge and the moral universe may also be reflected linguistically. In other words, factors having to do with the speech situation affect the information flow in spoken, but also in written (!) Tokelauan.[8] Note that this phenomenon would seem to confirm what Duranti predicts with his 'moral flow hypothesis'. On the other hand, when asking the second question of how the information is coded, we may also find examples of information that on first glance seems to be missing from linguistic representation, but which upon further examination is revealed to be rather a case of information that is differently coded. The following are a few examples of this, related to the omission of pronouns (see also Hoëm 1993).

Use of deixis 'instead of' pronouns

In these cases, the same statements with pronouns, though not strictly ungrammatical, are judged as unacceptable by native speakers. (For an explanation of the abbreviated linguistic terms, see the Appendix.)

Everyday speech
a. *Lea   mai*
   Said   DIR towards speaker or discourse topic [implicitly 'me' or 'us']
              i.e., 'hither'

te   *toeaina*
ART (sg. spec. ref.)   elder

'The elder said hither [to me/us]'.

b. *Lea   atu*
   Said   DIR. away from speaker or disc. topic [implicitly 'you,' 'her/him'
              or 'them']

au
1pers sg. pron.

'I said forth [to you/him/her/them]'.

c. *Fakatali   mai*   *koe*
   Wait   DIR 'hither'(implicitly 'for me')   2nd. pers. sg. pron

'You, wait hither [for me]'.

Formal speech
d. *Kua   ve   mai*   *ai*   *te*

TAM   tell   DIR hither [implicitly 'us']   ANAPH   ART(sg. spec.)

tahi   *Palehiva*
one   Palehiva (a kind of song)

'One Palehiva tells hither [us]'.

As these examples may serve to illustrate, despite the very frequent omission of pronouns in narratives, in many cases so-called contextual information can be gleaned from the system of demonstrative particles, which together with the directional particles makes it possible to convey very precise information about the *relative spatial position* of the characters in a narrative or the participants in a conversation vis-à-vis each other. This interpretation is supported by the observation that spatial relationships, both between the characters of a narrative and with regards to situating a narrative in geographical space, are frequently clearly marked and expressed in narratives.

Therefore it is a mistake to interpret the lack of pronouns in narratives simply as an omission of information. The information is not always omitted; in some cases, it is differently coded linguistically. Relationships between persons may be represented as spatial relationships by indicating movement and location, and the way in which this is expressed linguistically co-varies with the concerns of the speakers. Note that this interpretation would not have been possible to achieve within a framework restricted to a language-internal account of 'information flow'. As I stated above, in many of these cases it is possible to see a connection between the occurrence of elliptic traits and personal, moral concerns related to the maintenance of what one may call 'social face'. The variation in the linguistic presentation of actors, ranging from full reference to implicit reference to no reference at all, either by the use of proper names or titles, of pronouns, or of directionals etc., reflects variations in relations of relative status. It therefore seems valid also to interpret these traits as reflections of the social factors that Duranti covers with the concept of 'moral flow', and which I explain by reference to the Tokelauan moral universe and thus to the communicative practices associated with 'social face'.

I shall now examine how the flow of information in discourse varies across texts, and see whether it is possible to connect this variation to factors having to do with moral concerns, or rather, with the social control that is expressed as a concern with 'face' and which is exercised through the representation of agency as relations of command and responsibility.

Linguistic Representation of Relations of Command and Responsibility

Relations of command and responsibility between the interlocutors of a narrative are established not only through interpretive frames that serve as metacommunicative messages about how the narratives are to be interpreted, but also through the employment of various morphosyntactic and lexical resources that establish representations of agency.

Like Samoan, the Tokelauan language is a language with so-called ergative-absolutive case marking. An ergative-absolutive case marking pattern allows for the linguistic differentiation between the ascription of causal responsibility and control, as in the following sentence:

Na	*hapo*	*e*	*ia*	*te*	*polo*
TAM past, compl.	Vcatch	ERG	3pers.sg. pron.	ARTspec.sg.ref.	ball

'He or she caught the ball'.

In this sentence, 'he' or 'she' is linguistically represented as an 'ergative agent'. That is, in this language, a linguistic distinction is made between subjects that are agents, i.e., the subjects of transitive clauses, and subjects of intransitive clauses, which can be actors, experiencers and instruments.[9] The subjects of intransitive clauses are 'marked in the same way as the object of the transitive clause' (Duranti 1994: 123), that is, by the absolutive case (i.e., by zero marking or by the nominal particle *ia*). An absolutive rendering of the previous sentence could be:

Na	*hapo*	*te*	*polo*
TAM past, compl.	Vcatch	ARTsg.spec.ref	ball

'The ball was caught'.

Duranti describes how this system

> [O]ffers its speakers the possibility of explicitly and unequivocally assigning to a particular referent/concept the semantic role of Agent, to be understood here as *wilful initiator of an event that is depicted as having consequences for either an object or animate patient*. (Duranti 1994: 125. Emphasis mine)

As mentioned above, the significant distinction in a language such as Tokelauan is not between subject and object, as in English, but between subjects where the action encoded has causal consequences for someone or something and where responsibility for the action is therefore explicitly expressed, and subjects in sentence constructions where no such causality, responsibility or control is encoded linguistically.

This difference may be described as a contrast between a language where the relationship between subjects and objects (in the sense of things, or persons fetishised as objects) is marked grammatically, i.e., as in the case of English, and a language where the grammatically marked relationship is between actions carried out by humans that have consequences for others (persons or objects) and actions that are not represented as having such consequences. This linguistic difference may point to differences in cultural orientation. Crudely put, in the one, relations between people and things are marked grammatically; in the other, relations of command and responsibility between people are marked.

Information Flow Across Genres and Media

To examine how information flows may vary or resemble one another in different narratives, and to explore further to what factors we might attribute this variation, I shall present the following narratives: 1. An extract from a rendering of the history of the school on Nukunonu, Matiti, composed by the then Headmaster, Luciano Peres; 2. An extract from a life history told by the late Kula Fiaola to the Fakaofo village newsletter, *Vainiu mai Fakafotu*; 3. An extract from a statement made by the then Official Secretary of Tokelau, Casimilo Peres, to the people of Tokelau, in the all Tokelau Newsletter, now discontinued, called *Te Vakai*. Finally, I shall return to the narratives presented in the previous Chapter and discuss how the two women may be seen to present themselves and frame their stories in the light of the perspective developed here. The full texts and translations of the three above-mentioned narratives can be found in the Appendix of this work.

The first text was composed by the headmaster of the Nukunonu Matiti school, on the occasion of the New Zealand Governor General's visit to Tokelau. It was but one among many tokens of esteem presented by the community to honour and entertain the Governor General and his wife; other tokens included a Maori greeting ceremony (the Governor General being the first part-Maori in such a position to visit Tokelau), songs and dances, a ceremonial prestation of *hua* (green, drinking coconuts) in the meeting house, a trip around the village and to the outer islets, a reception at the administration office, and so on. As a text it is unique, both because the two other schools in Tokelau do not have such renderings of their histories, and in because renderings of local history do not usually come in such a form. The text was presented in written form on a board outside the schoolbuildings, and it was later painted on the wall of the school itself. (The greeting ceremony is represented on the front cover of this work.)

The newness of the text when compared with common forms of representing 'true stories from the past' (*tala mai anamua*) may lead us to analyse this text as one among many examples of what Eidheim has described as processes of 'dichotomisation' and 'complementarisation' (Eidheim 1971). He analyses those aspects of processes of ethnic identification through which a minority situation, structurally speaking, forces members of the minority group to single out elements of the minority culture as symbolic of their own ethnic identity. Through this process, elements of the minority culture (for purposes of contrast and comparison) are made commensurable with items in the dominant culture, and Eidheim demonstrates how the first step of this process, which he calls dichotomisation, consists of a 'setting apart' and the second step, or complementarisation, consists of a 'joining together' (T. Larsen 1989).

As an illustration of this process, we can take his example from the Saami minority vis-à-vis the encompassing Norwegian society. To assert the Saami identity, a trait such as joik, a particular Saami style of singing, is chosen as symbolising something uniquely Saami (dichotomisation), and then, by reference to the mediating category of folkmusic, it becomes comparable to other forms of Norwegian music (complementarisation). He demonstrates how the hierarchical nature of the relationship is such that it leads to an 'equalisation', in that the minority, or the group with less power, the encompassed group, has no choice but to 'itemise' its culture in terms of, and to match the inventory of, the encompassing culture. Thus a need to have a 'history' *of the same kind*, i.e., comparable with and equal in value to the majority culture, occurs as a result of structural conditions (see also Keesing 1992 for a similar argument).

It is an old truism that education is not culturally neutral.[10] Narrative one, that I have called 'Care for coconuts', could be read as an example of this, judging from the locally unusual use of chronology as a device to present a 'history'. In light of the above discussion about the relationship between information flow and context, however, we need to consider how the information flow of this narrative may relate to particular characteristics of this genre and its intended audience, and in what way such factors are reflected in the narrative structure of the text.

Narrative One: 'Care for Coconuts'

Taku Tala	*My history*
1904. Na talia ai e te Uluga Talafau te popo ake mai ke toto.	1904. The Ulugatalafau accepted the ripe coconut washed ashore so that it might grow.
1906. Haihu.	1906. Sprouting.
1909. Matala te lauhomo, kenakena,	1909. The germinating coconut's sprout opens, brown/yellowish,
lautovivi, laumatemate.	black leaves, dead leaves.
1912. Kua mauaka te pulapula.	1912. The coconut-seedling came to be well rooted.
[...]	[...]

When simply translated, on the basis of the information that is presented linguistically in the Tokelauan original version, this text is highly obscure. So, what characterises this text, and more importantly, how does it lend itself to interpretation? Given the prolific use of metaphor – note in particular the many references to various kinds and stages in the growth of coconuts – and the apparent absence of clues as to what this 'history' is actually about, it would seem safe to say that the text does not lend itself to classification as a prototypical 'autonomous' written text. However, as mentioned earlier, it is markedly chronological, and this in itself is enough to set it apart from most Tokelau narratives. Here it suffices to say that most Tokelau narratives concerning historical material do not in themselves carry any explicit references to time, nor do their narrative structure usually conform to a linear, strictly climactic developmental plot or scheme.

The rich use of imagery prevalent in this narrative is common in predominantly verbal genres, such as songs and speeches. The narrative structure of speeches, however, is such that interpretative clues are usually represented in the text – although not as a part of the sentence structure of which the image is a part, but rather in the post-positioned phrases.[11] The main textual figure, which serves to create narrative coherence throughout this narrative, is the imagery of the various stages of development of a coconut. The rich imagery draws upon local flora and fauna, and hints to the socio-political history that is to be found by adding the so-called 'knowledge of the world'. (See the version of the narrative in the

Appendix, where the text-external or contextual information is presented in brackets.) For somebody familiar with the events mentioned in brackets, the textual clues would probably be enough to clarify a large part of the *tala*. Another key for interpretation is the chronology, i.e., the dates. The name of the school and also the title, 'my history', can be seen as a framing device, i.e., as defining the main topic, but the imagery of the coconut is probably better read as providing the main structure of the text, for reasons that will be discussed below.

Thus, a preliminary conclusion is that the narrative structure of this text provides people outside of its immediate reference group with very few clues as to what the text is about. The syntax in the main follows the standard pattern of verb-initiality. For an illustration of this, consider how the sentences in the extract presented earlier all start with a verbal construction. On the semantic level, there are more clues as to what the text is about, but they are consistently not made explicit, except for one mention of the name of the school.

Does the difference between the implicit and the explicitly presented information, as evident in the difference between the first translation as compared with the translation with brackets (both in Appendix), consist then in adding the so-called 'knowledge of the world'? And if this is the case, is this added information in any way marked in the text? Have I, by talking to the author, gained contextual information which is implicit in the text that does not have to be stated explicitly because it is knowledge common to all members of the speech-community? As a step towards answering these questions, it may be helpful to note that the author was of the opinion that all of the members of the text's immediate reference group,[12] i.e., the teachers of Nukunonu, had few difficulties interpreting the text; it was mostly transparent to them. Visiting teachers from Fakaofo and Atafu also 'got most of it', but some of them had asked about the meaning of specific passages. It seems very likely that the degree of transparency diminishes rapidly as one moves outwards from the inner circle of those who are in the know. In this respect, this text-type shows identical characteristics with Tokelau speeches (*lauga*), which I have discussed elsewhere (Hoëm 1995) as an example of the social distribution of knowledge within Tokelau society.

In the search for interpretative keys in this narrative, I have carried out an inter-linear morphemic translation (see Hoëm 1995b for a documentation of this). The morphemic analysis, was guided by the question posed by Duranti in his 1994 work, namely, why this form now? I shall summarise my observations by means of this question, but I would like to stress that such a focus does not imply that the choice of linguistic forms by a speaker or an author is to be seen only as a result of conscious strategies. Habitual ways of speaking, and common phrases and forms, are often reproduced without any intentional depth on behalf of the speaker, just as is the case with most other forms of social action. This does not mean, however, that such habitual forms may not be expressive of culturally significant patterns; on the contrary, it is frequently in these naturalised practices that we may successfully look for traces of the deeply engrained cultural schemas or patterns.

As mentioned earlier, this text does not lend itself to classification as a prototypical written text, and one of the clearest linguistic indications of this is the almost absolute (one occurrence may be found in an embedded clause) non-occurrence of the linguistic form called the topic marker: *ko*. The focus on natural phenomena as the carrying structure of the text is common, and points to the high degree of inter-textuality mentioned earlier. In this respect, that is in the choice of central imagery (*ata*), this text bears a much closer resemblance to older genres within Tokelau expressive culture than a surface reading would lead us to expect. The unmarked syntactical structure, verb initiality, also strongly supports this impression.

The presentation of the text as a chronological history is a primary interpretative frame, but a more important interpretative key is to be found precisely in the imagery that focuses on natural processes of growth and decay. The socio-political events, which we would expect to be highlighted if we were to choose a reading according to the primary interpretative frame referred to above, are only hinted at, and this adds to the text's resemblance to other genres such as songs and speeches (see also Hoëm 1992). This text is highly elliptic, and the down-playing of agency (as defined above) is a prevalent trait. Interestingly, it is possible to observe how relationships of responsibility and command are represented, through the employment of various linguistic resources, in subtle and nuanced ways. In this text, relations of responsibility and command are mainly expressed in three different ways: through the use of ergative agents (2 cases); through strategies of what Duranti calls 'mitigated agency' – that is, through the use of the genitive construction, either in its stronger form using the *a*- or control form (7 cases); or through the use of the *o*- or non-control genitive form (6 cases).

It is possible to account for the use of these respective forms the following way: the two cases of ergative agency are used in combination with ceremonial address, thus creating an effect of distance and respect, and at the same time stressing the formal capacity of those addressed. This serves to legitimise their actions, and the ergative case is only used in this text with respect to absolutely uncontroversial, i.e., respectable and normative, actions. The shift between the use of the control and the non-control form is interesting; in the cases where they co-occur in the same passage, responsibility is shifted over to the actor to which the *a*- form applies. The use of both genitive constructions, described by Duranti as a strategy of mitigated agency, seems to soften the burden of responsibility by, as he says, shifting the focus on the action (or the patiens) rather than on the doer.

The cases where the control-form is used alone are all examples of actions that carry positive connotations, but where the event referred to is negative or controversial, the *o*- or non-control form is used. However, this pattern is not consistent. For example, we find an exception in the case of a 'difficult event' where the *a*- form is used. Granted that one accepts the interpretation of the author (i.e., that the churchworker's responsibility for the school was broken, not that it was continued), I attribute the use of the control-form to the acceptability of allocating responsibility to persons, groups, or things associated with the church or with God (for a similar point, see Duranti 1994: 144).

As a final illustration of what I have called the down-playing of agency, we can return to the lines where it is stated that 'the opinion that was put together', a phrasing typical of the narrative strategies so frequently used in this text. The interconnection between the information flow and the moral universe that we have seen illustrated in this text through the representation of agency is here expressive of hierarchical, respect and authority relations. The narrative point of view is present in the strategy of *speaking 'up' as one from a lower to 'higher' positions*. In this narrative, relations of responsibility and command are allocated to groups and houses, and through the strategy of showing respect through distancing, the project of seeking legitimacy for the institution on behalf of which the text speaks, namely the school, is realised.

Narrative Two: 'A Life and Blessings'

Unlike the first narrative, the following narrative focuses on an individual person. Moreover, the narrative genre is a life history. I wish to explore how this choice of topic and genre influence the information flow of this narrative, and also examine how the representation of relationships is affected. Again the full text and translation can be found in the Appendix.

Tala pukupuku o toku olaga ma fakamanuiaga a te Aliki na ko mauagia.	A short story of my life and blessings of the Lord that came to be.
Ko au ko K. Kula Fiaola na fanau mai au i te aho 30/4/24. Ko oku matua ko Fiaola ma Kula ni matua Kelihiano, nae galulue foki i te tofi tiakono,	I am Kula Fialola I was born on the day 30/4/24. My parents Fiaola and Kula Christian parents worked all the time in the position (of) deacons
mo tauhi kaiga nae fehoahoani malohi foki	for taking care of extended families and helping strongly

ki te Ekalehia ma te nuku	in the Church and the village
ma te komiti tumama,	and the sanitation (women's) comittee
ma akoako lelei ki matou te fanau.	and taught well to us the children.
E toka fitu (7) te fanau,	The children were seven,
e toka tolu (3) ia tama,	three were boys,
e toka fa (4) ia teine.	four were girls.
Na akoako lelei ki matou	We were taught well
i te Tuhi Paia mo te poto faka-iena	in the Bible for the wisdom found there
ona po (fakafetai ki te Atua).	in the evenings
	(thanks to the Lord).
[...]	[...]

This narrative is in the form of a life history, produced for the local newsletter *Vainiu mai Fakafotu in Fakaofo*. The piece is called '*Tala pukupuku o toku olaga ma fakamanuiaga a te Aliki na ko mauagia*' ('a short story of my life and [the] blessings of the Lord [that] that came to be'). Note the use of the term *tala*, the same term that was used to classify the previous narrative.

This is also an unusual text. It is unusual in the sense that it is of a new kind – the newsletters in Tokelau are probably among the first to publicly present such life histories.[13] The framing chronology is also recognisable from the first narrative, *Taku tala*, and it is striking that they are both classified as (presented as) being *tala* (tales or stories). Such an index of calendar time may occur in situations where it is important to present complementarity of the kind described by Eidheim (see also Keesing) and, given the sometimes striking use of dates in this second narrative as well, it seems reasonable to interpret this device in the same way as in the first narrative.

Looking at the other characteristics of this narrative, however, one sees a striking difference in the degree of explicitness. There is no need to look outside the text for further contextual information in order to be able to interpret the events that are referred to. One could say that this may be related to the fact that few, if any, socio-political events of the kind that inform narrative one are mentioned in this narrative. The text's explicitness may at least partially be interpreted as a result of the narrator's attempt to render what has actually taken place in her life in accordance with the norms of what is considered a morally proper (ideal) 'life'.[14]

In this narrative, there is no use of metaphor whatsoever, and the syntax is fuller in the sense that there is more frequent use of lexical words to describe so-called real-life events. The syntactical structure is also more varied, ranging from *ko*-fronted constructions (19 cases) to ordinary verb-initial sentences and to ergative ones (6 cases). The text is closer to what would ordinarily count as a prototypical written text, of an essay-like type, not unlike the women's' stories elicited by Vonen and Hovdhaugen (cf., Hoëm *et al.* 1992). There is one trait, however that is atypical of a written text, namely the 'thanksgiving' parts which may be interpreted as signifying the factor of 'involvement', which Chafe has suggested as a diagnostic criterion of a spoken text. We can find a parallel to this in Besnier's work from the atoll Nukulaelae in Tuvalu. In his work, he has shown that this factor features very prominently in personal letters in that society. The ergative constructions range from 4 cases of allocation of responsibility to official capacities, to a direct reference to the first person pronoun, 'I', in the line where the narrator wins a cup, and finally in the line 'used by the patients'.

The non-control form of the genitive occurs far more frequently than the control form (22 occurrences vs. 10), and the forms *ki* (DIR/PREP) and *i* (PREP) dominate compared with the directionals *mai* and *atu*. In this narrative, the anaphora have the standard co-referential pattern, in contrast to what we observed to be the case for the narrative 'Care for coconuts'.

The pattern of *ko*-fronting that is prevalent in this narrative could be interpreted as influenced by the biblical context referred to by the narrator. In the Tokelauan Bible there is a marked tendency to refer explicitly to agency, and a high frequency of *ko*-fronted sentences.[15] As R. Hooper has remarked (personal communication), the high degree of transparency in this text may also be related to the narrator's familiarity with the biographical genre from her visits overseas. In addition, A. M. Vonen (1993: 87) notes that the pattern of topic marking (*ko*-fronting) is commonly connected with elicited and/or expository texts.

To conclude, the contrast with the narrative 'Care for coconuts' is striking, and it seems clear that the difference in narrative structure is directly related to the dominant frame of the text. This second narrative is produced within a religious frame of reference, and no controversial events are referred to. These factors give the narrator a certain leeway in degree of explicitness, and legitimise a focus on herself as the narrative 'I'. There is no reason to restrict the allocation of relations of command and responsibility when it occurs within a context which is by definition dignified (*mamalu*): i.e., an old respected woman (*lomatua*), relating her life history to the readers of the local newsletter, thereby setting an example of a life-trajectory that it would be admirable for all to follow. She acquires the legitimacy to do so through her references to the religious context at frequent intervals throughout the narrative. In other words, the relationships that inform the relations between the interlocutors of this text are hierarchical, as in the previous text. However, there is a significant difference between the two in that 'Care for coconuts' speaks as *young to old*, that is, in spatial terms, as *low to high*, whereas 'A life and blessings' speaks as *old to young* or, in other words, as *high to low*. This, as we have seen, makes a significant difference with respect to the grammatical choices made in the two cases.[15]

Narrative Three: 'Why Go to New York?'

The final narrative represents yet another innovation, namely an expository newsletter item that by definition makes a clear break with the norms of dissemination of information described earlier. We shall examine how this genre affects the information flow and the representation of relationships in the narrative structure (again refer to the Appendix for the full text and translation).

Malaga a Tokelau ki	Tokelau's Journey to
Malo Kaufakatahi	the United Nations
Kupu Tomua	Introductory Words
Na fakatekia te tokalahiga	Many people were surprised
o tagata	
i te ahiahiga a na hui	by the visits of the representatives
o Tokelau ki Malo Kaufakatahi.	of Tokelau to the United Nations.
Ve ake ai foki he lagona,	and some probably also wondered
aihea nei te kua teki atu lava	why suddenly
ni hui kua olo	the representatives went
ki Malo Kaufakatahi.	to the United Nations.
Hove pe kua fakauiga	Maybe (they) meant (and)
ve ia pe manatu	considered (it to be) like that
kua i te takitakiga o Tokelau	in the leadership of Tokelau
ka iei he huiga i te tulaga	there would be changes in the position
ei ei te malo i te vaitaimi nei,	of the government at this time,
pe ona foki ko te Tokelau	or that it was also because the
muamua te kua kavea	first Tokelauan became
ma Failautuhi Fakapitoa	Official Secretary
ka olo ve ai oi lipoti	that (they) were going like that to report
na fakafitauli i te va	the controversial issues in the relationship
o Niu Hila ma Tokelau	between New Zealand and Tokelau
ki Malo Kaufakatahi.	to the United Nations.
[...]	[...]

The narrative that I have called 'Why go to New York?' is from the Tokelau newsletter *Te Vakai* and is an explanation to the people of Tokelau of Tokelau's political situation, composed on the occasion of Tokelau's first visit to the United Nations in New York.

This text resembles the previous 'A life and blessings', in that the subject matter is accessible and relatively transparent on the basis of the information given in the text. Compared with the first narrative (and the speeches presented in Hoëm 1992), one would expect a high frequency of ellipses, due to the clearly political nature of the subject. However, this is not the case. The main interpretative frame of the narrative, as presented in the first passage under the heading 'introductory words' and as repeated in the heading 'main theme of the visit', is to be found in the project of conveying new and vital information to the people of Tokelau. This project is unusual within the context of the traditional political institutions, but it makes sense within the institutions of the Tokelau Public Service.[16] Given the particular nature of the information presented in this narrative – information that it is not yet common knowledge – it would be virtually impossible to use the ordinary strategies of double meanings and veiled references here. That the presentation of this information is a difficult and politically sensitive task, however, may clearly be deduced from the sentence constructions.

The sentence constructions in this narrative differ from those of the previous texts in that many of them are excessively 'back-heavy'. It is almost impossible to know what most of the sentences or phrases are about (at least for a reader used to a different information flow) before the whole passage has been read, and only then is it possible to re-construct the meaning by retracing one's steps backwards. This stylistic pattern is one of many rhetorical devices in Tokelauan (R. Hooper 1987). It could be called 'informational postsupposition', in contrast with 'informative presuppositions'. As mentioned in my interpretation of the first narrative, this information structure is most common in the genre of speeches (Hoëm 1992). The informative presuppositions use ko-fronted or topic-marked phrases, introducing a new theme or topic into a narrative but presenting it as if it were known. This may have the felicitous result of blocking the way for a discussion of the matter in that something is already presented as a given, as an indisputable fact.

The pattern we encounter here seems to be somewhat the opposite, in that it goes far in its attempts to satisfy the readers' need for information. It is important to note, however, that the gravity of this task is balanced by writing in the most polite, self-effacing way possible. This effect is largely achieved through a strategy of embeddedness, mainly through the use of what in the *Tokelau Dictionary* are called 'reason clauses', introduced in this case by the conjunction ona, and by clauses of 'purpose and caution, introduced by the subordinating conjunction ke' (TD: xlvii).

Going again outside the text for clues as to what socio-political and cultural factors might inform the choice of such varied sentence structures, it is interesting to note how the topic of the text in *itself* influences the form in which it is presented. In this case, the text is about major political changes in Tokelau, presented by an informed person to the general public of Tokelau. His relatively young age and the importance of his position (as an Official Secretary he is the head of the Tokelau Public Service) place him in a somewhat awkward position in relation to the political leaders on the village level, and it becomes very important not to challenge their authority while establishing legitimacy for the choice of participants actually going to New York.

As mentioned above, there are no hidden meanings in the text. In contrast to the first text we analysed, the bureaucratic or modernistic view of a text as a means of conveying information is apparent here as a frame. However, the presentation is done in such a way as to ensure that Tokelau sensitivities are heeded. The absence of metaphor is also notable in this narrative when compared to the first narrative, 'Care for coconuts'.

The occurrence of ergative agents (16 in all) is in most cases allocated to the names of institutions or titles. An exception to this pattern can be found in the one line where 1st.pers.sg.pronoun 'I' is used, but on closer examination, this occurs in a description of the action of getting to know about something done by others; in other words, in this case, the responsibility for the action in focus lies elsewhere. The other exceptions are, interestingly, to be found in lines that express the allocation of responsibility and freedom of action to the people of Tokelau. As in the two other texts, there are many more instances in this narrative of the non-control possessive form than of the control form (60 to 17 instances). Again the control form is mainly applied to titles, institutions, and offices, whereas the non-control form is also applied to processes, principles and so on. The use of *ko*-fronting is present (23 cases), but it is not a striking feature of this text, as was the case with 'A life and blessings'. Instead, we find a relatively high frequency of *ki* (DIR/PREP) and *i* (PREP), thus adding to the impression of embeddedness described above. The references of the anaphoric constructions in this text are transparent, as were the ones in the previous text, and in this text the co-referential noun-phrases are consistently presented before and close to the anaphoric particle.

This text, then, when compared with the two previous ones, *speaks across or faces directly*. That is, it addresses all groups of Tokelauans, in a direct, egalitarian fashion. The strategies of hierarchy are adopted when a balance is sought between high and low, but the dominant relation informing the grammatical choices in this narrative seems to be level, or in Huntsman's terms, symmetrical.

Framing, Agency and Representation of Relationships

In the previous sections, I have analysed three narratives according to Duranti's hypothesis that a 'framing of characters and events' occurs 'in terms of their positive or negative value vis-à-vis community standards' (Duranti 1994: 121). Relations are assumed between grammatical choices and their pragmatic or metapragmatic functions, in that 'they do not only tell us about the events, they also say something about what the events mean to the speaker and what they should mean to the audience' (ibid.).

Through the uncovering of representations of agency in the texts, the most significant interpretative key in accounting for the variation in information flow is found in what I call relationships of command and responsibility. Another interpretative key is found in the main subject matter of the text (i.e., 'school-history', 'life history', and 'Tokelau's visit to the UN'), but as I have shown, this factor does not provide us with nearly as much information as that which is provided through a focus on the relationships between the interlocutors of the texts. In this sense, all of these narratives may be said to be couched in the language of face-to-face interaction, rather than of textual autonomy. This characteristic provides the dominant relations informing the narrative structure of the texts: that is, *speaking up, speaking down and speaking directly across*, respectively. These 'ways of speaking' reflect typical qualities of relationships. As mentioned in the Introduction, Huntsman has labelled these as complementary and symmetrical, and I describe them as 'sided' relationships of varying compositions of hierarchy and equality.

The themes of the narratives analysed so far in this Chapter can all be related to the experience of modernity: the first in its creation of history as a chronological object, and the second in its turning of life into an, again chronologically ordered, life history. The third narrative relates to the experience of modernity in the most direct fashion in that its topic is modernisation. It is also not coincidental that we find this connection with the experience of modernity in narratives that are presented in the written medium. This is not to say, however, that these texts conform easily to common notions about what is typically taken to characterise a written text, for example, traits such as 'detachment' and 'restraint'. This in itself should suffice to make us wary of making generalisations about oral and literate modes of communication on the basis of assumed inherent traits (see R. Finnegan 1992; E. Tonkin 1992).

Reflexivity is one of the concepts (besides authenticity) which is frequently attached to the oral:literate divide model, and also to the tradition:modernity dichotomy. Frequently, this is done in the rather coarse manner of attributing reflexivity to modernity and doxa to so-called traditional societies (see e.g., Bourdieu). An important exception to this is to be found within ritual theory that follows the lead of Victor Turner. Here, reflexivity is rather an inherent quality of the liminal phase of a ritual, where the actor is temporarily freed from the everyday constraints of his or her society before the next phase, which is re-integration. At the risk of distorting more nuanced analyses, I do wish to point out the difficulties connected with postulating *a priori* cultural 'locations' for reflexivity. First, whether something is used reflexively or not should probably be posed as an open question to be studied empirically. Second, it is possible to see reflexivity not as a qualitative measure of the limits of doxa and discourse at all (Bourdieu 1977), but more generally as the process of externalisation that I attributed to narrative earlier in this Chapter (see also Jackson 2002, Ochs and Capps 1996).

In my analysis of the narratives presented in this Chapter, we have seen how, underlying the 'information flow' in the texts, we find expressions of reflexivity in the monitoring of the relations of command and responsibility, a monitoring that I have previously described as informing the 'sided' character of relationships. If we now return briefly to the two extracts from life stories presented in the previous Chapter, this aspect of representation may stand out yet more clearly.

The Narrative Point of View

In analysing the narratives presented above, and in my rendering of the two life-histories presented in the previous Chapter, I have attempted to extract what, in technical terms, is called the 'point of view'. This term refers to the fact that every story is 'told from a vantage point' (Goffman 1974). Ochs and Capps comment that 'while point of view may be explicitly conveyed through soliloquies, asides, idioms, and other predications, it is implicitly realised though the structuring of narrative plots' (1996: 26). Furthermore, they add that: 'In forging story elements into a plot, narrators build a theory of events' (Ibid.: 27).

In the narratives analysed in this chapter, I have found that thematic choices have some impact on the information flow, ranging from highly elliptic (narrative one) to transparent (narrative two), with narrative three coming somewhere in between the two. However, the grammatical representation of relationships, as constructed by the narrator and in relation to a perceived audience, actually seems to dominate the narrative structure to a much greater extent. It is of course possible to argue that the subject matter of a narrative and who the potential recipients of that narrative will be do, to some extent, go together.

The question of how an audience or intended recipients of a narrative may influence the narrative in various ways is particularly highlighted when it comes to elicited material. There has been a long-standing discussion within anthropology about the use of life histories, in terms of what kind of data they may be said to represent. Life histories are typically elicited material. In Tokelau, it is not common for people to recount the stories of their lives to each other. People have a very high degree of familiarity with each others lives, though, and events that are perceived as significant or particularly telling about a particular person are frequently made the subject of joking and parody in skits by stand-up comedians on public occasions.[18]

Analytically, what makes life histories an important and interesting source of information lies in the fact that the story presented by the narrator is but one chosen version among several possible versions (J. du Boulay and R. Williams, 1984: 248). Thus, how the narrator shapes a narrative, selects events, assign values and reflects upon them, represents what I call interpretative keys. I collected and compared the two life histories presented in the previous Chapter on a thematic basis: they represent what may be called 'migration histories'. In the final Chapter, I shall draw on these stories and on many others to discuss fundamental patterns of orientation and social change. Here, I wish to reflect a little on the respective points of view in what I have called the narrative of leaving and the narrative of return.

The narrator of the 'leaving' presents herself as a typical Tokelau comedian. Her choice of a humorous rendering of her life history indicates that she perceives the whole of Tokelau as potential recipients of the narrative. This has consequences for her placing of herself in the text. She discusses all significant events in terms of social face (*mata*), and downplays her narrative 'I' as somebody who has little knowledge. These two main ways of framing her position are in agreement with common perceptions of what kind of behaviour is acceptable for a woman in her position, and goes some way to ensure her continued standing in the community.

The narrator of the 'return', on the other hand, had the outside recorder, the anthropologist, as her audience of one. She deliberately used the interview situation to reflect on her own difficulties, and placed herself at the centre of the narrative in a manner totally alien to the structure of 'leaving'. This impression is strengthened by her choice of language: she code switches between English and Tokelauan, using Tokelauan to depict typical experiences, such as walking along the village road and taking part in standard phatic exchanges (see also Hoëm 1993). This allows for a more detached rendering of features of village life. Interestingly, however, most of the material she chooses to discuss consists of issues related to social face and to dominant communicative practices in the atolls. The events she has selected for discussion are in fact linked together by this theme: how her relationship to local conceptions of relationships, and what is considered proper behaviour, gradually changes as a result of intense social pressure.

Her narrative has neither the framing nor the subject matter necessary to render it acceptable to a larger Tokelau audience in any direct way. However, in new genres and media, such as the second drama, *Mafine* ('Woman'), narratives such as hers are being told. The story of 'leaving' is intended for written publication, and is also ultimately dependent upon new media to reach an audience inside and outside of Tokelau. The second narrative of this Chapter, 'A life and blessings', is also presented orally, but is intended for written publication. The narrative 'I' is stated boldly and clearly, within the frame of 'old speaking to young', that is, from above to below. In comparison, the narrative of leaving speaks as 'young to old', and chooses a frame of humour to get away with such a subversive project. The narrative of return speaks, as does the narrative 'Why go to New York', directly across, but within a frame of 'non serious' or intimate activities, typical of situations associated with 'the back' (*i tua*) of the village. This spatial framing places the narrative of return in direct opposition to the spatial framing that the narrator of 'A life and blessings' speaks from, which is a typical 'front' (*i mua*), or formal setting. The narrators' respective rendering of relationships and her attitude to parting with information reflect this fact.

As mentioned in the previous Chapter, the two life histories presented there clearly express the trauma or 'culture shock' connected with the migration experience. This narrative plot, although important and interesting in itself, has not been the main focus of my analysis except as providing a basis for comparison. Rather, I have wanted to highlight *how the experience of displacement seems to activate fundamental orientations*. In my analysis of all of the narratives, I have pointed to how prevalent conceptualisations of place and position serve to inform, shape and make sense of subjective experiences of displacement and readjustment. The *conceptualisations of place and position* are related to what I describe as sided relationships, and as producing patterns of command and responsibility. The morally charged orientations that I extract from the two narratives presented in the previous Chapter are largely expressed in spatial terms. In Tokelauan, these relations are described in many ways, some of which are *hili* (high), *lalo* (low), *mua* (front), and *tua* (back), *loto* (inside) and *fafo* (outside), and they are also described in terms of face (*mata*)[19] or facing (*ala, feagai or hagatonu*). The significance of these terms and how they relate to the production of social spaces will be discussed further in the following Chapter. Here I have discussed how the framing of representations relates to social relationships. How representational frames also co-vary with culturally significant events, and thereby contribute to the production of social spaces, will be the topic of the final Chapter of this work.

Notes

1. See also Hoëm 1995 for a description of attitudes towards 'knowledge' and 'information' as a basis for the hierarchy of age.
2. Cf., Huntsman, Tuia and Thomas, 1990, Introduction.
3. Cf., *kupu*, word, in the TD: 169: '2). Statement, remark. [..] v. Be obedient, listen to commands. [...] *E kupu tahi te fenua nei*: There is only one authority in this land. [...]'
4. Cf., the comments to the narrative of return, Chapter three.
5. Such meetings of reconciliation are called *fakaleleiga* (literally 'making well or good').
6. As I have described elsewhere, this information pattern is not unique to communication in the Tokelau language, but I would argue that the frequency of such constructions is comparatively high in Tokelauan compared to the frequency in other languages.
7. This distinction is the basis for McLuhan's famous typology of 'hot and cool media'.
8. Cf., D. Parkin (1982: xlviii) on the relationship between power and knowledge

in the study of speech events. See also N. Besnier 1988 and 1989, on the relations between social context and written language in Nukulaelae, Tuvalu.

9. Note here that the distinction between subjects that are described as agents and subjects that are described as actors is made on the grounds of the difference in ascription of causal responsibility in the two cases.

10. See the work about Education in Tokelau and the Scholarship scheme, V.G. Sallen (1983) for a vivid description of the main differences in the nature of Tokelau versus the New Zealand based education.

11. For illustrations of this, see Hoëm 1992.

12. Not in the sense of main recipients of the text, but as one of its main groups of characters.

13. It may have happened occasionally in the schools or in mission letters, but not on such a scale, nor with characters with whom people were familiar.

14. See also Hoëm 1995, Chapter four on similarities and differences between Women's and Men's talk.

15. See also Besnier 1988 for a similar observation from Tuvalu, referring to written sermons.

16. See also Chapter five for a further discussion of the spatial concepts associated with these relationships.

17. For a description of these communicative patterns, see Hoëm 1995.

18. M. Lieber (1997) makes the same point on the bibliographic knowledge that atoll dwellers from Kapingamarangi communities have of one another, as compared to Kapinga residents in Honiara.

19. Also 'eyes', and 'centre'.

Chapter 5

Social Spaces

Symbolic orderings of space [...] provide a framework for experience
through which we learn who or what we are in society (D. Harvey 1990: 214)

Tulaga:
Site, location, position. Stand, platform, stage. Notches cut into a tree to
make climbing easier. Print, mark. Condition, state, situation. Status,
position, rank. Place. (*Tokelau Dictionary*)

Recent studies in cultural geography and the phenomenology of landscape (Harvey 1990; Lavie and Swedenburg 1996; Hastrup 1997; Fog
Olwig 1997) tend to stress the co-constructive nature of the relationship
between place and identity. Many of these studies share some underlying
assumptions and approaches to the relationship between locality and
belonging. In particular, it is possible to detect a common bias in the
many studies based on analyses of colonial and post-colonial situations,
as these relate to the institutions of the nation-state. Thus, theorisation on
the relationship between place and identity is coloured by the existence
(or the establishment of) national borders. This factor also leads to a classification and study of kinds of 'displacement' experiences (Fuglerud
2001). The tendency in so-called globalisation studies (found in studies as
varied as Hannertz, Bauman and Østerud) to focus on processes of fragmentation and disintegration may be seen as partly a result of this kind
of bias in the data basis selected for theorisation.

However, and as noted in particular by Karen Fog Olwig, this theoretical unity of focus has been achieved somewhat at the expense of the
theorisation of *movement* as an empirically varied phenomenon (Fog
Olwig 1997). Her own work on the processes of migration and identification represents a promising step towards such theorisation. Even so,
there is still a serious lack of information on processes of movement other
than that presented in studies which tend to see it as disruptive and
destabilising. Therefore, in this work, I have found it important to explore

how it might be possible to trace such dynamic patterns of movement and relations to place *in the contemporary Pacific*. In this Chapter, I shall concentrate on the atoll environment as social space, to explore further how acts of identification and representations of agency relate to movements within and between different social spaces and in relation to changing institutional frameworks.

As mentioned previously, Fox and many other scholars with him (e.g., V. Valeri, J. Charlot and M. Sahlins) have pointed out how local conceptions of identity in Austronesian societies are frequently represented in genealogical terms, as paths subject to processes of growth and decay. More specifically, the processes of growth and decay – or in Fox' terms, of social ascendancy or descendancy – are rendered through images that speak of sources or roots, bases or trunks, branches or posts. Across the Austronesian speaking world, spatial orientation is characteristically represented through the use of deixis (as we have seen in Chapter four), but also through what Fox calls topogeny, that is, through the identification of specific places in genealogical terms (Fox 1997).

I argue in this Chapter that the two aspects, of spatial orientation and the valuation of places in terms of their social history, are entwined in local practice. The connection that I have established in earlier Chapters, between spatial orientation and patterns of social relationships, may in other words be seen as an aspect of the social creation of events, as unfolding in, and in relation to, places that have particular significance attached to them. Furthermore, events occur as qualitatively different situations, associated with different places or areas in the atoll environment, compared to the difference between the formal and intimate situations I have described earlier, and between the centre and periphery in the villages.

In the Introduction and in Chapter two, I described how the local environment, in the atolls and in New Zealand, provides a basis for attachment, or in other words functions as a resource for acts of social identification in a manner akin to what I have described for language. In New Zealand, images of the home atoll, as represented in songs and in other forms of narrative, provide powerful models for what is considered the proper way of life, faka-Tokelau. In the same fashion, localities such as the Hutt Valley or Porirua in the larger Wellington area similarly function as points of group identification.

I argue that people have developed a particular awareness of the social environment that results in a prevalent '*sense of place*'. It is, however, not the case that this pattern of culture-specific directions or orientations is of such a nature that 'one's place' is simply experienced as a given, unalterable fact. Rather, what I here call 'directions' are constantly employed to produce common definitions of situation, making interaction possible by creating a context within which interaction may take place. Moreover, these 'directions' may also be employed as means of orientation when moving in life-worlds outside of Tokelau. I see this 'sense of place', then, as expressive of a prevalent concern with social relations. Furthermore, it is also possible to see this concern with relationships reflected in the language use of for example narratives, persons and relations between persons tend to be represented (most commonly by the use of deixis) as a movement in space and as situated in space. In other words, language and space are employed together as resources in acts of identification that produce processes of social inclusion and exclusion.

As will be apparent from the discussion in the previous Chapters, *negotiation* of status-differences is a pervasive trait of social interaction in Tokelau. Such negotiations may include balancing the concerns of an official position versus the dimension of age; or weighing the concerns of kinship, as between brothers, against the dimension of age; or striking a balance between the demands represented by 'village' and the 'family', to mention but a few examples. This empirical observation of a constant weighing of the demands and concerns related to one set of relationships against other, equally pressing concerns, may be explained by the fact that status differences, are, in most cases, not simply established a priori. This state of affairs may be attributed to numerous factors, such as the abolishment of the kingship system early in this century, the cognatic nature of the kinship system,[1] and the role played by the village as a whole in mediating the authority held by the formal political institutions, to mention but a few. In other words, social interaction is characterised by a 'focus on relationships', and this focus of interest is commonly expressed as a concern with place.

In his study of the social production of space, David Harvey (1990: 206) draws attention to the phenomenon that, as he says: 'Any system of representation [...] is a spatialization of sorts which automatically freezes the flow of experience'. His application of the term spatialization is thus very wide, and it seems to be used to describe an aspect of all representational activity. On the one hand, what I wish to draw attention to in this quote is the general quality of 'freezing', or objectifying the flow of experience. On the other hand, following Giddens' analysis of the 'duality of structure',[2] I also want to point to the 'constitution of the agent' that occurs in this process of objectification. In the previous Chapter, I described in some detail how such constitution of agency is achieved through linguistic representation.

The patterns that are the outcome of such processes may take on a doxic quality, and the patterns are then only possible to infer, for example from bodily hexis, but also from linguistic- and spatial representations. However, the doxic patterns are not possible to interpret satisfactorily without reference to other, more ideologically explicit or discursive aspects within the local knowledge horizon. This, then, is why, in the following, I shall use the different levels implied by Harvey's model of a 'grid' of spatial practices (Harvey 1990: 218) to further explicate the moral universe represented by the atoll life-world. I would like to stress that, in making an analytical distinction between social spaces seen as practices related to production and reproduction, and the representations of such practices, I discuss to a large extent the same empirical material. I make use of this analytical distinction to allow for a discussion of how what may be called material and cultural production are related, and of how, in a non-urban setting, landscape may come to provide a means for keeping activities separate that in a city may take place within different buildings, institutions and areas.

The Atoll Environment as Social Space

Harvey's *'grid' of spatial practices* is an analytical device constructed for the purpose of capturing some of the complexity to be found when examining the semiotic domain of space. As such, I find it useful for my purposes in this Chapter. However, much of Harvey's argument is shaped by a concern to establish the material experience of 'objective structures' (1990: 219) as engendered 'out of the economic basis of the social formation in question'.[3] As it is not my objective with this analysis to establish causal relations between the various spatial practices in a Marxist sense, but rather to throw light on the spatial dimension as a semiotic domain, we shall leave this aspect of Harvey's thought and instead make use of H. Lefebvre's (Lefebvre 1974/1991) characterisation of the three dimensions with which Harvey operates.

Harvey's three dimensions are (1) material spatial practices, (2) representations of space and (3) spaces of representation. Lefebvre (in Harvey's translation) describes these dimensions as 'the experienced, the perceived and the imagined' (Harvey 1990: 219), and he envisages a dialectical relationship between the three. Even though Harvey advocates the rendering of this relationship as causal rather than as dialectic, he concedes that:

> The spaces of representation [that is, the realm of the imagined] [...] have the potential not only to affect representation of space but also to act as a material productive force with respect to spatial practices. (Harvey 1990: 219. Insert mine)

Again, my objective is not to establish the relations, causal or otherwise, between these three dimensions, and I shall take the liberty of assuming that the relation between them is one of dynamic interwovenness, created by, and at the same time providing conditions for, the social institutions that we see reflected in individual life-trajectories. People's disposition in space is one of the means through which particular patterns of social relations are established, inculcated and (re)created. As such, they are part of the resources employed to constitute social events. Through a focus on the relationships between socially significant events and the field of action they are embedded in, we may learn more about how such resources are employed as integral parts of trajectories of action.

Material Spatial Practices

Following Harvey's definition, I shall take material spatial practices to refer to:

> [T]he physical and material flows, transfers, and interactions that occur in and across space *in such a way as to assure production and social reproduction.* (Harvey 1990: 218. Emphasis mine)

This dimension, then, is what is characterised as *'the experienced'* by Lefebvre.

The life world represented by the atoll environment consists of a very narrow band of land surrounded by the vast ocean on all sides, with hundreds of tiny islets lying like a string of pearls surrounding a lagoon. The orientation of interest and activity in the densely populated Tokelau villages has been described as centripetal, directed inwards, towards the centre of the village and towards the lagoon, rather than as centrifugal, towards the ocean and the world beyond (Huntsman 1969). Furthermore, Huntsman, in her detailed description of the kinship-organised subsistence activities in Nukunonu (based on her early fieldwork), notes the co-existence of two calendar systems, which she calls respectively lunar and solar time. She describes how '[t]he Tokelauan lunar calendar, based on the night-time position of celestial bodies, is still referred to in connection with fishing enterprises' (Huntsman 1969: 5). She concludes that:

> Despite the solar-time church bell announcing Mass, matins, benediction, and the Catholic calendar, the Tokelauan must adjust his activities to his own lunar calendar. *In the village, the two systems are adjusted to some degree, but out of the village the lunar calendar prevails.* (Huntsman 1969: 7. Emphasis mine)

The two calendar systems observed by Huntsman have their roots and rationale in two different spheres: one of these is the indigenous subsistence activity, while the other was introduced by institutions such as the Church and, to a lesser extent, the school and the hospitals. The two systems, with their respective ways of orchestrating village activities, still co-exist, but it is important to note that the activities associated with the solar-time calendar have gained very powerful 'backing' from the one institution that has expanded so dramatically since the time of

Huntsman's first fieldwork – the Tokelau Public Service.

As described in the Introduction, the amount of time spent on village work and the value placed on it today, as compared with the situation only ten years ago, is striking; it points to the rapid rate of change in the economic basis of Tokelau society. Today I would rather characterise the difference between the two systems that Huntsman found as a difference between time spent on subsistence-activities and time spent on 'office-activities'. 'Office-time' activities are those that involve the running of the various departments of the Tokelau Public Service. These activities are outward-oriented to a greater extent (although this may be said only to be a matter of degree), and have their roots in the monetary sphere. They are largely financed by aid programmes and lately also by revenues from Tokelau's exclusive fisheries zone. The two systems conflict in several respects, and there are many signs that indicate that they have opposing consequences with respect to social reproduction. In short, whereas the subsistence-oriented activities are geared towards reproducing large extended families and a very tight network of inter-family cooperation, the monetary-based activities tend to produce smaller, more independent units, and contribute comparatively little towards generating village cooperation. On the other hand, the monetary sphere is also closely connected with the demands for closer inter-atoll and national cooperation on a formal, institutional level. (See Hoëm 1999 for a description of the role of the UN and the New Zealand Administration with respect to the establishment of the local infrastructure deemed necessary for political independence.)

I have described this situation elsewhere (e.g., Hoëm 1995), with reference to the extensive work of Hooper and Huntsman, and I shall not attempt to replicate this argument here. However, it is important to note that the contradictions between the two systems of production are experienced within the confines of a very tiny land area by a group of about 1600 people. It is interesting to note how these contradictions are realised 'on the ground', that is, how the two production systems are visibly encoded in the atoll environment and in the physical appearance of the atolls.

Earlier in this work I have used the metaphors 'thinness' and 'thickness' to convey the contrast between everyday life and ceremonial occasions. In fact, village life may be seen as a cycle, fluctuating between 'lean' periods and times of abundance. In the lean periods, preparations are made for the lavish displays that characterise the periods of abundance; including goods, speeches, songs and other ritualised exchanges between the participating sides (whether this be the groom's side and the bride's side at a wedding, the atolls as sides vis-à-vis each other, the village sides, etc.). This fluctuating rhythm takes place irrespective of what I have called 'office time' and 'subsistence time', but the overall time spent on ceremonial activities and leisure has declined considerably with the introduction of 'office time'.[4] Furthermore, there is a conflict between wage work and unpaid work carried out by the village work force (*auma-ga*). The produce of the latter enters into the *inati*-system, due to the fact that the results are distributed equally amongst the entire population, including the waged TPS workers. The work carried out by the women's committees, producing gifts and food for ceremonial occasions and simi-lar activities, is also unpaid, and there are complaints about this imbal-ance. The strains brought about by this situation have generally resulted in a marked decrease in the amount of work carried out communally. Hooper and Huntsman note how:

> [In 1981, the village co-operative work] had become confined to the envi-rons of the villages and was concerned only with upkeep of the meeting houses and churches, or with tree-felling and the like. Communal fishing expeditions were no longer organised on an aumaga basis during the week, simply because the catch would necessarily have been distributed by the share system – and this included TPS members and their dependants as well as the rest of the village. (Hooper and Huntsman 1992: 101–02)

Today, Saturday is reserved for non-waged work, particularly for fishing expeditions, and it is also the day for collective preparation of food for the Sunday meal (*tonai*), as all work is banned on Sundays. The village work is mostly carried out by rotational groups of waged workers, thus going some way towards solving the dilemmas connected with adhering to the ethic of equal sharing inherent in the share- or *inati* system described in the Introduction. The Council of Elders still have the right to command the villagers' participation in communal work projects, and it is this kind of work that is mentioned in the quote above. But the major proportion of such work now is the preparation of gifts and food prestations for cere-monial occasions, and this work, apart from the fishing, is mainly carried out by women.

The rhythm of 'subsistence time' village life is punctuated by meetings. The Council of Elders hold weekly meetings in which they define the weekly schedule of activities, and plan the tasks for the rotational work-ers. The women's committees usually hold weekly meetings as well (see Hoëm 1995 for a description of the respective groups' activities), and fre-quently these meetings concentrate on the organisation of work projects, such as mat-weaving instigated by the Council of Elders. Activities cen-tred around the churches also take up a significant proportion of the time. Youth and sports organisations also have their meetings and times of practice and games. The main subsistence-time activities carried out by men are fishing and house maintenance, and the female chores are prepa-ration of food, child care and cleaning (washing clothes, sweeping away the leaves from the coral stones around the houses and so on). When it comes to the distribution of food, the actual task of carrying the coconut-frond baskets and plates laden with food from one household to another is done by children. The village councils appoint trusted men as *tauvaega*, distributors of the inati to every single person in the village regardless of age and gender. The *inati* goods are distributed by the *tauvaega* from a central place in the village called the *laulau* (platform, plate or table), and the share-groups are, in this context, designated by the names of children, who again are the ones responsible for taking the goods back home.[5]

In the 'lean' periods, distribution of food takes place on a daily basis between households. In the prototypical case, this takes the form of a flow of resources from a brother to his natal household where his sister (the *fatupaepae*, the 'cornerstone' and distributor in the extended family, as described in the Introduction) resides, and of prepared food from the sister to her brothers' households. The catches of fish made on village workdays that exceed a certain amount (everything below that amount goes to the boat's crew), and all catches of *ika ha* (sacred or tabooed fish), are distributed by the *inati*. Ceremonial occasions[6] are, in most cases, centred on the lavish display of food, and all participants are presented with a *laulau* (food mat) laden with food. The participants sit in a circle along the posts (*pou*), supporting the roofs of the open houses or along the walls. After tasting the food, they hand the mats out behind their backs to the children who stand outside of the meeting house, and who then carry the food home. It is considered shameful for an adult person to walk on the road carrying (given) food.

As was discussed in the life histories presented in Chapter three, the roads (*ala, auala*) in the villages are the public areas *per se*, in addition to the formal arenas represented by the meeting houses and the village green (*malae*). It is common for competing sides or, for example a married couple after the wedding ceremony, to circumambulate the roads (*tamilo*), circling around the village, singing songs, sometimes carrying baskets laden with goods for food prestations. Other kinds of 'walking on the roads' are restricted, as we shall see in this Chapter and as we have also learned from the earlier analysis.[7] The *vavao* (curfew) imposed by the Council of Elders – that is, the time of evening prayers when people are restricted from walking about the village – is expressive of the same concern with control of movements in public space.

Early in this century, at the decision of a resident District Magistrate, the villages were realigned on an urban grid plan (Huntsman 1969: 3). Huntsman writes:

> Most houses were initially confined within the established grid, with cookhouses concentrated at the ocean shore, where the prevailing wind would carry the smoke out to sea. Boat slips, boathouses and outhouses were at the lagoon shore. (Huntsman 1969: 3)

The older villages were centred around houses (*fale*), described as 'men's houses' and closely associated with the *pui kaiga* (or clan-groups), of which there were nine on Fakaofo, seven on Atafu, and four on Nukunonu. The named land-divisions are still recognised today, but the houses have long since gone.[8] The houses are remembered by references in the *fakalupega* (or village ceremonial address), and they function occasionally as groups on certain ceremonial occasions.

At the centre of the villages lies the *malae* (the village green), where the meeting house is located. Close by lies the church (except on Atafu, where the church is further away), the administration building (the office), and the cooperative store. On all three atolls, the hospital and the school are located further away. On Fakaofo, these institutions are placed on the more recently settled islet of Fenua Fala. The visual impression of the villages has changed quite dramatically in recent years, mainly due to two factors. The first is the increase in tidal waves and hurricanes, which has led people to adopt a 'seawall project', covering the stone walls protecting the ocean-side of the village-islets with meshed wire as a further protection against threatening seas. The second is the UN-sponsored housing scheme, in which, through loans, most families are able to partake, and which has resulted in the almost universal abandonment of Tokelau-style housing (using thatched roofs and open walls) in favour of New Zealand-style houses with water reservoirs and roofs of corrugated iron.

As I mentioned in the Introduction, the recent decades have seen the rise of socio-economic divisions that have their basis in wage-employment in the Tokelau Public Service. Whereas earlier there were differences between the extended families, in terms of the size of the land areas they possessed, the ownership of land did not in itself make for prosperity. The prerogative to command able-bodied persons to gather and process food seems rather to have been the critical factor, and this control was ultimately in the hands of the Elders. In other words, throughout most of the period since the abolishment of the kingship system in 1915, Tokelau has not experienced marked variation in the material status of its inhabitants. Nowadays, such material differences are present, however, and socio-economic differences are easily detectable when comparing the two-story *papalagi* houses containing video-players, freezers, microwave ovens and other consumer goods with other, more modest abodes with no such amenities. The public buildings in Tokelau villages include the meeting-house, the cooperative store, the church,[9] the school, the pre-school buildings and the adult training centre, the women's committee house (in Nukunonu only), storage sheds and outhouses placed over the lagoon. The *kaiga* (extended family) dwellings usually consist of one main building plus a cookhouse or *umu*. The cookhouses are ideally placed at the 'back' (*i tua*), towards the ocean side.

Married couples may sleep in the cookhouse or in the main house depending on the composition of the household; grown brothers and sisters will avoid sleeping and eating in the same house if at all possible. The women are associated with the inside of the house, and in fact women spend most of their time (away from 'office work') in the close vicinity of the family homestead. The men are outdoors most of the day, working either in village work groups or with members of their natal household, or doing office work, and they usually only return to the house of their wives for food and rest. That the island is small does not mean that it is always experienced as such however. This point was brought home to me when listening to a man describing how he felt so lonely and homesick after having moved to his wife's family home upon marriage. He had in fact moved approximately 50 metres, but, as he related it, this seemed like an unbridgeable distance.

The structure of the houses has changed more than once since the time of the 'ancient dwelling houses', described by H. Hale in 1841 during the United States Exploring Expedition's visit to Tokelau as 'of oblong shape with eaves sloping nearly to the ground' (Macgregor: 122). Lister describes these houses by saying that '[t]here were no walls, but a low fence or railing formed a definite limit to the inside of the house', and Macgregor continues: '[a] low terrace of coral pebbles retained by a curbing of coral slabs was laid under and around the house. The house floor of coral pebbles was raised above the foundation terrace'. Interestingly he comments on how:

> Inside, the house was divided into two parts for sleeping. There was no material boundary, but the side on which the men slept was the *fasi* [?], and the women's side, the *faitotoka* [door]. (Macgregor 1937/71: 123, inserts mine)

Today, there are no such conceptual boundaries between the men's side and women's side of the houses that I am aware of. It is more common for unmarried men to sleep outside of the houses, while the unmarried women are placed inside the house, and away from the door rather than near to it. Visitors will be offered a mat (or a chair) to sit on, much in the fashion described by Macgregor (1931/71: 124); however, it is important to note that the conceptual difference between high and low, discussed in the previous Chapter, plays a role in the placing of a visitor in- or outside a house. Children, who are the messengers between households, approach houses by standing outside the door, crouching so as to be physically lower than the person who receives the message, and they do not enter the house at all unless explicitly asked to do so. Visitors also pause outside or in the doorway, usually sitting on the doorsill, and do not take a seat inside before being directed to a suitable place according to the status of the person and the nature of the visit.

The same pattern is repeated when entering the house where a public gathering is held, and in most cases this leads to significant 'delays' in the timing of the proceedings as people hesitate outside the building in the vicinity to avoid being first to enter and thus having to assume responsibility for placing themselves. This dilemma is usually resolved when persons of unquestionable authority (a very old Elder, the priest, the *faipule* etc.,) enter – allowing the rest to follow in groups and pairs, placing themselves 'below' these important persons, or with them, if urged to do so.[10]

Inside, the houses are rather empty by *papalagi* standards. There are boxes and suitcases for storing clothes and other valuables, and piles of mats and pillows or mattresses that are spread out for sitting and sleeping. There is usually a little space set aside for religious pictures and photographs of graduations, weddings, and so on, and a box or chest with a mirror and toiletries. In addition to this, since the mid-eighties many houses have had video players, and most possess freezers that are powered by the village's diesel-fuelled generators that usually run for intervals during the daytime. Placed so that they mark the boundary between inside and outside, the posts supporting the roof of an open Tokelau-style house are comfortable to lean against, and the posts of the meeting houses are reserved for higher-ranking persons. The houses are square or oblong, and in almost any communal gathering, people sit around the walls, facing inwards, with the open space of the floor in the middle. The most respected persons sit in the 'highest' side of the house, and the relative importance of the persons present may be assessed by degrees outwards from the highest to the lowest. The absolute lowest position is occupied by those who sit outside the house where the meeting is held, and with the introduction of walled meeting houses (Atafu has the first one), this group of people is now literally left out of the proceedings, for the first time in history. However, the spatial arrangements in terms of bodily positioning follow the same pattern in the '*papalagi*-style houses'.

Finally, the atolls are broadly divided into different kinds of land areas, according to the material spatial practices described in this section: communally held land, church land, land areas held by extended families in the villages (*kakai*) and land areas held by the extended families on the outer islets (*uta*). The general term for land is *fenua*, and this term may also refer to the people of the village. It is also used about countries. The other general term for land is *kelekele*, used in the sense of soil, earth, dirt, which, interestingly, is also used to refer to blood. With this, we have already moved into the level of perception and symbolical representations, and we shall now turn our attention to such representations of space.

Representations of Space

With this dimension of Harvey's 'grid' of spatial practices we enter into what Lefebvre defines as 'space *as perceived*':

> Representations of space encompass all of the signs and significations, codes and knowledge that allow such material practices to be talked about and understood [...]. (Harvey 1990: 218)

As mentioned above, regulation of the use of the atoll environment as a whole is traditionally vested in the Council of Elders, in such a way that, for example, the power of commanding the opening up (*taga, tatala*) and restriction of access (*ha*) to the family-held land areas (*lafu*) is ultimately in their hands. The immediate control of the moral aspects of the social environment is more in the hands of women.[11] These two factors combined mean, among other things, that where one is and what one does there is, for the most part, under communal direction and scrutiny, and that what a person does is always carried out under the eyes of everybody and, as mentioned earlier, kept in check through constant phatic-talk exchanges such as: 'where are you going?', 'I am going to...' (Hoëm 1993).

Symbolically, the village (*nuku*), seen as collective space, represents the front of the village, whereas the ocean lies at its back (*i tua*). A main distinction is made between the socially controlled and well-ordered areas, the villages (*nuku*), and the 'bush' areas (*vao*), that include everything on the main island that is not village, i.e., the wilderness.[12] As Shore also observes for Samoa, this distinction may be seen as a symbolic elaboration of a spatial contrast between 'frontness' and 'backness'. Shore argues that these spatial categories are associated with pre-Christian and Christian notions about the division between *ao*, the day (side), and *po*, the night (side), and he further associates these divisions with the division between what is *tapu*, under ritual restriction, often interpreted as sacred, and what is *noa*, the unrestrained, free or profane. In Tokelau, it is in the 'back', particularly in the bush, that danger lurks, where people (especially women) are vulnerable to attacks by spirits or ghosts (*aitu*).

As mentioned above, the Elders have the power to regulate the activities in the village, the evening curfews and so on. The controlled (i.e., *tapu*, or *ha*, restricted), dignified, and, above all, quiet behaviour associated with the village areas is quite different from what may take place in the uncontrolled, wild areas in 'the back' (i.e., *noa*, unrestricted activities). At the centre of the village lies the *malae* (the village green), where the meeting house is situated; symbolically, this is the area associated with special, restricted (*tapu*, or *ha*) activities.[13]

These spatial conceptualisations are used extensively in reference to much wider, moral categorisations. A prototypical example of a situation defined as 'restricted', apart from the brother:sister relationship, is an occasion of oratory taking place in the meeting house, i.e., at the centre of the village.[14] As mentioned in the previous Chapter, in such speech making, knowledge is often displayed in such a way that it is only perceptible to those who are in the know. The main part of the audience, however, though physically present and sitting there quietly, apparently listening, may be mentally far away and cannot be counted on to be able to recount the contents of the speech. It is none of their concern. Examples of situations which are said to be 'of no account' (*mea tauanoa*), and where behaviour (also verbal) is accordingly unrestrained, are the one-sex only groups doing work in areas lying outside the village, and night-time drinking parties.[15]

When I use the term 'knowledge', such as when talking about the (often veiled) references made in speeches, I mean what Tokelauans refer to as traditional knowledge (*poto tuai*). That is, as mentioned, knowledge relating to areas of specialisation, such as fishing and navigation – i.e., charts of wind directions, positions of the stars, movements and seasons of fish – and, not least importantly, genealogical knowledge and the knowledge of what is called the real, old Tokelau language (including spells, sayings, legends, songs, and so on). The possession of such specialist knowledge has been crucial for survival in this environment, and the assumed possession of such knowledge provides much of the rationale for the age-hierarchy.

Furthermore, genealogical knowledge ultimately refers back to the 'houses' discussed earlier in this Chapter and their association with specific land areas. In this way, and as it relates to issues of conflict over land areas, historical knowledge is intimately associated with specific geographical areas.[16] In this respect, the landscape can be said to be perceived as a socio-historical map, or in Fox's terms, a toponomy (Fox 1997). This is illustrated by what happened when Tokelau history was introduced into the schoolcurriculum, and the teachers invited Elders to come to the schools and teach the subject to the pupils. The Elders responded to this by taking the children on what they called an 'historical tour' around the atoll, during which the Elders recounted the historical tales connected with each place they stopped.

Most of the knowledge of the atoll landscape that is connected with historical events is preserved in songs and presented in speeches held at public gatherings. It is important to note that this knowledge of the socio-historical map of the atolls is not socially neutral.[17] As referred to in earlier Chapters, for a certain period in history the three atolls were at war, and Fakaofo gained overlordship and extracted tribute from the other atolls. Many of the landmarks are related to the old order, as they are considered to have been before the 'days of war'. Other landmarks are associated with things that took place during the wars, and to bring up any of this knowledge may disrupt the harmony of the occasion and may ultimately threaten the present-day relative political stability. The Elders are entitled to handle this knowledge, for example in their role as arbiters in the case of land disputes. This kind of knowledge is often displayed jokingly at feasts; although these occasions are by definition not 'serious', they may have political consequences (Hoëm 1992). Accordingly, a great deal of careful calculation goes into deciding how one is to present enough to show that one is in the know, which one has to do if one wishes to gain a certain standing in the community. On the other hand, one must be careful not to tell so much that one gives it all away (or rouses unwanted animosity). This mechanism of inclusion and exclusion, creates a difference between those who are in the know and those who are not (anchored as it often is in knowledge about family groups and ties to specific land areas), and as we have seen (particularly in my analysis of narrative one, 'Care for coconuts' in the previous chapter), this communicative practice naturally generates linguistic opacity.

What I would like to convey through this description, simplifying somewhat, is an image of how people have strong ties to land (*fenua*), and more specifically, families have strong ties to their particular land areas. Furthermore, these land areas and the respective families' ties to them are of historical significance.[18] As I just mentioned, the Elders are custodians of this knowledge. This means that they are the ultimate authority on 'who belongs where'. In practice, however, in any given situation, every person has multiple choices for affiliation, and this provides the system with some inbuilt flexibility. To cope with this open-endedness, there are some general principles of inclusion and exclusion that applies across situations – i.e., leadership structures, the hierarchy of age and gender relations. This furthers the situational allocation of roles of restraint, command, and intimacy, and leads to a constant concern with status negotiations, producing a prevalent 'sense of place'.

This sense of place is expressed in a multitude of ways, each reinforcing the other, much like what V. Turner refers to as condensed meaning (in his discussions of what he calls dominant symbols, Turner 1967: 28). The polysemy of the term *tulaga* illustrates clearly how land, land areas, particular places and social positions are conceptually associated. As referred to in the introduction to this Chapter, some of the semantic references of the term include 'place, site, location, or position'; it may also mean 'stand or platform', 'print or mark', 'condition, state, or situation'. Furthermore, it signifies 'status, position, or rank', and finally, it refers to 'place'.

Seeing the land as a toponymy, as genealogical history, of inter-atoll and inter-family rivalry, is one level on which this connection between land, land areas, and social positions is expressed. The island seen as a gradient of more or less formal, or central, and more or less informal, and peripheral areas, is another.

Seen from the perspective of the most immediate kinaesthetic or physical level, and as described earlier in this work, people are concerned with what Goffman, and Tokelauans, call 'face'. This concern is expressed in concepts of frontness and backness, above and below, and inside and outside. The dimensions above and below are used to express relationships of a hierarchical nature, which may be seen in bodily posture, ranking of seating arrangements and of village areas and social situations. Relationships based on gender divisions, but also between 'offspring of brothers' (*tamatane*) and 'offspring of sisters' (*tamafafine*) within the extended families, have their most obvious expression in the distinctions that we have seen expressed in Chapter three, made between 'outside' and 'inside'. This relationship is characterised by physical avoidance. As discussed in Chapters three and four, a man and a woman are not supposed to 'face each other' outside of marriage. Relationships of equality are characterised by physical proximity and are expressed as producing equal, competitive 'sides'. These then may 'face each other' in interaction, thus showing a comparative absence of restraint and defining either intimate or competitive relationships.

The local distribution system (*inati*) is geared towards taking care of those who do not have any direct ties to land.[19] A stranger, in the sense of one who has no personal ties at all (a *tino kehe*), is someone for whom there is no room, and there are examples of strangers having been asked to leave the atolls, the reason given being that there is no way to support them. The definitions of situations and the classification of persons as insiders or outsiders according to 'place' (e.g., family- or atoll-affiliation) vary, and through interaction, the different perceptions of 'place' (land, landscape, and social position) are established as conceptually salient and strengthened by the way they overlap and reinforce each other. Thus a specific life-world, and a particular cognitive and moral orientation, is built up.

Spaces of Representation

The third and final dimension in Harvey's 'grid' of spatial practices is the realm of imagined and imaginary space. He says:

> Spaces of representation are mental inventions [...] that imagine new meanings or possibilities for spatial practices. (Harvey 1990: 218–9)

In Lefebvre's terminology, this would be space as *imagined*, and in Harvey's scheme, this dimension would include spaces of desire, visions and dreams. In his description of the fragmentation of post-modern urban landscapes, he easily separates the three. Finding more difficulty with separating these dimensions than he seems to have, I take this as an indication of the interwovenness of these dimensions in Tokelau spatial practice. This problem will already be apparent from my interfusion of aspects of symbolic representation with my description of the level of material spatial practices. However, I find his 'grid' useful as a heuristic device, in that it may help us to distinguish between the experience of spatial practice, the representation of spatial practice, and people's reflections on the two. It is to the level of reflection to which we will turn our attention in this section.

The sides (or *faitu*), are, as described earlier, by definition occupied with 'things of no importance', i.e., 'unrestricted' (*tauanoa*) activities. They meet for recreational activities that are competitive, such as cricket and dancing. These activities are characterised by the active participation of everyone present, and 'the knowledge', which in the strict sense is a domain solely controlled by the Elders, which is also, through songs, dancing and clowning, made the object of reflection and negotiation by and for everybody.[20] That is, negotiations of power relations enter into these communal festive gatherings, but in the main through the playful inversion of relationships in skit making and clowning. It is in these situations, characterised by boisterous physical activity, rather than in the intellectual discourses represented by the oratory of the Elders, that people's tacit knowledge is given expression, in a form that invites and encourages reflection. By focusing on the performative aspect of these gatherings, we see how a fine line is drawn between *the exercise of power* and the *playing with power* described in Chapter one.

The institution of the sides is not based on kinship. As such, it serves to provide a neutral arena that carries the potential for bridging the opposition between other factions in the community that have everything to do with kinship. It does not carry any associations to the symbolic oppositions of gender and authority, or centre versus periphery, that are found in the villages. Precisely for this reason, it constitutes an alternative, neutral arena for handling these oppositions which are intrinsic parts of village organisation.

The behaviour I have described as a balancing of 'thinness' and 'thickness' varies situationally. This situational variation, although mainly expressive of negotiation of social relations, is also connected to physical locations. N. Besnier, in his description of gossip on the Tuvaluan atoll Nukulaelae, contrasts what he calls 'anti-poetic discourse' that takes place in locations such as cook-houses and on the beach, with the seat of 'high culture' represented by the meeting house. He concedes that no such local term (as anti-poetic discourse) exists, but argues that, in terms of the community's aesthetics, such evaluations do. However, he adds that it is possible to obtain alternative forms of social prestige (as opposed to the prestige that is sought through the formal political institutions), for example, as a valued conversationalist (Besnier 1994: 1–5).

Besnier's distinction between 'anti-poetic discourse' and 'high culture' is observable in Tokelau as well, and the difference is frequently used as a ploy in skits. Presented in the meeting house, and therefore by definition 'clean', *mama*, as we saw in the example presented in Chapter one, a 'dirty,' *kelekele* or *mataga* (disgusting) thing may be humorous. The sense of what is fitting in the situation is preserved by virtue of it being a humorous item. If, however, a person enters the house on such an occasion and behaves 'anti-poetically' out of context, for example, by exhibiting drunken, boisterous behaviour or by not being properly dressed, this is truly *mataga* (disgusting), and a reason to feel shame and to be castigated, *ma*. Similarly, behaviour which is presented as the norm in contexts associated with what Besnier calls 'high culture' and that I have called 'the front', such as chastity, may be ridiculed in situations 'at the back'. Thus, a woman in her thirties, presenting herself as a virgin, and being proud of this during a session of informal talk between women, received not the praise she considered her due, but only laughter and the comment that, if this truly was the case, she was like a box with a broken lock.

I have included these examples to show that there is a link between 'restricted' and 'unrestricted' behaviour and place, but also to illustrate that it is not possible to infer what kinds of behaviour would be judged as fitting and aesthetically pleasing merely from the distinctions between 'clean' and 'dirty'. Rather, it is a question of striking the proper, humorous balance between the two. As described in the case of the theatre group, the main challenge of their presentation stemmed not from the topics they presented, but from the fact that their performance was presented in a *serious* manner.

I would argue that the main arenas for airing grievances in earnest, for what Besnier calls 'anti-poetic' or 'anti-hegemonic' discourse, are located in the back, for example, in the outhouses, cook-houses and on the beach, and that in arenas such as the drinking parties (which are invariably accompanied by songs and guitar playing), desires, dreams, and visions of alternative practices are expressed.

Whether such alternative visions, articulated in 'the back', ever come to be realised as what Harvey describes as 'a material productive force with regards to spatial practices' is an open question, but I would venture to say that in terms of local conceptions, this is dependent first upon the visions being presented in 'the front', for example, in the meeting house, as the theatre group did, and second, upon the creation of an atmosphere of openness and inspiration (*matagia*), thus clearing the air for an acceptance by the participants of the 'message contained in the gift'.

Codes of Behaviour and Life-trajectories

I have so far seen social spaces in the light of three analytical levels. I have described how, in discussing practices associated with production and reproduction, the institutions associated with subsistence activities and 'office' activities tend to produce different patterns of social organisation. In discussing the representation of social spaces, the distinction between inside and outside come across as particularly relevant for the ordering of gender relations. The distinction between front and back (and high and low) relate to the creation of relations of authority and social hierarchy, and are also reflected in the distinction between formal and intimate settings. In discussing places of articulation, I have shown, in this and in previous Chapters, how narrative structure, topic and form of performance and interpretation vary according to the dimensions of outside and inside, front and back, above and below.

In other words, new media and genres of representation frequently reflect the tension inherent in the different practices of social production and reproduction, and as we have also seen relate closely to long standing patterns of representation, communicative practices and the associated arenas provided by the atoll landscape.

In conclusion, I shall return yet again to the subjective experience of codes of behaviour, thereby highlighting how some individuals, who are differently socially positioned, experience and express the tensions between the old and the new which are presently encompassed by the concept of a 'Tokelau way of life' (*faka-Tokelau*). The following is an extract from an old woman's narrative of her life in Tokelau, describing how she perceives the differences between life now and earlier. Her narrative clearly illustrates how a particular spatial orientation is inculcated.

> The only life of the female child [was] obedience and attention. My life, oh dear me how scared I was of my parents. I was rarely beaten by my father, but [he] would instruct (*fakatonu*) [me] 'you are not to go wandering about'. But I would go, and I would come back and get a hiding by my parents because I didn't obey what [I] had been ordered. And [I] would be told '[you] know the good thing is obedience'. […] The only life of the Tokelauan female child, all of her lot (*tofi*) is staying in the house. How different the situation is now, isn't it? Now, in these times, when the knowledge has come[21] […] The children, the male child is respectful towards the female child. He is talking [respectfully] … but now, no! Because now the cleverness is so great?

To elucidate the different 'ways of going' that were referred to so frequently in the extracts from narratives I presented in Chapter three, and in the quote above, I shall turn once more to the basic principles of orientation, as they relate to everyday life and thus to the moral universe within which Tokelauans live.

Indigenous ideas of truth and beauty are intimately connected with notions of quantity, as for example, expressed by the concept of *katoa*, 'wholeness', 'fullness', or 'richness of detail'. Such behaviour, as described in the practice of bowing down when passing in front of a person, has a duality to it, in that on the one hand it is an expression of proper restraint, as it is a behaviour which creates what has been described as 'thinness' (Levy 1973; Marcus and Fisher 1986: 49). On the other hand, in behaving thus, one shows oneself to be a person with a true spirit, and in this way one gains a quality of wholeness, or thickness, i.e., a position (*tulaga*), a certain standing or command (*pule or mana*), in the eyes of others.

Returning to the discussion of social personhood and 'the concept of person' (e.g., Shore 1982: 136), this, in Tokelauan terms, comprises, on the one hand, all the 'sides' (*itu*), in the sense of relationships, that are seen to make up the social personae, and which the person partakes in. Moral evaluations of these 'sides' relate strongly to the person's active engagement in these relationships. On the other hand, as the concept of personhood relates to ideas about individual identity and innate characteristics, a person is thought to inherit certain traits or skills or uiga, a word that also signifies 'meaning'. Thus, a man is said to 'always come too late', and this is explained as a trait he has inherited and that 'runs in that family'. Another woman may be considered a 'funny person,' and this is also explained as being a quality she has inherited.[22]

Such characterisations are common, and are part of the shared knowledge in the communities. We may see in this how the basic principles of orientation, coupled with such characterisations, can affect a person's standing in the community in such a way as to permanently shape that person's life-trajectory. In particular, it is interesting to observe how such characterisations may affect the individual's experience of him- or herself. In reflecting on this issue, I do not propose to venture into an ethnopsychological analysis, but examine this area of experience in terms of social organisation and through its social consequences.

The following is an extract from a life history told by a middle-aged woman who has lived in Tokelau all her life and who entertains no dreams of going elsewhere. She has been on a short visit to New Zealand, and explained that even though it was nice to see her family again, she didn't like it there. She said that this was because she is used to a life of hard physical activity in Tokelau, and that she found life in New Zealand too passive. 'You put the clothes in the washing machine, you buy food in the shop ... There is nothing much to do and I don't enjoy just to be sitting there doing nothing'.

Yes, I then, I was born in the year 1935. In other words, my years are 56 at this time. In my life, my childhood, I [was] a child [who] was guided by my parents so that (I) should know [*iloa*] and do my behaviour [*fai taku amio*] and my character [*uiga*]. I came to respect and [to be] afraid of the grown-up people. I was a child [who] was beaten. I was beaten by my father so that my life should be good. My father didn't want there to be any bad stories of mine arising. I [was] a child [who] learned, I [should] break off [i.e., stop], [being] a child [who was] beaten.

I value [this] highly, but [this is] another time. I was beaten, I learned, [this is how I think of it now], now, in this time now, in my adulthood [that has] come [to me]. [I] came to know the lesson of my beating, with the guidance of my parents so that I should manage to do the good things. My life is not a life allowed independence [*tuku haoloto*, uncontrolled, be free to do what one wants²³], where I would rule, [in case] I had not learned and followed the guidance, the situation is like that.

Well, my growing up and my living, the character of that is to me, I am scared of the grown-up people and I feel the obedience, the willingness to any activity the grown-ups were doing in me because of the guidance of my parents. [...]

My life is a peaceful life. Our relationship inside of [*i loto o te kaiga*] our family is a peaceful, quiet relationship. There is not a sadness or anger, there is not a thing that worries me. Everything [for] me, [I am] just living in the contentment and live happily. It is like this too my being with the children. There is not a thing [which] is done to my burden. [It] is happiness for them and [it] is happiness for us, it is not a thing, for the belief of mine and our family is fellowship with Jesus, because [of this] there is happiness for us.

This narrative tells the story of how this woman learned her 'place', within the family and within the community. Through negative sanctions, such as being scolded and beaten, she has learned to keep a proper balance between the 'inside' (*loto o te kaiga*), i.e., represented by the house and the family, and the 'outside', represented by the 'activities of the grown-ups', i.e., village tasks. The threshold is guarded by instilling obedience (*uhitaki*), and she speaks of how her life is peaceful (*filemu*), governed by content (*loto malie*), and thus how she leads a happy life (*ola fiafia*). The price she pays for this, she says, is that she cannot roam freely, that her life is controlled, and that she cannot rule (*pule*) herself.

Although there is a certain ambivalence in her narrative in her expressing an awareness of an alternative (which she may have mentioned so as not to show herself ignorant of the alternative represented by my way of life, and also so as not to offend me), she seems to accept these terms happily, as indeed she 'should', according to the moral logic of her story. It is true that, looking at her situation from the outside, she seems happily adjusted. Her standing in the community is good, and she is respected. She has achieved a socially acceptable balance between 'wilfulness' and conformity. She is funny, but not 'a funny person'²⁴ – that is, she is not a clown. She is religious, but not to such a degree as to be seen as a hypocrite; she always lends a hand in village affairs, but not to the extent of neglecting her own family or for 'selfish', i.e., power-seeking, reasons.

In contrast, the following extract is taken from the history of a person who also 'stays' (*nofo*), but who is not happily adjusted to community life.

She is 33 years old, female, and talks in the following way about her life in Tokelau.

> The Tokelau life is beautiful. It is good, if you walk good, if your behaviour is good, but there is one thing that is wrong with me. My parents didn't accept [lit. accept to] me.[25] My life is like this at the present, I live a life of confinement. [...] I only stay in the house, take care of my baby, do the chores, to just sit (*te nofo lava*). It is not like my former life, I went to the people's houses, going with no particular purpose (*eva tauanoa lava*), talking [about] the things that have arisen in the stories,[26] but not just sitting in the house in case there might be something for me to do. Looking after our family.

To sum up, there is a certain duality in the behaviour expected in most situations, 'restricted' as well as 'unrestricted', in that a *loto nuku* (a village- or cooperative spirit), and a *loto maualalo* (a modest or humble 'heart'), are necessary to be positively valued, which tends to produce a certain 'thickness', in the sense of a certain standing in the community. For one's words to have any power, for one's actions to have any 'efficacy', in short, to have any flexibility and control over one's life-situation, it is not enough to be obedient (*uhitaki*), it is not enough simply 'to go straight' (*eva fakatonu*). One must, if one is a man, know how to temper the exercise of power or *pule*, with sensitivity to the needs of others, that is, by *alofa*, compassion, love, and generosity. If one is a woman, the balancing act is much the same, except that it is mainly cast as a question of achieving a harmony between the demands of the 'inside', of the family (*loto o te kaiga*), and the demands of the village, 'outside' of the family. As we have seen from the above statements, one is judged differently if one *eva ho* or *eva tauanoa* (goes 'outside' without having a specific purpose) than if one *eva ki na mea* (i.e., goes to participate in the preparations for the ceremonial gatherings, and to contribute to these activities).

Men who place themselves at the centre of attention, without being counted as having earned their right to a place there through everyday respectful behaviour and contributing to village affairs, are branded as *fiapule* (i.e., 'wanting to rule'), and thus are not taken seriously. Those, who, on the other hand, are only respectful, who show a meek demeanour and who do as they are bid, without ever showing any ambition of their own, are equally likely to be made the butt of jokes. Thus too 'high' and too 'low' are both not quite striking the correct, the most attractive balance in life.

A woman who puts herself forward, without having attained a position (i.e., being in publicly accepted command of a certain area of knowledge, such as for example, weaving, dancing, or cooking), which gives her the legitimacy to lead others with this quality, or who is seen as using such a position for her own purposes, is labelled *matamua*, as forward (literally 'face-first') and hence might not earn much support (Hoëm 1995). A woman who is very shy, on the other hand, or *matamuli* (literally 'face-last'), is not of much use when it comes to taking an active part in village affairs.

Generally, obedient, shy or passive people end up with a heavy burden of manual work. This earns them respect, but not enough to earn authority or influence in family or village matters. They fulfil the ideal of *filemu*, of being quiet, but for the occasions where a certain forcefulness, a *matagia*,[27] enthusiastic, outgoing, inspired behaviour is called for, this is simply not enough.

Describing the 'neo-traditional social order', which in their terminology is equivalent to the *faka-Tokelau*, Hooper and Huntsman (1992: 52, 53), present an adage, which sums up what they call 'Tokelau's principle of gender complementarity'. The adage says: 'The woman stays: the man goes on the path' (*Te fafine e nofo: te tagata ka fano ki te auala*). Whereas this adage basically refers to the common practice of men moving to their wife's household upon marriage, Hooper and Huntsman point out that it also indicates that women's lives tend to be 'sheltered and relatively sedentary', i.e., she 'sits' or stays (*nofo*), while men's lives tend to be more active, i.e., he 'goes' (*fano*).

In other words, when their lives are contrasted, as in the adage above, men are associated with the outside and women with the inside. As an increasing number of people are employed in the Tokelau Public Service, this association, in as much as it had its basis in a certain division of labour, tends to be weakened, and the pattern of interaction changes somewhat.

Whether one ends up 'staying' or 'going', the feeling of being stuck in a place, which socially or geographically is not of one's choice, varies considerably from person to person. As we have seen in the contrast between the last two life history extracts, the first woman is largely content with her lot, in that she is where she wants to be, whereas the second feels imprisoned. In fact, through repeated infringements of village rules, she has gradually put herself in a position where she no longer has any say at all in matters such as where she lives. As mentioned in Chapter three, the ultimate sanction for 'not going the proper way' is what is called *tu noa* ('just stand' or 'stand without support'). This implies 'house arrest', in the sense of social isolation (Hoëm 2000). A person who has been punished in this way has to stay in the house constantly and is not allowed to go anywhere else, except to the church and to the toilet. It is not forbidden to receive members of one's household or other legitimate visits, but it is not possible for a person in such a position to have any social life outside of this. Such punishment is usually reserved for infringements which are of a sexual nature, but which must have additional aggravating circumstances (i.e., not a situation where a solution would be to order the culprits to get married or else pay a fine), or for cases of repeated drunkenness and violence.

The person in the first narrative presented in Chapter three does not describe any event in her life as having come about as a result of being ordered (*fakatonu*) to do one thing or another, compared with the person in the second narrative in the same Chapter. She has behaved in such a way as to leave her with a feeling of herself having made the choices forming her life-career. Note that I am not attempting to assess whether this is 'really' the case or not, or whether she has had to make enormous sacrifices which she has glossed over in her story. Looking at it from the position of an outsider, what is striking are the contrasts between the narratives. In the narrative of return, the narrator, in an introductory section not included here, clearly states that she did not want to come to Tokelau in the first place, but that it happened as a result of her overstepping the boundaries of 'ways of going' in New Zealand, i.e., she went 'outside' to engage in 'unrestricted activities'. At this point, her brother intervened, and decided that she was to start saving up for her return to Tokelau, taking her parents there with her. Although having led a rather independent life up to that point, she did not feel herself to have any say in the matter any longer. She had, so to speak, 'used up her moral currency', and once the intervention was a fact, it was too late to do anything about it.

Such dilemmas of choice (or a lack of choice) are experienced to an increasing degree by the younger part of the population, and the problems and difficulties that this entails are what the drama group tried to address. On this background, I would like again to finally point to how, what may on the one hand be seen as an increasingly common experience of the effects of globalisation, for people from Tokelau and related to the Tokelau communities overseas, this experience is inextricably tied up with a particular sense of what it is one's (and other's) proper *place* to be.

To move between social spaces (in terms of authority and leadership, but also in relation to gender) is not always easy: in particular because to exercise authority over any kind of local resource, that is, through ties to land and positions (*tulaga*), first of all demands *presence*. As we have seen, the members of the theatre group Tokelau te Ata wished to address some of the difficulties involved in moving between different social spaces. On the one hand, in their plays and also in their self-presentation to the New Zealand communities and to the atoll villagers, it is possible to see acts of identification that employ imagery that Fox describes as common for the Austronesian area. On the other hand, it is also clear (as is also indicated by his model), that these acts of identification also express, and create, distance, discontinuity and exclusion.

For a final illustration of the dynamics of the processes of inclusion and exclusion involved in such acts of identification, we may return yet again to the presentation of the play *Tagi* to the larger Tokelau community in New Zealand. In Chapter one, I described how some voiced their objections to the opening scene of the play where the individual actors come forth as their genealogical connections are called out. The objections were that the genealogies were wrong, or partly wrong; the fact that the group had chosen to 'link' or 'connect'(*hohoko*) themselves through one of the possible 'paths' (*auala*) that they have in common, instead of through others, was a major source of contention. As described earlier, one community leader stated to some members of the Nukunonu community that they shouldn't 'worry about that lot. They are from Atafu'. (The theatre group were otherwise considered to be from Nukunonu.) In other words this man, who belongs to the 'traditionalist faction' of the community, tried to use the group's tools against them. His arguments drew legitimacy from the fact that social recruitment to localised communities in different parts of the larger Wellington area is atoll (and congregationally) based. Thus, his comments had the potential of setting a large number of the community against the theatre group and undermining its credibility, as most people are 'for their own' and compete against others, at least when it comes to sports or cultural performances. The group's way of linking themselves genealogically was, however, deliberately chosen to show the community that (in the group's view), even such deeply rooted emotional identifications as the one with one's home atoll (which their adversaries played on) can and indeed, must, be transcended if Tokelau is ever to develop a common sense of nationhood and purpose.

The opponent and his supporters then proceeded to create their own theatre group, in an open challenge to the Te Ata group, thus creating a mirror 'side'. In response to this, the Te Ata group decided to take their play (and the new one, 'Woman') on a tour to the three Tokelau atolls. Interestingly, the group members felt that they strongly wished to avoid the controversies surrounding the genealogical part, when coming to the social spaces represented by what they called the homeland, in contrast to their intention with the opening part of the play as presented in New Zealand. Upon arriving at each of the atolls, the oldest man of the group went to consult with an elder known for his proficiency in genealogies. Thus, the first scene represented different 'paths' (*auala*) when performed in different places, linking the cast members to Atafu, Nukunonu and Fakaofo on the respective atolls. This relativistic and detached attitude towards atoll affiliation is highly unusual. As far as I know, it went unnoticed by the very few spectators who travelled to all three atolls during the tour.

In what I have described, it is possible to see how the imagery mentioned by Fox is still used and reflects social dynamics. Furthermore, we see how the actors' representational 'play' with possible different ways of identification has its clear limits, in as much as real processes of inclusion and exclusion are at work. We have here at least two different frames of reference informing acts of identification. One is within the competitive striving for honour and ascendancy between the atolls (coached in terms of standing *latupou*, and leaning branches, *lafalala*) that demand primary allegiances to geographical place. The other framework is provided by the so-called 'Pan-Pacific Movement' and the demands of the institutions associated with the emerging nation-state. This last framework is also the point of reference for the activities of the theatre-group.

In terms of the overarching patterns of social organisation that constitute the conditions for, and limits on, movement and acts of identification forming peoples' life-trajectories, we may ask what kind of *connectedness* do the patterns I have outlined represent? We learn of processes of social association and differentiation, spoken of in terms of such concepts and images as positions and places, paths and branches, and the hooking up or joining (*hohoko*), of groups or sides. But what then does this joining mean, and on what level does it take place? For example, what about the relationships to others, to other ethnic Austronesian-speaking groups, and what about to other 'others'?

I would say that in most contexts, geographical locality, village community and kingroups are still very much the dominant frames of reference. As we have seen, this is also the case in the New Zealand communities. Even if the atolls are in fact quite ethnically diverse communities, with inhabitants tracing their ancestry to places such as Samoa, Tuvalu, Kiribati, Germany, Cape Verde, New Zealand and so on, in most situations this aspect is downplayed. In the more recent context, where macro-factors contribute to force social groups into more frequent contact, it is still important to hold common practice, current ideology, preference and choice up against each other in order to get an idea of long-term patterns and consequences. For example, it is probably too early to be able to see whether the movement of a new generation from New Zealand to Tokelau leads to permanent settlement there, or whether this movement is part of a larger current going elsewhere.

The rationale for the patterns of movement, which lend the patterns a specific shape, is ultimately connected with attempts to achieve social control over the flow of goods and information. As mentioned earlier, a person who is without any ties to local land is, in Tokelau terms, a *tamamanu*, a 'fledgling', widow or orphan, one in need of the support of an established local group or *kaiga* in order to be able to survive. This dependency, and ties of 'feeding' and nurture, are established through the connecting 'channels' of branches and paths. This then creates the conditions for the real politics of distancing and proximity that not only govern everyday life locally but also inform the macro-political relations between Tokelau and aid-donor institutions.

Finally, in the sharedness of the patterns of communicative practices, of concepts, in representations of linguistic agency and in the idioms informing ways and means of identification, we see a continuity and commonality between many groups in the Pacific. These patterns have the potential for being open-ended (see e.g., Sahlins 1985). They have developed from systems of social stratification, and yet they constitute patterns of movement, patterns that have so far proved to be incredibly dynamic and flexible. We see this in the pre-historic expansion into the Pacific region, but we also see it in the contemporary movement into still new areas with incredible speed (Summerhayes 2000). Here, ancient orientations are established in new places and new social spaces are added, bringing new acts of identification and new forms of expression (C. Macpherson, P. Spoonley, M. Anae, eds. 2001).

Notes

1. Hooper and Huntsman's (1976) descriptions of how people 'count' their genealogical relations differently according to task/situation and accessible resources may further serve to illustrate this point. Describing the Tokelau kinship system, they write: 'Tokelau social structure conforms in kinship terminology and marriage regulations to those systems which are labelled "Crow–Omaha". In regard to the latter, the marriage rules, though negative (as in complex systems), are phrased in terms of social groups (similar to prescriptive systems). However, the descent system, which is thoroughly cognatic, does not conform to the "Crow–Omaha" ideal type.' (Hooper and Huntsman 1976: 270.) When stating that the incest prohibitions are expressed in the idiom of social groups rather than in terms of genealogical relationships, they point out that whether one is counted as *kaiga* (family) or he *toe kaiga* (no longer family), is decided on pragmatic grounds, i.e., according to whether the involved parties hold land together or not (and if they do, and still wish to marry, the landholdings have to be divided), rather than by any absolute application of rules.
2. I.e., his analysis of how: 'Structure enters simultaneously into the constitution of the agent and social practices, and "exists" in the generating moments of this constitution' (Giddens 1979: 5).
3. Here he refers to Bourdieu (1977: 95).
4. See Hooper 1993 where he notes how in 1967, three months were set apart for side-activities around the end of the year, whereas now the time allotted amounts to a few days.
5. See Hooper 1982, for a description of this.
6. See also the Introduction, on *fiafia*, feasts.
7. An interesting historical illustration of this practice is found in Macgregor, where he relates the story of 'one Ellice Islander': 'He and his family were looked upon as foreigners and were not allowed full social privileges of the island; they were called *alatafatafa* [i.e., road by the latrines, the outermost circle of roads on the village of Fale, Fakaofo], which is said to mean people who had to keep at a distance from the council house while the chief's meetings were in order.' (Macgregor 1937/1971: 28, Insert mine.)
8. The houses on Fakaofo are recognised as nine or ten, on Atafu, after the resettlement there, according to Macgregor (1937/71: 54) there were three men's houses besides the houses of the seven *pui kaiga*. On Nukunonu there were four houses. See also Hoëm 1992, Chapter two, on the different houses.

9. See Besnier 1991 for a discussion of seating arrangements in Church as radically different from other gatherings (and school).

10. See also the description in Chapter one of the process of entering the meeting house during the presentation of the plays.

11. See Hoëm 1995 for a description of the relationship between women and men with regards to their respective domains of control and their institutions (Women's committees and the Councils of Elders).

12. An illustration of the ideal of calm, harmony and well-orderedness associated with the presence of strong authority, particularly connected with the village areas is found in *Matagi Tokelau* where the Elders of Fakaofo present their version of Tokelau history, saying: 'Noise in the village was strictly forbidden and there was no shouting there. We also know that whenever a family wished to crack open a coconut for food they could not do it in the village; instead they had to take it to the *Puga-foa-vaka*, a coral head far out in the lagoon and crack it open there. Such was the dignity of Fakaofo. Nobody could escape punishment for breaking village laws, and the punishment could be as severe as death' (1991: 45–6).

13. This is not the case on Nukunonu where the *malae* is placed on Motuhaga, in a reclaimed swampy area, said to have been formerly used for punishments, called the *taihala*.

14. See Hoëm 1992, Chapter two.

15. Parallel examples are to be found in Besnier 1994. In Tokelau, the ultimate example of words of no effect/account would be those uttered when possessed, *ulufia*. See Hoëm 1995.

16. This observation is also made in *Songs and Stories of Tokelau*, where reference is made to a song, *Teumata*, which is described as an '[A]ncient geographical song that takes a journey around the atoll of Nukunonu counterclockwise, starting at the shore by the village settlement. Sites are mentioned by name and by a well-known attribute of each place – 'rich drinking coconuts', 'sweet smelling blossoms'. The woman Teumata, who is pictured making this journey, is thought to be an exile leaving the land, or remembering it, but today her identity is lost. The song is a *vale*, a memorial song, sung at funerals and other solemn gatherings' (Thomas *et al.* 1990: 16).

17. There is, for example, a set of songs about each atoll and their particular treasures, for example, Fakaofo has water, Nukunonu has *kie*-pandanus and Atafu has *kanava* trees, all highly valued resources. (See Hooper and Huntsman 1985 and *Matagi Tokelau* 1990 and 1991.)

18. On this, Huntsman and Hooper write: 'Places around the atoll and in the village, and offices with specific prerogatives and duties, are associated with [...] stocks [*pui kaiga*, also referred to as 'clans'], which separately and together maintain the social order' (1985: 138, insert mine).

19. This may happen through marriage, if able-bodied relatives have died or left so that there is nobody there to take care of the person, who is then called a *tama manu* (lit. little bird. Widowed or orphaned person).

20. See also Hoëm 1992b, for a discussion of the particular role played by songs as a medium for externalising political relations.

21. She is probably referring to developments within the field of education and to all the projects aiming at 'developing Tokelau'.

22. In addition, a person is also thought to exhibit personal emotional dispositions, *loto*, much in the same manner as Mageo (1998) describes in her analysis of models of selfhood in Samoa.

23. Compare Shore 1982: 158, on the use of this concept in Samoa (i.e., *sa'oloto*).

24. See Chapters one and three about clowns.
25. That is, they didn't approve of her behaviour, the way she 'walked'.
26. I.e., the stories going around in the village, gossip. See Hoëm 1995 for an analysis of the role of such stories in the process of the making and unmaking of an individual's reputation or 'name'.
27. See Thomas 1986 for a further discussion of this concept. Cf., also Levy 1973.

Epilogue

The material presented in this work mainly concerns three topics: theatre, social relations and social spaces. By choosing this focus, I wish to highlight the dynamic relationship between expressive culture, or issues of representation, and political processes. This perspective makes it possible for us to examine how identities, personal as well as cultural, are shaped through the frames, institutions and arenas that we allow to be established for their manifestations.

In presenting this perspective, I have described how communicative practices, in the Tokelau atoll societies and in the Tokelau New Zealand communities, are informed by a general, and largely shared, sociocultural orientation that tends to produce a pervasive 'sense of place' and takes the form of 'sided' relationships.

The work of the theatre group Tokelau Te Ata has been used as an illustration of how some common aspects of political processes in the contemporary Pacific, such as nation-building, infrastructural change and increased regional migration, may be experienced on the ground. In particular, I want to stress the theoretical insights we gain as anthropologists if we pay close attention to how performances are produced, not only as special social events but also as part of everyday interaction. By doing so, our theoretical perspective shifts from observing socio-cultural patterns as taxonomic structures to viewing them as temporary manifestations of a continual negotiation of social relationships involving a multitude of small acts of identification. In other words, we no longer simply chronicle 'the culture' or 'the social organisation' of a field site. Instead, we treat these patterns as part of local identity politics and as ideological constructs. This is not to say that social institutions, such as gender roles, leadership structures and the nation-state, to name just a few, do not have a social reality. If anything, we shift our attention ever more closely to the processes whereby such institutions come into existence and how they are manifested in peoples' lives. However, by examining how people negotiate the interpretative frames that serve to govern interaction in formal and informal social settings, our descriptions gain the aspect of insiders' perspectives that Herzfeld calls 'cultural intimacy' (see Introduction).

To recognise and describe the tensions that exist between representations of identity produced for external consumption, such as in 'cultural performances' as part of Pacific Islands' presentations to the wider New Zealand public, and representations produced for a closer circle of 'social intimates' is important. Thanks to Herzfield and others' dedication to the comparative study of how national ideologies emerge, the existence of these kinds of representational discrepancies are familiar to us. As he observes, discrepancies between images of representation produced for external and internal consumption are universally occurring phenomena, and tend to take predictable shapes when related to the establishment of a nation-state. It is common knowledge how the ideologisation of historical narratives, and linguistic roots and ties to land, emerge as a result.

What is interesting and unique about the material presented in this work, however, is that it allows us to observe that a similar tension between different levels of representation may also exist *within* the sphere of social intimates and in relation to images produced for internal consumption. Typical examples of this are provided in the first part of Chapter one, where we see how local acts of identification may shift from claiming allegiance on the basis of ties to a land area, to ties to a side of the extended family, to a village side, to an atoll and so on. Another illustration of such shifts in representation is found in the story of the theatre group taking their plays to the homeland, and how they shifted their representation of what they were doing from taking a message to bringing a gift. These shifts in representation seem to vary according to the composition of people present at an event, and also according to what kind of social space the event represents.

The more general theoretical lesson we may draw from these and other similar examples described in this work is that the comparative study of identity and the politics of representation has much to gain from seeing social events and associated communicative patterns as the outcome of multiple life-trajectories. By doing so, we get a perspective that allows us to describe and analyse how locally held conceptions of agency, personhood and morality go together to produce common general patterns of orientation. As a counterbalance to the tendencies of reification inherent in such an approach, we also need to keep a focus on the processes whereby such basic orientations are produced and maintained, negotiated and changed. This main theoretical perspective is not culture-specific and may in principle be applied anywhere. As a result of this and similar exercises in the field of comparative ethnographic studies, we may discover that there is still more for us to learn about the conditions and factors that govern human life, and that there are many unexplored – and some not yet even invented – venues representing limits and possibilities for the realisation and expression of personal and cultural identities.

Appendix

Linguistic Terminology and Abbreviations

ABS	absolutive
ANAPH	anaphoric pronoun
ART	article
CAUS	causative (*faka-*)
COLL	collective (*ha-*)
compl.	completed action
cont.	control
contin.	continuous action
DIR	directional (*ki*)
du.	dual
EMPH	emphatic particle
ERG	ergative
exc.	exclusive
FUT	future
GENR	general tense-aspect-mood particle
HUM	human numeral classifier (*toka-*)
inc.	inclusive
LOC	locative (*i*)
NEG	negative particle
NOM	nominaliser
nsp.	nonspecific
NUM	numeral classifier
p.	particle
PAST	past
PERF	perfect
pl.	plural
POSS	possessive

PRES	presentative (*ko*)
PROG	progressive (*koi*)
Q	question particles
sg.	singular
sp.	specific
=	morpheme boundary

Translations of *'Tagi'* and *'Mafine'*

The translations presented below of the two plays are based on Sulu Aukuso's transcription of my tape recordings of the original, Tokelauan versions. In the process of translating, I have edited the content as little as possible. I have not attempted any but the most basic standardisation of writing conventions, and largely follow her transcription. The () parentheses represent my own interpretations. The [] parentheses contain stage directions. Question marks that occur in the text indicate that part of the text is inaudible on the tape and thus missing from the transcription. Note in particular that the translations are not always written in standard English, but stick closely to the Tokelau/Tokelau English version. A comprehensive literary version of these texts is a task that would demand and be the prerogative of a Tokelau author/playwright.

Text 1: *Tagi* ('Lament')

Part One

Scene 1 [The reciting of individual genealogies.]

[The orator]
The dignity of our extended family (*kaiga*): the mothers, the fathers, the friends, and the children of Tokelau. Our group here are going to attempt to bring you our entertainment or story, directed towards our homeland, Tokelau. Our story too, with all respect, is going to be in the Tokelau language. Respects (to) the Faleiva ('Nine-house' or Fakaofo), respects (to) the Falefa ('Four-house' or Nukunonu). Respects (to) the Falefitu ('Seven-house' or Atafu).
From the eldest (ancestral) couple who were Tonuia and Lagimaina grew the houses (that) are seven. From there came the offspring Vaovela, Laufalii, Fekei, Pio, Levao, Laaua, Malokie.
From the offspring of Vaovela dwelling here, Tonuia, Lagimaina, who were the ancestral couple, (came) Vaovela, Hakalia, Moti, Tuilave, Teuila, Ioana, Heto. [Heto walks forward.]
There is the sister of Tuilave, Muia. Muia, Katalina, Valelia, Eheta. [Eheta walks forward.]
In (recounting) the process of bringing forth children, (we) once more turn down to Tuilave … going down – Teuila, Ioana, there is the *tamafafine* (offspring of sister's children) and the sister of Ioana. Kaloline, Pule. [Pule walks forward.]

From the offspring of Laufali, the ancestral couple Tonuia and Lagimaina, Laufali, Malifa, Malae, Pou, Malia, Akata. [Akata walks forward.]
From the offspring of Fekei, the ancestral couple, Tonuia and Lagimaina, Fekei, Lepeka, Tioni. Tioni living together with Fipe, the offspring Hiohe, Huliana, Sulu. Hiohe descended, Tahi, Teofilo, Nila. [Nila walks forward.]
Sister of Hiohe is Huliana. Huliana, Pahi, Akapito. [Akapito walks forward.]
Pahi's sister, mother Huliana, Ana, Tioni. [Tioni walks forward.]
From the three Hiohe, Huliana (and) Sulu, Huliana's sister. From Sulu, Taunehe, Sulu. [Sulu walks forward.]
From the offspring of Pio, the ancestral couple Tonuia and Lagimaina, Pio, Fafie, Teaile, Hakalo, Taupe, Tekata, Loha, Luifala, Ateli, Huhana. [Huhana walks forward.]
From the offspring of Levao, Levao, Iakopo, Naomi, Ehekielu, Akenehe, me – Falani. [Stands up.]

Scene 2 [Individual/Collective statements of purpose]
[Falani] I, in this 'party of swimmers', try to search for some answers to the question of where my culture is heading and for my efforts in this direction to be so that the culture may flourish.

[Heto] Our story is done in Tokelauan to allow the use of the voice or the Tokelau language and so that I may manage to stand firm in the custom of the Tokelau.

[Nila] I want to know the doings of the old times; I too want to take care of my Tokelau culture.

[Tioni] Trees and the creeper … (a) root that way, (one) root that way, another branch that way. The call of the warrior: you look for the trunk that stands fast. The trunk I look for is Tokelau.

[Akapito] In this time there are lots of things that are easily forgotten. It is like this for me too, and therefore I come here. There are little things that are lost to me that I now have come to look for.

[Pule] I have joined the group for this play, so that I may get to know the things that happened to my ancestors in earlier times.

[Eheta] I am here so that I might get to know the beliefs of my ancestors.

[Sulu] Who am I now? I have come because I wish to know, and I want to come to possess it.

[Akata] Be Greeted! I value my Tokelau. Wanting to have my Tokelau from bottom to top, top to bottom.

[Huhana] I have come like this; I want to join making stories in the Tokelau way.

[Song.] *O My Child*

You don't understand the language anymore
but you recognise the words

O my child.
The future of our village.

Let me move towards
what the words are that you speak to me.
Because my eyes have caught the light
of the different colours of this life.

Who then is capable of bringing
the heart and the spirit
by which my village beautifies itself?

So that my body here can be brought alive
by the sweetness of this life.

You don't understand the language
but you still remember the words.
O my child.
The future of our village.

Scene 3 [Origin stories.]
[Orator] Excuse, this is a story from a folk tale. In the days which have gone past, (there were) stones, sea, ocean, reef, the group of brothers, Mauimua (Maui-front), Mauimuli (Maui-last) and Mauiloto (Maui-middle). The group of brothers went fishing. Crack, fissure! The boat shifted a little. ?
Palu (a species of fish) palu, the group was fishing for palu. Mauimua was fishing. He was fishing. Now the baskets were full of the palu. Mauiloto ... the boy was playing in the stern. Kapoa (species of fish?).
?... in his group. The palu area.
Crack! Your Palu of ?
so that you may bring down an oily palu, a palu.
Shihu! Oh the area of coconut trees, area of coconut trees is roaming in the ocean...?
Fishing of the day, a stone, the stone, what is ....?
Shift a little over here, shift up here, shift over here too.
Fishing of ... what (is) this?
The nonu root appears. -
Kapoa, kapoa, kapoa, kapoa (a species of fish)
Hi! Kanava (a kind of tree) is roaming in the ocean. Tokelau surfaces. Mauimua, Fakaofo, (the) trunk of the group, trunk of the coconut tree. Mauiloto, root of the nonu, Mauiloto, emerges Nukunonu, Kanava for Atafu, emerges Mauimuli. Let the night be good!

[Orator] In the old days, there was an aitu of Fakaofo (whose) name was Fenu. The aitu of Nukunonu was Hemoana. One day, Fenu thought like this.

[The aitu Fenu] Now I am going to take the water of Nukunonu (and bring it) here.

[Orator] He then went to Nukunonu. He went with his clam-bucket (and) drew up the water of Nukunonu. And he ran away to Fakaofo. He ran away, but the thing who was Hemoana (an aitu) arose.

[The aitu Hemoana] I am going to go and pinch Fakaofo's pandanus leaves.

[Orator] That is how it was in those days. Fakaofo became well off with its water and Nukunonu with the pandanus leaves.

Scene 4 [Pre-palagi, pre Christianity time. A village scene of warriors fighting while women and children stay home to cook, weave, baby-sit, etc. Women are crying because of the fighting between warriors. A warrior presents gifts for Tui Tokelau.]

[Lefotu the Atafu warrior, in an extreme manner] ... Drink blood!

[Pio the Fakaofo warrior] Pio is first. Fakafotu! (bring forth)[1] Tui Tokelau ['King of Tokelau'] Fakaofo.

Lefotu?

Accept.
Crack!
Hey you, hey you.

[Pio] Pio was from Fakaofo, Tui Tokelau from Tokelau. Come, come, come, come, come to? Shift over.

Your originating from this day.

[Pio] Your day
Shift down. Shift down
Tui Tokelau, Pio got the strength ... Shift, shift, shift down
The 'bowing down' (a humiliation and placation ritual) is complete.

Move along down, move along down. Bow down to Tui. Shift, shift down.

Down, down, down, shift , crawl.

Go you, get lost.

[The warriors set out to fight again, but one woman intervenes, criticising the warrior culture.]

[Woman] Oh, oh, oh, quarrel, strife! Look down, you are like the warriors of yours. First the quarrel, strife. Look, look to Tokelau, women and children have died in the wars. Where is the village-spirit of yours? Where are the things that are good for Tokelau, if you are that. The warriors, what a quarrel, conflict, strife.[2] Get yourselves moving, go fishing, bring some fish, look at the women and children who want to eat. What a crew of pigs!

Scene 5 [The other women agree and collectively (including men) they present an image of ordinary, nurturing village life.]
[Women and children singing as they go about their work.]

Spin(?) the tip behind
The oar, the oar
Bring up a lot
The oar, the oar
Lash down the eel
The oar, the oar

[One of the men keeping an eye out for the boy climbing the coconut tree]
Keep steady boy. Grab so that you are steady boy and don't fall down.

[Another man asks] What has happened to the sea?

[Elder answers] See there. Look to the sea. We shall be too late. The scoop net is inserted on top of the exploring boat.
Yes.

[The men take the boat out fishing. They are going fishing, singing as they go.]

[Elder] You, the lines(?, could be the back of islets). You.
Come.

[Song] The ? shorten the guy rope (of a traditional sail) than (?) as
(Hii-) Fish with a hand line or rod and hook boat, boat, ... (??)

[They have caught enough so the elder decides it is time to go home. Singing. They give some fish for Tui Tokelau and the rest is taken to the women.]

[The boy] The fish.

[Woman, fatupaepae, 'distributor of goods'] Eat the eyes of the pone. Well done. Take (this) for your work, but come back and gut the fish ... Oh light the earth oven.

[Man praying to Tui Tokelau] Tui Tokelau go to your heaven, go to your ocean, a skipjack sea, a pala sea, a coral sea. Go to your reef inland of channels, a hand-fishing sea, a pone sea, a spotted surgeonfish sea, a kamutu sea, a se ..., a se ... What is this?

Part Two

Scene 1

[Everybody] What is this? A house?

Is the boat going?

Oh, look!

Oh, oh, see!

I want to see.

Go over there!

We want to look!

Go over there!

[Women and children are hidden away while the men check out what the 'thing ' is. One girl dares to disobey orders, and sneaks out for a peep. The papalagi (the foreigner in the boat) sings.] Oh my darling, oh my darling, oh my darling Clementine...

[The papalagi] We came across a small island heavily planted with cocoa trees. There was a large lake in the middle. The inhabitants were a fine swarthy looking people. They paddled out and as many as could come alongside came alongside. And they offered us some tokens, which didn't amount to very much, and in return we gave them some meagre examples of the gifts of civilisation with which they were well pleased.

[The men receive the gifts with much happiness.] Ha ha ha. Oh, look. Give (me) my things.

[The papalagi] We named the island the Duke of Clarence after your majesty's brother and then we sailed off. [Singing] 'Oh my darling, oh my darling... '

[When the men come back to land they gather women and children around to tell them of the house that sails on the sea.]

[A man] Come and gather here, congregate, come.
[One woman asks] What is it?

[A man] Come here, gather here. Sit down. Come here come here come here.

[One woman replies] Oh my!

[A man] Sit down sit down listen to me. Listen to me concerning our visit to the boat that appeared here.

[All] Yes what is it? What is it?

[A man] An exploring boat.

[All] What?

[A man] A superior boat, a big enormous boat. The travelling people came from the sky, (they were) some Gods.

[One of the crowd] (They) came from where?

[A man] We also saw the chiefs and the 'second in command', the spirits and the ogres gutting people. Look at these things which they brought. They are from them, (they) are forbidden for the women.

[While this is going on the child that sneaked to peep at the men and the papalagi, manages to take her mother away from the gathering to tell her that the men are wrong. First dialogue.]

[The child] Come please.

[The mother] What is it?

[The child] Come so that I may talk to (you). The taulelea (the able bodied men, the work force of the village) are mistaken.

[The mother] What are you telling me?

[The child] Only what I saw. That they are some gods are really lies.

[The mother] Shut your mouth, don't (you) know that the taulelea cannot be mistaken?

[The child] I saw people who are like us, but their clothing and their colour is different. It is not some Gods.

[The mother] That is none of your business.

[The child] The taulelea are mistaken.

[The mother] No!

[The mother will not try to understand her daughter, so she just takes her back to the gathering where the men are still going on.]

[A man] They explained and expressed that the things are forbidden for women to touch.

[Somebody from the crowd] Why?

[A man] It is forbidden for women to touch the things. You understand, these things are especially for Tui Tokelau and men.

[Elder] It is forbidden, forbidden, forbidden, forbidden. Is it understood? Fish-hooks, sacred things.

Scene 2 [The coming of Christianity.]
[Another boat appears again.]

[Somebody] Is (this) … a house?

[A male villager] Welcome, hello, hello.

[The priest] Greetings Children, greetings. I come to tell you that the one true God is Jehovah.

[Samoan priest, an interpreter for the papalagi priest] I have come to tell you that the Lord, only he is the true God.

[Somebody] Ask whether there are any fish-hooks.

[Male villager] Du you have any fish-hooks?

[Papalagi priest] Jehovah created the whole world.

[Samoan priest interpreter] Jehovah created the whole world.

[Papalagi priest] He created all the sea, all the birds, all the trees, (the) sky, he created all good things.

[Samoan priest interpreter] He created the world, the sky, the trees, everything he has made.

[One woman wants a closer look but she is pushed back again.] Oh, I want to look.

[The papalagi priest carries on] He created man in his own image.

[Samoan priest interpreter] He created the people like Him.

[Papalagi priest] Sinful.

[Male villager] Fish-hooks?

[Female villager] In what manner then?

[Papalagi priest] Jehovah is the one true God.

[Samoan priest interpreter] Jesus, Jehovah is the one true god.

[Papalagi priest] Then evil men crucified him.

[Samoan priest interpreter] Bad people went and crucified Jesus.

[Papalagi priest] In his death he gave his forgiveness.

[Samoan priest interpreter] In his death, his death he forgave us.

[Papalagi priest] Jehovah is the one true god.

[Falani] Jesus, Jehovah he is the true God.

[Samoan priest interpreter] All others are demons. [Walks over to (the statue of) Tui Tokelau and hits him trying to destroy him.] They're monsters.

[Village people pull priest away, not liking what he is doing.]

[Female villager] Kill the person!

[Papalagi priest] You are sinful people. You go over there!

[Somebody] Look, (what) he is going to do with Tui Tokelau.

[Female villager] Oh, what a noise! Get the hell going! What a noise!

Listen, listen, pay attention.

[Papalagi priest] And if you take no notice of the truth you shall be condemned in hell forever more.

[Samoan priest interpreter] If you don't steer right to the true words you shall burn in the fire in Evil everlasting, for ever.

[Papalagi priest] All over the world people are turning to the one true God.

[Somebody] Tell (him) that (he) should go.

[Papalagi priest] Now the truth has been brought to…

[Male villager] Where are the fish-hooks?

[Papalagi priest asks his interpreter] Where are we, where are we?

[Samoan priest interpreter] Tokelau

[Papalagi priest] Oh Tokelau. I'll leave you with my… Let us all kneel together.

[Samoan priest interpreter] Please, we, bend – (your) knees down.

[Papalagi priest] Our father who art in heaven…

[Somebody] Who is he talking to?

[After prayer men ask for fish-hooks again]

[Male villager] Where are the fish-hooks?

[Papalagi priest] I'll be back.

[Male villager] Where are the fish-hooks?

[Papalagi priest leaves]

[Samoan priest] First let us pray.

[Elder] Gather here, congregate. Do the prayer. Get down.

[Samoan priest praying] Our Lord we are sinful people to our disgrace. For we are praying to you, our Lord, the highest in the heaven, all the things in the world are created by you. Forgive these sinful people. Amen.

[He gives out fish hooks, then the chief of the village decides, yes they will become Christians, but one woman disagrees and says so. At the end of it she gets a hiding for challenging (authorities).]

[Young woman] You are telling us to change religion? Who is he? Who is the papalagi who came telling us to obey his God, but did he see this Tui Tokelau?

[The women try to shut her up because she is in for a hiding.]

Beat, beat.

[The child] Oi, raise (the head). What is it?

[The child is looking up.]

[She gets a hiding and is taken away, but calls out.] You are obeying, you will be taken as slaves for the papalagi.

[She is ignored, so it is village life again. Then another boat appears.]

Scene 3 [The arrival of the slave-traders.] [The slave ship arrives. The men are enticed on board. The young men are trapped, a young boy is thrown off. He reports to the women and children. There is crying everywhere, hysteria etc.]

[Slave raider] Oh! The village oh!

[Somebody] What is it?

[The boy] The taulelea have been taken by the boats.

[A woman asks in disbelief.] What?

[Another cries] Oh how painful ... my father!

[Somebody cries out] Aaaaaaaaa Tui Tokelau!

[Women and children cry on the beaches, crying for their sons, fathers, brothers, grandfathers.]

[A mourning lament, or *haumate*, (lit. 'come death')]

'The taking'
Taken, have taken
The strength of the land
Come here to your mat
Lie down in the meeting house
Oi! Oh!

Lost, have been lost
By the taking of the sails
(We could) not take farewell
You have gone elsewhere
Oi! Oh!

Lost, have become lost
A generation of Tokelauans
Give here turn here
so that I can once more see there
Oi! Oh!
       Your men

[While lamenting, orator reports about the slave-traders]
In February in the year 1863 came the first man-stealing ship to Tokelau...
The strength of the land (the men) was deceived, by some cloth, down into
the bottom of the ship and was locked inside its hull. Two hundred and fifty
three were the number of people who were taken by the man-stealing ships.

[A statement from the girl that no one would listen to.] Look to what an end
this came to. The papalagi came and took the strength of the land. A time of
crying alas, a time of mourning. How is Tokelau going to proceed? Who is
now a Tokelauan. Let us be strong and build Tokelau. Let Tokelau live!

Part Three

Scene 1 [Orator chants the political genealogy (of): how Tokelau came to be
a part of New Zealand.]

In the year 1765, appear the first 'group of gods' of Tokelau ... (it) was the
first ship of the papalagi. There in the year 1877, the flag of Britain was
raised on Tokelau. There were periods of man-stealing ships, of ships
spreading the gospel, of ships 'roaming about aimlessly' that went to
Tokelau. Useful for what purpose? The children of Tokelau fished with
scoop nets on top of the reef edge on the ocean side.
In the year 1916 the 'village' of Britain brought Tokelau into the lands she
ruled. Tokelau, Ellice Islands, Kiribati were ruled together by the government of Britain. To what end? To be in the back. Merged together to do
things together.... But the elders dwelled making their weavings.
In the year 1925, Britain and New Zealand made a decision that Tokelau
should come under New Zealand rule. Again, there was a merging together. Samoa, Cook Islands, Niue, Tokelau were merged together without a reason under the supervision of New Zealand.
In the year 1948, New Zealand decided to bring Tokelau inside of its ruling
boundaries. Tokelau and New Zealand were merged together. In 1962
Samoa became independent, in 62 New Zealand asked Tokelau do you want
to shift (allegiance). (The options were) Australia, Britain, America, Samoa,
the Cook Islands.
The elders of Tokelau decided to send a group to the Cook Islands. They
decided that they wanted to group with New Zealand.
The meeting of the country, of ... the Tokelauans together say that that is
perhaps their first decision concerning this matter.
In the year 1966, Tokelau was caught under a hurricane, it blew and blew
and blew. The elders decided that the land could not manage, that Tokelau
had no resources to take care of its people, and that we had to be carried to
New Zealand.
That is the reason why Tokelauans came to gather on this soil. A land for her.
Well wishes for the night!

Scene 2 [Individual accounts of journey to New Zealand.] [Background
songs.]

Good-bye you, farewell you
My dear my dearest
And ornament (with flowers), sing to you
of your song
waking you.

The difficulty
The saying good-bye
It is difficult
The parting

Well I came to do a mistake
in my happiness
But I forgot
Meet but again leave
Be here
The love so that it may get wings
So that I may go there
To bring you to your family

Oi, alas the difficulty
The bitterness of the love
You come, had better go
You don't want to go there

[Individual accounts of the journey to New Zealand. Told by the Tokelau New Zealand born.]

[Youth] I went abroad from Tokelau in a ship. The ship sailed to Samoa, to Fiji, the Cook Islands and arrived in New Zealand. The first thing I saw in Auckland was the lights. How beautiful the lights in Auckland were.

[Youth] When I arrived in Auckland the first thing I felt was the coldness of New Zealand. What is the place I have arrived at? A new life. For what? For me.

[Youth] I was very happy that I should come to see a different life from Tokelau. On the other hand it was sad to think of my parents, extended family and especially the country where I had lived.

[Youth] I did not want to go to New Zealand, oh poor Tokelau. What shall I do? My family decided that I should go, so that I may work and donate money to them so that I may help taking care of my family.

[Youth] I came to understand that I was the oldest child in my class. How terribly difficult it was to talk the palagi language. The children were laughing at me. Five came here.

[Youth] The years I went to school, they were happy years for me, because the children who came from other countries were friendly towards me and wanted to make friends with me. One boy from Tonga I became friends with. He was like a boy from Tokelau, in the way he acted.

[Youth] The people are nice, the best thing is that it was money for me to go to New Zealand. But (if) I don't work, I don't (cannot) live in New Zealand. It is not like Tokelau, (where there) is lots of fish and popo (eating coconut) (that you) don't have to buy.

[Youth] The sunset is slow … The people here, (go) to there, to there, to there. Where are they going?

[Youth] Poor Tokelau! Tokelau is caring for the family, the people are caring. But here, you look after yourself only. Alas (for) Tokelau.

[Youth] Because of my parents are, ...now what..., what is it that they do in Tokelau? I lie down on my mat, thinking about what they are doing. How cold it is here. What a ..., is a difficult life or a happy life? I am finding out about it.
[Youth] Alas, it is painful that there are lots of things which are good in New Zealand, but Tokelau is better for living for me. I feel sorry for my parents. I convey my love to you two.

Scene 3 [Party scene and skits of first experiences in New Zealand. School holidays!]
?
?
[One man] Where have you been?

[Another man] I have spent my time at the wharf. It is no fish biting.

[One man] Is there no fish?

[All] Clap. Cheers, cheers!

[Song, 'come on baby lets do the twist ', some get up to dance.]

[Somebody says] Sit down Tioni.

[Tioni] Alright, alright.

[The side singing] Over to you! Over there! (Standard way of ending a specific kind of Tokelau song.)

[A woman] How you make much trouble, don't you know how to dance?

[After the song, Falani] Keep on with your dancing, (while) I recall the days I went to school.

[Tioni] Ha, ha

[Akapito] Oh

[Falani] Yes, Kima and Hitolo and Iaheto (went to) the St. Joseph('s College) in Masterton. I don't remember the story about us.

[Huhana] What year was this?

[Falani] Which year? In 1964, yes, it was in 1964. I was in school and the brother superior came and asked me, Falani, you ... swim? (I answered, in my broken English) 'Oh yes, me good swim. I come from Tokelau'. (He said) Come here and be our group, Heto, you come here. Heto, Iaheto, Hitolo, I am Hitolo. You come here. Where is the person who can be ... Come you.

Yes, me, yes

[Falani, demonstrating what it was like] The audience are sitting down there. Come here, come here you. Remember that that is the side of the swimming pool, he is the person of the swimming pool.

Yes, yes, are you ready. Yes.

[Cheering and laughter by the party]

[Falani] Hitolo's hand reached the side of the swimming pool. It was like he had won. (He) surfaced, looking at the people who were watching [diving down, going for the whole (distance)].

[Laughter]

[Tioni] Well done. He is telling his story but I remember the story about him.

[Falani] Don't, don't.

[Tioni] You tell your story. Yes, is about Falani.

[Falani] I am hurt.

[Tioni] In the school, oh, do the people know how to jump for diving?

Yes, yes.

[Tioni] Yes, like that. We were doing our diving at school, and the brother superior went like this, 'Falani'? 'Yes bro'. 'Do you know how to dive?' 'Yes bro, I dive in the island'.

[Somebody] Oh, what a noise.

[Tioni] The palagi children went like this [whistles], beautiful eh? But the 'snake there ' went just like he did in Tokelau, like the children in Tokelau do. 'Hey brother I'm ready.' The brother superior came, 'you ready?' 'Yeah ready'. [He dives Tokelauan style; the one that stays down longer wins. Laughter!!!]

[Huhana] Wait, wait. So that I may tell the story of Tioni. Tioni had just come from Tokelau, he was twelve years. It is like this, it is not a story about him. Because he had just arrived, us from Tokelau.

[Tioni] Don't do a lie story.

[Huhana](We) were sleeping on top of the mats …

[Falani] You, stop making noise!

[Tioni] Sorry!

[Huhana] … we were sleeping on top of the mats in Tokelau. The school had a break and we came to the house where we lived. The night went, (we) were sleeping on top of the sofa, the persons were distributed on their sofas. (We) slept, slept, but one night we heard (a) bang! What is it that is saying bang? Tioni had fallen down. It was like this, for Tioni was rolling over like that, like that, he didn't know a palagi sofa.

[Song. 'I have a band of men and all they do is play for me'.]

[Huhana] Oh, oh stop please the party, stop the party! Drink your beer, the lady here feels she is going to give birth.

[Sulu] (They) are sending her, home to their houses. Home time, home time. Good bye!

[Akapito] Go and call for a car.

[Nila] A taxi?

[Akapito] A taxi, a car, be quick.

Scene 4 [The first child is born and begins to grow up within the papalagi culture. This becomes disturbing and scenes of cultural erosion begin to take place, climaxing in one problem child being taken away.]

[Female child] I am the first born Tokelau child in New Zealand.

[Father] Wait here, I am going to work.

[Mother] Good-bye you.

[Father] Good-bye!

[Nurse, knocking on the door] Good morning, I am your plunket nurse. Now, we do things differently here. Discipline and hygiene, that is what we are all about. After all we are no longer climbing up coconut trees. [Pushes baby away and baby cries. Nurse mimes regular feeds, recommends milk powder and bottle, leaves. The mother is confused. The baby crawls forward, watches TV, begins to imitate TV.]

[The TV] Hi, I'm the TV, you'll be seeing a lot of me.

[Mother] Hello!

[Father, comes home from work] Hello!

[Mother] Are you hungry? Do you want to eat?

[Father] Is there any supper for us?

Scene 5 [Headmaster Scene]
[Headmaster] Come on girl, enough TV, time you started school. What is your name?

[The girl] Hei.

[Headmaster] I beg your pardon?

[The girl] Hei.

[Headmaster] I'll call you Hai, yes I will call you Hai. You must remember when you come to school I do not want to hear any of your mumbo jumbo Tokelau language here. Alright? Do you hear me? English is the word, English is the language you must learn in order to get somewhere in this world. Do you understand? Good, don't forget.

Scene 6 [Friend Scene]
[Girl on the street] Hey … hey you … coconut, coconut.

[The girl, Hei] Yeah.

[Girl on the street] Got any friends? You look lonely here.

[Hei] Yeap.

[Girl on the street] They're small ones, eh? Well do you wanna be my friend?

[Hei] Yeah.

[Girl on the street] You've got no friends at all. You wanna play ball at the park? I'll teach you.

[Hei] Can I just go and ask my mum 'cos I have to go home.

[Girl on the street] It is only … you just finished school. Don't worry, you'll be home in plenty of time.

[Hei] But...

[They play in the park]

[The girl on the street] That's it … yeah. Got any money?

[Hei] Yeah.

[The girl on the street] How much have you got?

[Hei] Two dollars.

[The girl on the street] Oh … a … that's enough, we'll play spacies.

[Hei] Spacies?

[The girl on the street] Down town, it is not far, yeah you don't know.

[Meanwhile back home]

[Father] Where is, where is Hei?

[Mother] She has gone to play in the park.

[Father] What?

[Mother] She has gone to play in the park.

[Father] How many times did (I) tell the children not to go and play at this time? Look at the time. What!

[Father goes to look for Hei] Hei, Hei, Hei, Hei ... come, come.

[Father drags her home, gives her a hiding, mother protesting.] You are not fed up (with this)?

[Mother] This is enough.

[Father] Are you not tired of the hiding?

Scene 7 [Child watches TV. Uncle arrives, drinking begins. Mother and father go to sleep. Uncle molests child.]

[Uncle] Hello!

[Father] Yes.

[Uncle] Ha, ha, ha!

[Father] Where have you been?

[Uncle] I have been at the pub.

[Both] Cheers, cheers!

[Father] Where have you been?
?
[Father] You know the way (i.e., how it is), make your party like this, I am going to rest because I am working tomorrow. OK?

[Uncle] Yes, go then.

[Father] Good-bye you.

[Uncle] Good-bye.

[Uncle] I sleep on the sofa here.

[Father] Yes.

[Uncle] Good-bye, good-bye you two, good-bye, good-bye you two.

[Uncle makes sure that they are asleep, then goes over to Hei.]

[Hei] Hello uncle.

[Uncle] Hei, hello. Drink?

[Hei] No, no, ... NO! Leave me alone! [Scene is blacked out.]

[The following morning.]

[Father] Hei, make tea for me... Hei ...

[Hei reacts by screaming at her parents, then she runs off.]

[Hei] Why did we come here? I hate you.

[Mother] Oh, what is it? (I am) tired (of this) (this) stinks.

[Street kids take Hei on board. Police takes her home. Father gives Hei a hiding. This time the mother cops in too. Hei runs away again.]

[Man from the welfare] I'm from the welfare. Your child is at risk. You 've got to be very ...

[Father to Hei] How many times have you been stopped? What?

[Street kids gather. Heavier this time. Welfare brings her home, indicating that they are removing her from home. Father gets stroppy.]

[Man from welfare] I warned you, you've taken no heed. There is a need to take her into care.

[Mother protests.]

[Mother] Oh, oh, what is it then? Why is it like this with us? Everything has become broken up in all ways. The families ... why then did we come here? Oh Tokelau.

Scene 8 [Reciting of speeches and sayings about family.]
[Orator] Look at the situation which we have arrived at. Look at the position of the fatupaepae. She is the one caring for the family. Look at the thing which has happened to us here since we came to New Zealand. A culture to be handed to the children? A culture to be handed to the tamafafine? Where is our culture, Tokelau? Is it our exile in New Zealand? .... Stand up, stand up, stand up. Remember you, you are the fatupaepae, you, you who are the strength and take care of the family. Come you the ... Tui Tokelau ... we are searching, searching for a road for you. Searching for you (for) the things that are useful so that we may finish this.

[Another man] Spirit of the bottom of a basket, the fishing boxes (treasures) ... abandon the (negative) values of the culture. The values that are wanted (positive), are a road for us. The sayings from the culture   (is that) 'the offspring of parents are the children, the product of children are the parents'. Well being (to you all).

[A woman] The child of the bird lives on fish. The child of the fisherman lives on the words. The child is like a little fish, it bounces away (from) your hand, it is difficult to catch it again.

[A woman] Tokelau parents. We have come from Tokelau, our culture (is) from another place. We have born children in New Zealand and the culture of New Zealand is on one side of the cord. The children face (this situation), making a commitment, concerning which culture they are going to walk in. We speak the Tokelau way, the Tokelau children speak the New Zealand way. But we, the parents have to make balance between the two cultures so that we may live happily... we and our child. Good luck to us!

[All come together to sing the final song.]

Fatupaepae of the family
Sharing out, distributing the meal
Sharing out, distributing the fish-share
Tamatane of the outer islets
Tamatane of the boats going fishing
The positions may stand fast
by the words of the ancestors.

[All together] So that there may be life for Tokelau.

Text 2: 'Mafine' (Woman)

Scene 1 [Tima arrives home (in Tokelau) after having been away at school for several years. She comes off the boat with a papalagi woman. Men are working unloading the cargo. Tima's mother and aunt await her arrival at the beach.]

[The orator]
Respects (to) Tokelau. Respects to the young ones, respects to the white-heads, the old ladies and the elders. Respects to you, the strong bone, respects to the children, respects. We steer gently in front our *tauhunu*-tree (good for making bailers for canoes, sweet smelling) towards light and understanding. We (are) moving over gently. This is an attempt by us, our party of swimmers, some reflections of ours. We go and compose our story, a tale. Spur the actions, look with a good disposition at our country, our tradition, and especially at the position of women. That is the name of our story. Woman. We are now going (to do it). Respects.

[Singing the tuala (opening song)]
Spread out the sitting mats for the night call
Well, yes (in reply)
Spread out the sitting mats for the journey
Enters, is (ritually) opened
Her leaf-skirt
Well, yes
Enters, is (ritually) opened
The pearl shell pendant

Well, yes.
Yes, a mother-of-pearl shell.

[Tima's mother] Soon now my child will arrive.

[Men] The boat, the boat.

[Tima] Hey, that's my mum. I think its my auntie with her. [Tima runs towards her mum. Kisses and hugs her.]

[Tima] Mum, mum.

[Mum] Oh my poor child.

[Tima] You, how well (you look)

[Mum] Tima, it is not like this how the girls of Tokelau do (their) loincloths! [Puts a lavalava around her.] It is not nice to wear trousers! [Auntie and Tima react, but don't say anything.]

[Tima] O mum, this palagi woman has come to work in Tokelau. This is my mother [introduces her mother to the papalagi]. Hey, that's my auntie. [Kisses and hugs her auntie. Introduces the papalagi. The papalagi wanders off while Tima, auntie and a little girl walk on home. They meet Tima's brother on the way. Tima rushes up to hug and kiss him, but the brother stops her hug in mid-air.]

[Brother] Wait then! (What you do) is like running loving to your brother.

[Tima] Hello.

[Brother] Welcome. Your journey has brought you here? Yes, (it is) good to go first to the house (for you), so that I can first do my chores, and then we meet in the house?

[Tima nods her head.]

[Brother] Good-bye.

[They walk on home.]

Scene 2 [Tima goes for a walk around the village.]
[Tima] Mum, may we go for leisure, like this and then we come back again. It is good, we are returning quickly.

[Mum] Yes, return quickly. Farewell then.

[Tima] How Tokelau has changed. Tokelau used to be large in those days, but no! How small it is. The Church too, it is not a very high and large building, look at the small house. How it has changed. Whose is that house? [She ask some of the children.] Look how (they) stare at us from inside of that house.

[Young man 1] Tima, hey. [Meets up with a young man on the road. Greets him with hugs and kisses. Her brother sees and shakes his head in disapproval.]

[Tima] Hi, how are you?

[Ym1] How are you?

[Tima] (I) am well. And you, are you working?

[Ym1] There are lots of things from the outer islets to bring here.

[Tima] Yes, if you had gone to New Zealand, your shoulders would not be painful for nothing, of the aimless carrying of the bags because people have come here.

[Ym1] You are lucky. You have become a papalagi girl.

[Tima] And how beautiful life in New Zealand is! How hot your land is.

[Ym1] It is good to 'leisure around' like this, no?

[Tima] Good-bye then.

[Ym1] Good-bye, good-bye.

Scene 3 [Mum and dad decide that Tima is to stay home in Tokelau with them.]

[The orator] Our story is still moving along. Tima's thoughts and desires when she came to New Zealand were of her beautiful Tokelau. It was what she was thinking about and cherished in her heart and soul. Is it the same now? Is it the same, the Tokelau that she has cared for in her heart and the place that she then came to? She has entered into her tradition/culture and it is still new, but the dark days are beginning to appear, the dark days. We are going on.

[Tima's father. Praying] Our Lord, our God, there is none but you. Only you are the object of our thanks, and again thanks for the bringing here in our hands our dear child. We didn't know when we would ever be together again. Our, our Lord, accept our thanks. This prayer of ours is sent towards you there above. In the name of the Father, the Son and the Holy Ghost. Amen.

[Tima's father address his family] Mother, our child has arrived. Look! Are you proud? You can be proud, she has arrived and the schooling in New Zealand has ended, she has come back to where she came from. She has come to work in the Public Service of Tokelau. So that (she) can make our name good. So that she can bring money, bring money to the family. We two have become old, there are no people here, because all our children have long been gone to New Zealand. You have come, you may think, that you don't go abroad again, you are not going abroad. We two have become old, there is not a child in our hands, they have all gone abroad.

[Tima's mother] Tima, you must listen well. I am your mother and I am going to convey the decisions and the stories that will make your life a good one. Now your father has finished speaking to you. We two are old, there is not one person here that takes care of us, we cannot do a thing. Being in New Zealand is over for dear little you. Look, now there are only us two. Your mother and father, I have grown old too, there is not a thing (I can do). You are going to stay here and look after us. Obey us Tima, your well being is what we are saying to you.

[Tima's brother] Respects to the father, respects to the mother. Tima here, you listen to the words of the father and the mother. Obey them. Have compassion. Look, they have become old. Embody your love in obedience. (We bring) to you the wishes that you are to stay here and carry out your duties as a sister in the family. In this time, Tima, pay attention to me, you are not to go and familiarise yourself indiscriminately with the boys that are strolling along on the road, this situation is not agreeable to me. Stop going and doing that this day. Do you understand?

[Tima] My parents. And my brother too. Please, please (understand) that what you are telling me, how difficult, oh what a difficulty it is. You tell me that I am to go to New Zealand to look for a life so that I can find my place to live in this life, because we are not unchangeable. (But then) suddenly you are telling me that I shall abandon my schooling and that I shall stay here and take care of you.

[Father] It is enough of this cleverness!

[Tima] It is not, it is not like that. My schooling is not completed. There is still work, there is one more step that (I) have to take, so that I can get the course that will allow me to work. Please understand, to me the idea is that I shall return to take care of you. If there is no work for me, I must go and finish my schooling, please my father and my mother.

[Father] And the school is where? And the schooling is where?

[Tima continues] Please give me a chance. I can still return and look after you, when I can obtain my own food. My brother, please explain to the parents, you are the one of us that can understand this opinion.

[Father] To the school then? Well! Stand by me.

Scene 4 [Tima runs off to the beach. She speaks her thoughts, while at home … a marriage arrangement is made.]

[Tima] The beauty of Tokelau. How beautiful Tokelau is. The breakers of the waves of the ocean, but Tokelau is sheltered by the trees. What a nest, how beautiful. But to be retained here. What a slavery! How my parents don't understand me. I cry because I also have the feeling that I should stay here and take care of them two. (They) don't know the hardship and the sweating (that is connected with) schooling. Alas, the sun is going down and bringing different colours as it goes. But it is standing fast and retained in the souls of people that the beauty is like this. Poor me, I am turned upside down due to criticism and scolding and I do not know what to do.

[While Tima is doing this, a marriage proposal goes on at home.]

Scene 5 [The marriage proposal.]
[The orator] If you go shopping, you pay money for the thing you want. Do you recognise the buying that goes on now? The youth of Tima is sold, and her strength. (They) want to obtain a strength from outside the family for the family, (and so they) buy it. Tokelauans, what is the price of our daughters now, how much do we use to sell them for? What then is their price? How much is the price of our daughter? Are we still familiar with this? We are still going on (with the play). Respects.

[Father] Remember, you remember that I am the father of the family, and another couple have come and discussed with me, arranged nicely inside of our village, so that you may make your family. You are going to go and live with the man. There is not another decision that will be reached about this. Your situation is that you are not going to go abroad, you are going to stay. The knowledge that you have gone to bring here from outside is sufficient. You don't want to listen to your mother, you don't listen to your father, there is not one more word I convey to you. The custom here is that you listen to your parents and make your family.

[Mother] Tima, our decision-making is over. The decision is that you are going to make your family, be a good child, a strong child, a child that stands up for her family. Bring the strength of that child to take care of us two, cooperate with your strength in all things. There will be not a thing to worry about (then). This is the decision that we have made.

[Tima] My parents, this is the thing that you want. You want (me) to bring in some money, but where is your love for your child, that is me. How am I going to fare? You just stay. What about what I want? But it is not just that I want something, this thing that you are doing is wrong. You have not come to seek my best. Why is it like this that my family is not nice and have come to this? It was not because of this that I came here. My father, it was not for this that I came here. I came to visit you two. It was not this thing that I came for. Oh, these people are crazy. Please tell me that I am dreaming.

[She runs away. Meets up with the young man who proposes to marry her.]

[Young man 2] Tima, hello.

[Tima] What are you doing here? What did you come for?

[Ym2] Have your parents told you of the thing that we came about in the night?

[Tima] I don't want to listen to that thing, I don't know what you want. We don't know each other, you don't know me, I don't know you, so go somewhere else, leave me alone.

[Ym2] Know that you don't have to worry about a thing. Know that I have loved you since the day of your arrival. Know that we two are going to live together and I am going to care nicely for you. You don't have to worry about a thing. It is also agreeable to our parents that we two are going to live together.

[Tima] Leave me alone okay? Just leave me alone. I think you've gone mad. You've gone mad.

[Ym2] Tima, please, love me. Oh Tima. [On his knees.]

[Tima] Get away from me, get away from me, leave me alone, get away from me.

[Ym2. Threatening] Just you wait until we are married!

[Tima meets her aunt and asks her to intervene for her.]

[Tima] Auntie, auntie, come here please, help me.

[Aunt] What is it?

[Tima] I have come to visit my parents, but what a different thing they are doing to me. Oh come, please come. Please auntie, explain this because they don't want to listen to me.

[Aunt] Tima, alas my poor child! I know well the difficulty of what you have come to and I have arrived at. But Tima, it helps to remember: it is right that you have lived in New Zealand and become grown up in New Zealand, your cultures are now two. In my opinion it is necessary for you to keep dear your Tokelauan culture, and don't throw it away. But the thing that you are telling me, you must not worry. I shall go and talk to your parents and tell them this, do you understand? Lets go to the house.

Scene 6 [The Family Council.]
[Song]
Congregate
Oh Tokelau
Congregate
Congregate in the malae (meeting-ground) of the land
Oh, read out the words of the village
The love of my heart and soul
has become occupied with.
Your men.

[The orator] Alas, how beautiful the words of the palehiva (songdance) are. That Tokelau congregate in its malae, are the ways of the country. – Following the words of the village tradition. Alas for the beauty of the spirit and the words of the song! But the family of Tima also make their congregation. Their family-meeting is now beginning. Each person with his noose, his noose for unmated hens. It is the 'harvest' of Tima, so as to tie her up, so that she may stay. We are continuing.

[Father] Well, our family has congregated. It is doubtful whether there are any questions, because it is the living custom told by my father that the daughter shall listen and there is no other view of the family concerning this decision. All the sides[3] agree to this, don't they? Is there another meaning that needs to be expressed here? No, there is not another opinion. The family is to be made. That is how it is to me, my opinion as the head of the family, that the family is to be made. I don't want to listen to a feeling about this, I don't want to listen to her thoughts concerning what we have arrived at in the family. The wedding is to be held.

[Mother] There is not another thing that has arrived here. There is not another change that will change this thing. It is finished. The decision has been made. The thing has ended. You make your wedding. Don't stare like that with your eyes Tima. You listen well, the decision is over. The two families' family have taken care of this thing. The wedding of yours will be made. Come here to us and look after us two. Do the things I have to do for me.

[Brother] Respects to the father. Respects to the mother. Tima, now when the family is gathered together, you listen to the thoughts of the father and the mother that they are truly taking to you. But alas my dear sister I have one word to tell you, I live inside this family and you are safe there too. Tima, obey, obey the father, obey the mother, obey the family. Your life will then become well. Respects to the father, respects to the mother.

[Aunt] Our family, please! This Tima here has come crying to me, to ask me to come and speak to you. What is it that you are worried about, in letting Tima go and look for our best. When she is finished with that, she will return and come here and take care of you, the old ones. You don't need to worry. Tima is only 19 years old and is only a child.

[Father] She can manage to take care of us.

[Aunt] Let Tima please go and finish her schooling. The little bird will come back to you.

[Mother] It isn't your business, don't come and meddle with that thing. It is in our power to decide. The child is mine and not yours. My story has been made, the decision has been made, and her father agreed to it.

[Father] Yes.

[Mother] This thing shall be done. Now shut your mouth.

[Tima] Wait, wait then! My ears hurt from the listening to your story that you have made. There is not a person who asks me what my thoughts are like.

[Mother, to the aunt] Look there.

[Tima] Please, please, listen to me. I love you. If you love me, we should talk together to arrive at a good decision. My father, please, give me the opportunity. I have not done enough preparation on that side. My brother, please help me. Auntie, come here, say what you think so that that group can understand, please.

[Brother] This is wrong.

[Father] Is there another word? Decision: the wedding is to be made.
[Aunt] Tima my child, look at what I have achieved! There is an unwillingness to cooperate so that poor me is angry. Tima, have patience, there is not a thing I can do.

[Song]
I am awaiting the wind
the wind of life
I am awaiting the wind
the wind of life

The compass
sets the direction of my way
my way, my behaviour.

Scene 7 [Tima is on the beach speaking her thoughts and meets up with Tioni, the teacher.]

[Tima, speaking to herself] Why then, why is it that there are two things that I keep dear, my parents and my country. But when I came here, they did the things that make me angry and are so uncooperative towards me when I have come to be with them. My dears, my parents, they gang up against me and make public this thing, but when (we) came, I didn't know, I didn't know where I was going. The fish of the ocean, the coconut-palms, the sand, please help me. I don't know what I shall do. How I want to escape! Where is a place I can escape to? It is better that I go unwillingly. I do not any longer feel any suffering.

[Teacher] Tima, hello.

[Tima] Hello. Who are you?

[Teacher] I am Tioni. Don't you remember that we met at the tournament that was held in New Zealand?

[Tima] Oh, yeah. Have you been long here?

[Teacher] A little time, six months, I am a teacher at the school, the school of your auntie. Hey, I hear you are getting married.

[Tima] Oh the listening to their stories! Maybe you know Tokelau the prison, the best penitentiary in the world. All the prisoners of the world are coming to Tokelau because it is impossible to escape from here.

[Teacher] You have become bitter in your view of Tokelau.

[Tima] Why are you not angry?

[Teacher] Um, I think I know what you mean, but I think we need to be trapped.

[Tima] What do you mean?

[Teacher] Well you want to travel the world, maybe you want to go to America, to Britain, maybe worse, even marry a papalagi. You want to be free in all things. What is the true meaning of your wanting the freedom. Tima?

[Tima] So that I may do what I feel, so that I may go to school, so that I may have my things.

[Teacher] Yeah, but don't you know? The cultures that you know are two now. You originated earlier from Tokelau, you went to New Zealand. Which one do you choose Tima?

[Tima] I am only 19.

[Teacher] So? You've had more privileges than 90 percent of third world people. We need people like you here Tima. Your auntie needs you.

[Tima] What for?

[Teacher] Because there are lots of changes that she is doing in the school. Books are printed in the Tokelau language and she is also teaching the children to be creative. But there is another side, the people who don't agree with what she is doing, but that cannot be helped. People who work in the community, well they need to make a sacrifice, they need to be trapped otherwise... this is our meaning no, when coming to the difficult things it is a shock (but we have to) stand and pay attention.

[Tima] But we still need to be personally happy.

[Teacher] Yes, you are right.

[Tima] Are you married?

[Teacher] No. [Taking his glasses off, moves towards Tima touching hands. Her father sees them, and attacks Tioni.]

[Father] Hey, you, bloody hell! [Gives the teacher a hiding. Tima runs home, packs her clothes, but the village priest turns up.]

[Priest] Tima! What is it that you are doing Tima? What are you doing? Are you alone the only person who understands that thing? You have learned in your schooling that you are a child and that your greatest ambition should be Jesus and God.

[Tima] Yes, o Father.

[Priest] Have hope. In the days when you were a child you were taught first to fear God, first to obey your parents.

[Father] Yes.

[Priest] You should take care of the things that make your life peaceful. Prepare your heart, you cannot achieve calm until Jesus takes you.

[Father] Yes.

[Priest] Jesus is the way by which you achieve the good things. Obey. Go to your parents, keep your life peaceful, good through obedience. Go then.

Scene 8
[The orator] Carry on this way (thinking): God will show up, Jesus will appear. We think that we shall meet with the things we desire, but they are in the power of others. We say that that is the will of God, (we believe) that is the desire of the word of the Gospel. What is it that we are accustomed to? A question: (Maybe) because is it common for us to use His words as a way through obstacles for the things that we want, we carry on. We wait for God to appear to set everything right. Maybe our spirit consists of waiting and postponing our actions in order that someone shall make the choice for us? The answers are yours. Respects.

[Family gets Tima ready for the wedding, men sing their chant to Tima.]

[Men]
Isa, isa, isa!
(You are) black, but want to be a papalagi
(You) don't accept
to be a Tokelau girl
(You) are tired of the ancient things
Her mouth speaks!
(She) is precocious, wanting to be clever.

E, e, e!
The power speaks
Obey the kicks
suffocate your knowing
So that (you) may go the way of the men
Give up what originates from the Samoans
(Give up) what thing the palagi do

You are a fatupaepae.
Do chores all the time!
Drink the bitter drink of quietness!
This is the lot of Tokelau women.

[Tima] Look here, look here! Poor me, I am like a caged person, I live in this life that other people are programming. (I) am grown, but don't know what to do. But I am stuck with what it was like before. Stuck with accepting whatever it is that they do to me. This is me, this is I.

[Final song]
Obedience makes strong (they say)
Little me will not be calm anyway!

I expect with confidence
that a Tokelauan will understand.

Ch.
Alas, the ancestors!
Alas, the message sent
The things chosen.
Look well after those
Because they are what Tokelau drink.

Well being to women!
(they) are the strong bone
who constitute the base of Tokelau families.

Well being to women!
(they) are the backbone,
a flower ornament, a wreath
beautifying[4] Tokelau.

A note on transcription of the following three narratives. The parentheses have been inserted in these narratives by the authors. The brackets contain information added by me.

Narrative One: 'Care for Coconuts'

Taku Tala

1904. Na talia ai e te Uluga Talafau te popo ake mai ke toto.

1906. Haihu.
1909. Matala te lauhomo, kenakena,

lautovivi, laumatemate.
1912. Kua mauaka te pulapula.

xx 1920??
1940. Na lahi ai na falitega valevale

na fai ki te pulapula,
e te kau Halevi.

1946. Kua fatio te taume.

1954. Muaki muamua
e taufa popoga ki Hamoa.
1955. E he motuhia lele
te falitega a te kau Halevi.

My history

1904. The Ulugatalafau accepted the ripe coconut washed ashore so that it might grow.

1906. Sprouting.
1909. The germinating coconut's sprout opens, brown/yellowish, black leaves, dead leaves.
1912. The coconut-seedling came to be well rooted.

1940. There were all kinds of arrangements
made for the coconut-seedling
by the group of Church workers (lit. The Levi family).

1946. The spathe of the coconut tree craned its neck.

1954. First bearing of fruit,
a bunch of four is picked for Samoa.
1955. It is no longer existent
the arranging of the group of Church workers.

Lalau, tapue, velevele.

1956. Toe tu te muaki,

e tautolu, toe popoga
foki ki Hamoa.
1959. E kitea pea
te fetoku o te ola
1960. Na kave ai na tino
ke akoako fakapitoa
ki te tauhiga ona pulapula.
1964. Toe muaki foki te niu.

Taufa, toe popoga ki Hamoa.

1965. Hatala te kau Ikavai

ke kaumai ni taga kelekele
mai Niu Hila.
1969. Kae pa mai loa
te taga kelekele mai Niu Hila.
Kae atafia na galuega
a te taga kelekele.
Hui foki na foliga o te niu.

1971. Lapa te uila,
tanumia ia Pohiko,
kae oho ia Matiti
ofaki ki ona hapiga.
1974. Toe kave foki
te onogafua hua ki Niu Hila.

1975. Na atafia
ai na galuega
a te tagakelekele,
ka liu ai te foliga o te niu.

1976. Na opotia ai na lagona

ve lava e hili ka tapue
te niu i te pulu
ma te atigi apa.
Na fakataufai ai,
ko na hua
e popoga ki Niu Hila
e mokomoko atili.
Na falite fakatahi ai
na niu e tolu a Tokelau.
Na fakalauefa ai te David Lange
te auala ki Matiti.
Kae kikini te kaiao Tokelau.

Na amanakia ai te PAHINA

Bind with dried pandanus leaves,
trim, place a tin around.
1956. Once again flourished the
bearing of fruit,
a bunch of three is picked
to go to Samoa.
1959. It is seen nevertheless
of the coconut seedling.
1960. People were taken
to learn to specialise
in the care of the coconut-seedling.
1964. Again the coconut tree bears
fruit.
A bunch of four is again picked for
Samoa.
1965. The group of Elders
rummaged
to bring some bags of soil
from New Zealand.
1969. And arrived here then
the bags of soil from New Zealand.
And came to understand the work
of the bags of soil.
The appearance of the coconut-tree
changed.
1971. The lightening flashed,
Boscoe was covered over,
but Matiti rose
to nest in its place.
1974. Again took a bunch of
six drinking coconuts to New
Zealand.
1975. Came to realise that
[because of] the work
of the bags of soil,
the appearance of the coconut-tree
was going to change.
1976. The opinion that was put
together
was that it is better to protect
the coconut with the coconut husk
and the tin container.
It was then discussed
whether the drinking coconuts
being picked for New Zealand
were too young nuts.
Then put things in order together
the three coconut-trees of Tokelau.
David Lange expanded
the way to/of (?) Matiti.
But swung hard the green
fertilising leaves of Tokelau.
Then expected with confidence

he alelo eoo atu.
Kanapa, kanapa, kanapa,
kua hegia lele na mata
o te Uluga Talafau,
te Kau HaLevi, te kau Ikavai,

te kau tauhi Pulapula,

te kiwi,
i te pupula fekai a MATITI.

the white pearlshell lure
a tongue of the skipjacks.
Flash, glitter, flash.
The eyes of the
Ulugatalafau
the group of Church workers, the
Elders
the group caring for the coconut-
seedling
the New Zealanders
became very startled by the fierce
brightness of Matiti.

My history [of the school].
1904. The Ulugatalafau [the Ulugatalafau or Two-Couple, is Nonu and Alo. This is part of the *fakalupega* or ceremonial greeting for Nukunonu, one of the three atolls of Tokelau] accepted the ripe coconut washed ashore, [i.e. the school], so that it might grow [i.e. develop].
1906. The prefix *ha-*, refers to family, [and taken together with] *ihu* or nose, [is said by the author to evoke the image of sprouting, 'just like a nose.' Together then, this refers to the 'starting of education.']
1909. The germinating coconut's sprout opens, [this is how one shoot, i.e. of the school develops.] Brown/yellowish [is how another shoot develops.] Black leaves [like a black naped tern, means that this shoot is sick.] Dead leaves [reflects the fate of that shoot. This phrase taken as a whole refers to 'the different things coming from abroad resulting in changes in the community.']
1912. The coconut-seedling came to be well rooted. [This means that the school became well established.]
1940. There were all kinds of arrangements ['It was a lot of various kinds of displeasure' about what was] made for the coconut-seedling, [i.e. the school,] by the group-family-Levi, i.e. the Church workers: the Catholic father, cathecists and nuns [who were responsible for the school in Nukunonu at this time.]
1946. The spathe of the coconut tree craned its neck. [This refers to progress within the field of education.]
1954. First bearing of fruit, [in that] a bunch of four [i.e. scholarship students] is picked [i.e. chosen to go for further training] for Samoa.
1955. Is no longer existent, the arranging of the Group of Church Workers [their responsibility for the school was broken]. Band with dried pandanus leaves, trim, place a tin around. [I.e. the responsibility for the school was taken over by the community, and they began with 'protective measures' towards the school.]
1956. Once again flourished the bearing of fruit, [i.e. scholarship students] a bunch of three is picked to take to Samoa.
1959. Is seen nevertheless the slackening off of the life of the coconut seedling [the school. This is said to refer to the scholarship students in Samoa and their problems.]
1961 The people were taken [abroad] to learn to specialise in the care of the coconut seedling. [I.e. to train as teachers.]
1964. Again the coconut tree [the school] bears fruit. A bunch of four [i.e. scholarship students] again picked for Samoa.
1965. The Ikavai-group [respected people, here referring to the New

Zealand Government,] rummaged in order to bring here some bags of soil, [i.e. Education Advisors], from New Zealand. [This refers to the first time Education Advisors were sent from New Zealand.]

1969. And arrived here then the bags of soil [Education Advisors] from New Zealand.

1970. And came to understand the work of the bags of soil [Education Advisors]. The appearance of the coconut-tree [i.e. the school] changed. [This refers to the change when the school came under the government, and the growing progress at that time.]

1971. The lightning flashed, Boscoe covered over, but Matiti rose to nest in its place. [There was a change in that the old schoolhouse, the J. Boscoe building was abandoned, and the school moved to a new site and changed its name to Matiti. Matiti is the name of a star, hence the reference to rising.]

1974. Again took a bunch of six drinking-coconuts [scholarship students] to New Zealand.

1975. Came to realise that the work of the bags of soil, [Education Officers] the appearance of the coconut-tree [school] was going to change.

1976. The opinion that was put together was like is better to protect the coconut-tree with the coconut husk and the tin container [i.e. whether use of local resources would be preferable. This led to the office of Education Officers being terminated.]

It was then discussed whether the drinking-coconuts [scholarship students] being picked for New Zealand were too young nuts.

Then Tokelau's three coconut-trees [atolls] put things in order together [i.e. cooperate about education. 'For the first time, education in Tokelau was put together as one thing.']

The David Lange expanded the way to (?) Matiti. [The then president of New Zealand came to Nukunonu and opened the new school building which was then named after him.]

But the green fertilising leaves of the *pukakakai* Tokelau, which are put around the *pulaka* to make it grow well, swung hard. [I.e. The local workers were doing very well, working forcefully.]

Then expected with confidence the white pearl shell lure, a tongue of the skipjacks [i.e. the Tokelau language]. ['At this time Tokelauan was developed in the schools. The feeling that this was important, and a feeling of pride in this was coming strong.']

Flash, glitter, flash, [The school flashes with its brilliance.] The eyes of the Ulugatalafau, the group of Church workers, the Ikavai group [New Zealand Government and Administration], the group caring for the coconut-seedling [the teachers], the New Zealanders, became very startled by the fierce brightness of Matiti.

Narrative Two: 'A Life and Blessings'

Tala pukupuku o toku olaga ma fakamanuiaga a te Aliki na ko mauagia.	**A short story of my life and blessings of the Lord that came to be.**
Ko au ko K. Kula Fiaola na fanau mai au i te aho 30/4/24. Ko oku matua ko Fiaola ma Kula	I am Kula Fiaola I was born on the day 30/4/24 My parents Fiaola and Kula

ni matua Kelihiano,
nae galulue foki i te tofi tiakono,

mo tauhi kaiga
nae fehoahoani malohi foki
ki te Ekalehia ma te nuku
ma te komiti tumama,
ma akoako lelei ki matou te fanau.
E toka fitu (7) te fanau,
e toka tolu (3) ia tama,
e toka fa (4) ia teine.
Na akoako lelei ki matou
i te Tuhi Paia mo te poto faka-iena
ona po (fakafetai ki te Atua).

1939 – Na feagai au
ma te Faifeau Samoa
ma te Faletua
ko Teleso ma Siniva
i te tauhaga e ve ona takua i luga.
Na hauni malaga te Faifeau
ma te Faletua
mo te uhugafono ki te fono tele
a te E.F.K.S. i Malua.
Na ki la lavea ai ki matou
ko ni tama ma ki maua
ma Lufo Sili na teine,
ma to la fakamoemoe
e kave na tama ki Maluafou
ka ko maua e kave ki Papauta.
(Ni aoga uma a te Lotu).
Na malaga ki matou
ia Ianuali i te 1939,
taunuku ki Samoa
ma nonofo fakatahi pea
ki matou ma te faifeau ma te Faletua
ma te fanau i to la kaiga
i Vaimoso ma Malie.
18/3/39. Na fakaulufale loa
ki maua ma Lufo
ki te aoga
i Papauta Girls High School
koi pule ai te tamaitai Peletania,
Ko Miss E.A. Doons ma ni
faiaoga Samoa
nae fehoahoani ki ei.
19/3/39. Na kamata loa
te aoga nae fiafia lele
ki maua ki ei.
5/5/40. Na fakaofi ai au
ma Ekalehia
e te Faifeau Samoa ko Saaga
mae aoga pea

Christian parents
worked all the time in the
position [of] deacons
for taking care of extended families
and helping strongly
in the Church and the village
and the sanitation [women's] comitte
and taught well to us the children.
The children were seven,
three were boys,
four were girls.
We were taught well
in the Bible for the wisdom found there
in the evenings
(thanks to the Lord).
1939 – I met
with the SamoanPastor
and the wife
Teleso and Siniva
in the year that was mentioned above
Prepared to travel, the Pastor
and the Wife
as delegates to the big meeting
of the Theological College in Malua.
They two took us there,
some boys and us two
[I] and Lufo Sili were the girls,
and their purpose
was to take the boys to Maluafou
and take us to Papauta.
(They were all Church schools).
We went
in January of 1939,
arrived in Samoa
and lived all the time together
we and the pastor and the wife
and the children in their family
in Vaimoso and Malie.
18/3/39. Then were enrolled
we two [I] and Lufo
at the school
in Papauta Girls High School
the leader was a British Lady
Miss E.A.Doons and some
Samoan teachers
assisted her.
19/3/39. Then began
the school and very happy
we two were with it.
5/5/40. I was confirmed
into Church
by the Samoan Pastor Saaga
and went on with school

ki te tauhaga 1943.	to the year 1943.
28/11/43. Nae manuia pea	28/11/43. Went well
te nofo akoakoga	the schooling
na fai ai foki te toe hukega	and did the examination
i te mahina tena ko Novema,	in that month, November,
na manuia la te hukega.	the exam was good.
Na filifili au ke fano	I was chosen to go
ki te hukega ulufale	to the entrance examination
mo te falemai,	for the hospital
na manuia foki taku hukega	my test was good
ma kamata loa taku aoga	and then began my training
fakateine tauhi-mai	[as a] nurse
ite tauhaga 1944.	in the year 1944.
I te tauhaga 1944 nae fiafia pea	In the year 1944 I was happy all the time
au ma taumafai ki te aoga	and did my best at school
ma te galuega.	and the work.
1945. – Nae vena lava	1945. – Exactly in the same way
ona aoga ma galue	schooled and worked
i na tauhaga lava iena.	in those years.
Ia Hetema 1946	In September 1946
na fakaavanoagia au ke hau	I got the chance to go
ki Tokelau aua na pehia	to Tokelau because were affected
ia Tokelau katoa i te flu	all of Tokelau by the flu
i te tauhaga tena,	in that year,
omai ai ki maua ma	came we two [I] and
te fomai Samoa	the Samoan doctor
ko S.M.P. Ropati Viliamu	The SMP Ropati Viliamu
nonofo ki maua i Fakaofo nei	we two stayed here in Fakaofo
kae fano te lualua	and the boat went
oi kave na vai	and took the medical supply
a Nukunonu ma Atafu,	to Nukunonu and Atafu
nae faigaluega pea ki maua	and kept working we two [I]
mo te fomai tenei i Fakaofo.	for this doctor in Fakaofo.
Nov. 46. – Na feoloolo ai	Nov. 46. – It improved
te famai oi toe foki ai	the epidemics and returned
ki maua ki Apia	we two to Apia
ia Tehema i te 1946.	in December in 1946.
1947 – Na fakaauau pea	1947 – Continued
taku aoga fakateine tauhi-mai	my nursing school training
i te kamataga o te 1947.	in the beginning of 1947.
I te mahina la ko Iuni	In the month of June
na fai ai te hukega paahi	did the certificate exam
ko toku toe tauhaga tena	that was my last year
ma taku toe hukega tena.	and that was my last exam.
Na manuia ma maua ai	Was good and got
toku tuhi paahi i te mahina	my exam certificate in the month
ko Aukuho kua kavea ai au	of August, I became
ma teine paahi fakateine	a certified nurse
tauhi-mai o te falemai i Apia.	of the hospital in Apia.
10/10/47. Na hikitia ai au	10/10/47. I was transferred
oi faigaluega i te falemai	to work in the hospital
i Musumusu i Fagaloa	in Musumusu in Fagaloa

mai ia Oketopa kia Novema.
Toe hikitia ai au
ki Poutahi i Falealili
oi faigaluega ai lava
e pa kia Setema i te 1948
fakatahi ai ma na Toeaina
ko Sese Faiva ma Tala Lapana
ni (dresser)
ma Lufi Kilifi
ma Vaepa Poasa
ni teine fehoahoani.
Na faigaluega pea mai
1948–49 i te tauhaga la 1948
e tokalua oi oti ia failele
i te fakaikuga o te tauhaga.
I te kamataga o te tauhaga 1949
kua kamata tokalahi mai ai
na fafine fananau, nae manuia

i te fehoahoani mai o te Aliki
(fakafetai ki te Atua).
1950 – Nae galue pea
i te falemai i Fakaofo,
aho 23 Novema na toe hikitia

ke galue i Apia.
11 Fepuali 51. Na fakaipoipo
ai au kia S.M.P.Iosefa Mapusaga,
na fakapaia e te Faifeau
toeaina Metotisi ko Kalo.
8 Aukuso 51. Na fakamanuia
ai toku kaiga ma maua taku
tama he tama ko Logotahi
te igoa e 7lbs 40 ounces
te mamafa (fakafetai te Atua).
Fakafetai foki kia Samuelu
ma Naomi ma te kaiga
te alolofa, fehoahoani.
1952 – Na galue pea
i te falemai i Fakaofo
(tauhaga fanau o Logotahi)
fakafetai ki te Aliki.
1954–55 Na pehia ai
e famai ko te fiva hamahama.
1956 – Na toe foki ai au
ma galue i Apia na maua ai e au
te AWARDS te ipu.
He ipu e maua e te teine paahi

e galue lelei.
(Fakafetai ki te Atua).
1957 – Na pehia ai te
famai mihela i Fakaofo,

from October to November.
Again I was transferred
to Poutahi in Falealili
and worked there
until it came to September 1948
together with the Elders
Sese Faiva and Tala Lapana
who were dressers
and Lufi Kilifi
and Vaepa Poasa who were
nurse aides.
I worked continuously from
1948–49, in the year 1948,
there were only two births
at the end of the year.
In the beginning of the year 1949
the number began to grow of
of women giving birth, and went
well
with the help of the Lord
(thanks to God).
1950 – Worked on
in the hospital in Fakaofo,
day 23 November was again
transferred
to work in Apia.
11 February 51. I got married
to the SMP Iosefa Mapusaga,
were blessed by the Pastor
Methodist Elder, Kalo.
8 August 51. Was blessed
my family and got my
child, a boy, Logotahi
the name, was 7lbs. 40 ounces
the weight (thanks God).
Thanks too to Samuelu
and Naomi and the family
for the love, the help.
1952 – Worked on
at the hospital in Fakaofo
(Logotahi's birth year)
thanks to the Lord.
1954–55 Was affected by
the epidemic it was the yellow fever
1956 – I returned again
to work in Apia, I got
the awards, the cup.
A cup is obtained by the certified
nurse
working well.
(Thanks to the lord).
1957 – Was affected by the
measles epidemic in Fakaofo,

na tutumu uma na fale
o te falemai ma te Falefono

kua fakaaoga e na tauale.
Fakafetai ki te Atua
na vave uma tenei famai.
I te fakaikuga o te 1957
na valakaugia ai au ke fano
galue i te falemai i Nukunonu.
1958–59 Nae galue pea
i te falemai i Nukunonu.
1960 – Na toe fano ai au
ki Apia mo te Refresher Course.
1961 – Toe foki ki te falemai

i Nukunonu ma toe faigaluega
ai lava mai te 1961–64.
1964 – Na toe foki ki Fakaofo
ma galue ai i tena tauhaga.
1966 – Toe foki ki Nukunonu

ma galue ma feagai ai

ma te agi o te afa matagi
ma te galu.
1967 – Toe fano ki Fakaofo
ma galue ai ma fakauku ai
te Faleha.
1968–69 Toe foki ki Nukunonu

ma galue ai.
1970 – Na uhufono ai au
i te fono a te Atunuku
nae fai i Fakaofo.
Na maua mai te avanoa
maia Mr. Webber mo oku
ke fano ai ki Apia
ke fai he tonu lelei
mo Logotahi aua kua uma
kae ka kave fakahikolahipi

e te Ofiha ke aoga i NZ.
(Te Atua fakafetai).
1971 – Na teka kehe ia Logo
kae toe hau ki Tokelau
ma galue ai.
1972–74 Na toe fano
ki Nukunonu ma galue ai.
Na olo ai maua
ma Huka ki Samoa mo NZ

i he avanoa na fakataga
e te ofiha ona ko Huka

were full all the houses
and Maluatea [the Pastor's
residence]
were used by the sick.
Thanks to the Lord
this epidemic was quickly over.
In the end of 1957
I was invited to go
work in the hospital in Nukunonu.
1958–59 Worked all the time
in the hospital in Nukunonu.
1960 – I went again
to Apia for the Refresher Course.
1961 – Again went back to the
hospital
in Nukunonu and continued to work
there from 1961 to 1964.
1964 – Again returned to Fakaofo
and worked there in that year.
1966 – Returned again to
Nukunonu
and worked and faced [the
consequences]
of the blowing of the hurricane
and the tidalwave.
1967 – Again returned to Fakaofo
to work and to inaugurate
the Church.
1968–69 Again returned to
Nukunonu
and worked there.
1970 – I was a delegate
in the meeting of the Country
held in Fakaofo.
The opportunity was gotten
from Mr. Webber for me
to go to Apia
to make a good direction
his schooling in Apia
but was going to be taken for
scholarship
by the Office to go to school in NZ.
(The Lord thanks).
1971 – Logo went away
and (I) returned again to Tokelau
and worked there.
1972–74. Again went
to Nukunonu and worked there.
We two went [I]
and Huka to Samoa for New
Zealand
in an opportunity permitted
by the office because Huka

nae he malohi.
1983 – Na toe foki mai au
ki Fakaofo ma galue ai.
1984 – Na litaea ai au
kae faigaluega pea
aua e lavaki te kau faigaluega.
1984 – 24/4/90. Na fatoa
malolo mai au mai
te galuega faka teine tauhi-mai
ma kua i te kaiga.
(Fakafetai te Atua).
E tuha ai nei kua 53 ia tauhaga
na faigaluega ai i te
Hoifua Maloloina o Tokelau
Ma kua tuha kua 66

nei ia tauhaga o toku olaga.
Fakafetai lahi ki te Atua
ki to atafai mai kia te au.
K.K. Fiaola.

was not well.
1983 – Again I returned
to Fakaofo and worked there.
1984 – I retired
but continued to work
because there was a shortage of staff.
1984 – 24/4/90. For the first time
I rested from
the work as a nurse
and am in the family.
(Thank the Lord).
It amounts to 53 years now
that [I] have worked for the
Health Department of Tokelau.
And at the same [time?], have
become 66

now the years of my life
Thanks very much to God
for your kindness towards me.
K.K. Fiaola.

Narrative Three: 'Why Go to New York?'

**Malaga a Tokelau ki
Malo Kaufakatahi**

Kupu Tomua
Na fakatekia te tokalahiga
o tagata
i te ahiahiga a na hui
o Tokelau ki Malo Kaufakatahi.
Ve ake ai foki he lagona,
aihea nei te kua teki atu lava
ni hui kua olo
ki Malo Kaufakatahi.
Hove pe kua fakauiga
ve ia pe manatu
kua i te takitakiga o Tokelau
ka iei he huiga i te tulaga
ei ei te malo i te vaitaimi nei,
pe ona foki ko te Tokelau
muamua te kua kavea
ma Failautuhi Fakapitoa
ka olo ve ai oi lipoti
na fakafitauli i te va

o Niu Hila ma Tokelau
ki Malo Kaufakatahi.
E fakailoa hako venei atu e au
ko he fuafuaga ke toto
ma fakamautu te agaaga

**Tokelau's Journey to
the United Nations**

Introductory Words
Many people were surprised

by the visits of the representatives
of Tokelau to the United Nations.
and some probably also wondered
why suddenly
the representatives went
to the United Nations.
Maybe [they] ment [and]
considered [it to be] like that
in the leadership of Tokelau
there would be changes in the position
of the government at this time,
or that it was also because the
first Tokelauan became
Official Secretary
that [they] were going like that to report
the controversial issues in the
relationship
between New Zealand and Tokelau
to the United Nations.
I shall explain it correctly:
it is an arrangement to cultivate
and firmly establish the nature

ote galulue fakatahi
o Takitaki o Tokelau
ma Malo Kaufakatahi
kae ke talanoa atu foki
e uiga ki te ahiahiga talu ai
a Malo Kaufakatahi ki Tokelau.
Na he vaega mai
te pulepulega katoa
te taukave tautahi
e Tokelau ma ona takitaki.

Kautu o te Ahiahiga
Ona he fenua i lalo
o te taukikilaga a Niu Hila,
ko Tokelau ei te hili
ona fenua i lalo o te pulega
a Malo Kaufakatahi
ko te Komiti Fakapitoa
la i te tulaga o te Tuku Aloakia
o Te Tutokatahi
ki na kolone taikokole
ma ona tagata,
pe fakapukupuku veia
ko te Paoa ei te Komiti
Tokahefulufa (C24).
E kikila totoka te Komiti
ko tagata o ie nei fenua
e tatau ona tauhihi
ki te fakafoega aia
a te Ofiha o Pulepulega
ma kafai e mafai
ke tutokatahi fakapolitiki
ke vena foki te ekonomi.
fenua tenei.
Ona ko to na tulaga
e tatau ai ia Niu Hila
ona lipoti ki te komiti
i tauhaga uma
(e uiga ki na atiake i Tokelau)
mo na fuafuaga
a Malo Kaufakatahi
e uiga ki na atiake
kua fai i Tokelau.
i te 1974
na fakamamafa ai
ka he toe amanakia
ma pulepulega faka Niu Hila
mo Tokelau kae ka tuku
ke pulepule faka Tokelau.
I te vaitaimi tena ko Tokelau
nae i lalo o te taukikilaga
fehoahoani a Maori ma
Ofiha o Ailani ka ko fakaikuga

of the working together
of Tokelau's Leadership
and the United Nations
so that [we] also can discuss
the meaning of the recent visit
of the United Nations to Tokelau.
[This] was just a fraction [of]
the full mandate [authority]
that was carried alone
by Tokelau and her leaders.

Main Topics of the Visit
As a country under
the supervision of New Zealand,
Tokelau is the highest
of the countries under the authority
of the United Nations
Decolonisation Comittee
concerning the recognition
of Independence
to the small colonies
and their people
in short
this power is with the Comittee
of Twentyfour (C24).
It is the Comittee's firm position
that for people of these countries
it is necessary to adhere to
the steering
of the traditional political authorities
and if [they] manage
to become independent politically
Tokelau is in this group of countries.

Because of its status,
New Zealand have to
report to the comittee
every year
(concerning the development in Tokelau)
for the arrangements
of the United Nations
describing the developments
The meetings that were held in Wellington
in 1974
stressed the importance of
not relying on
the New Zealand way of government
for Tokelau, but to allow
for governance the Tokelau way.
In that period Tokelau
was under the supervision [and]
help of the Office of Maori and
Islands Affairs, but all decisions

uma e pule mai e Ueligitone.
I te 1977 na fai ai te huiga
ma ko te fakafoega
ma te pulepulega o Tokelau
kua taukave e te Ofiha o
Matakupu Tau Fafo,
ko te Failautuhi,
ko Ulu Fakatonu ia o Tokelau.
Kua toe fakaleleia ai
na tonufai ma ko te mamafaga
ona tiute tau pulepulega
o Tokelau kua tuku mai
e Ueligitone ki te
Failautuhi fakapitoa i te Ofiha
o Matakupu Tokelau i Apia.
Ko he fuafuaga kua maneke
ai te tulaga o Tokelau.
Kua kitea ai te galulue
fakatahi o Tokelau mo ni

latou lava ma te fakapolo-
kalamega faka Tokelau
ona pulepulega, kua heai
he faka Niu Hila.
Kua iei he fuafuaga
mo he tino kua fakamaonia
hana fakaikuga,
ko te fenua tena e he toe
takua he kolone,
e Niu Hila.
Na kikila totoka ia Niu Hila
ite atiake ona tulafono (polihi)
i te vaitaimi tena.
Na fetaui lelei lava
iena fuafuaga.
Ve la ko te fakatuuga ote
Kaufaigaluega fakamua
a Tokelau,
e tu tautahi lava ia
ma ka fai na talanoaga
e fakakautu lava ki te
lumanaki o te Malo o Tokelau.
Ko fuafuaga ma
manatu kautu ia o te Pule
ke fuafua na polokalame atiake
fakakautu kafai kua he toe
kavea te fenua ma kolone.
Kua fakailoa e Niu Hila
te matakupu tenei ki
Malo Kaufakatahi
ke fakafetaui ma fuafuaga
a te UNO ka ke

were governed by Wellington.
In 1977 a change was made
and the steering
and governing of Tokelau
was made by the Ministry of
Foreign Affairs,
the Secretary
was the Administrator of Tokelau.
Then still better
decisions were made and the bulk
of government duties
of Tokelau was transferred
by Wellington to the
Official Secretary at the Office
for Tokelau Affairs in Apia.
This was an arrangement that improved
Tokelau's status.
It was observed that Tokelauans were
working together for themselves and
for the
making of Tokelau programmes

for its governance, which was not
the New Zealand way.
An arrangement has been made
for the people to confirm
its decision,
that this country is no longer
to be counted as a colony,
by New Zealand.
New Zealand looked carefully
into the development of the laws
in that period.
Fitted very well
those arrangements.
Such as the establishment of the
Tokelau Public Service,

which is independent
and will take part in the discussions
that are central for the
future of the Government of Tokelau.
These are the arrangements and
main suggestions of the Government
so that the development programmes
are arranged to apply if the country does
not continue to be counted as a colony.
New Zealand made known
this subject to
the United Nations
so that it could fit with the arrangements
of the UNO so that

fakahaoloto ai ia tagata
o te fenua ke filifili lava
e latou na atiake faka politiki
ma ekonomi mo te lumanaki

kae ke kui malie atu
ai na huiga o he kolone
mo he tutokatahi vaelua
pe he malo tutokatahi.
ki tana lipoti te valakaulia
ni hui o Malo Kaufakatahi
ke toe ahiahi mai ki Tokelau
ke kikila ki na atiake kua fai
i Tokelau kae ke fakalogologo
foki ki manakoga o tagata
mo o latou lumanaki.
Mai ite 1976 ki te 1986
tuha kua tolu ia ahiahiga
a Malo Kaufakatahi ki Tokelau
ma e tofu lava te tauhaga
ma te lipoti a Niu Hila
ki te tulaga ko te aia
o tagata Tokelau ke filifili
Nae iei ni vaitaimi faigata
i te va o Malo Kaufakatahi
ma Niu Hila na faigata ai
i te komiti ona talia
te manakoga o Tokelau.
Kua uma te fakailoa
e Niu Hila te tulaga o Tokelau
ki Malo Kaufakatahi,
veia e kehe mai lava
ona e he lava na atiake,
ko tona aganuku e fakafaigata
ki Malo Kaufakatahi
kua hili ai te he toe kavea

ma kolone.
Kua fakaali ho tenei matakupu
e te Fono fakamua
ma te kaufono i Tokelau
ki te UN.
Kae faigata lele ke talia
kona e fakalogologo
te tahi tino ki te tahi tino.
Ei ei foki lava ni ie tahi
fakafitauli e lavelave
na tulafono ate UN
i na matakupu venei.
I te ikugafono o te
Fono Fakamua ia Hetema
1986 na fakamaonia ai

the indigenous people could be free
to choose
themselves the political
and economical developments for the
future,
so that can proceed gently
the changes of a colony
towards a bilateral independence
New Zealand included
in its report an invitation
that some representatives of the UN
visit Tokelau again
to look at the developments made
in Tokelau and to listen
also to the wishes of people
for their future.
From 1976 to 1986
three visits were undertaken
by the UN to Tokelau
and each year there was
a report from New Zealand
concerning the status of the right
their own future.
There were some difficult times
in the relationship between the UN
and New Zealand when it was difficult
in the committee to accept
the wishes of Tokelau.
When the reporting was over
by NZ on the status of Tokelau
to the UN
it seemed to be different
because its development was not enough
its traditions were making difficulties
for the UN
it would be best that it was not an
longer
a colony.
Repeatedly informed about this topic
the General Fono
and the Village Councils
to the UN.
But acceptance was difficult
because everybody talked to
everybody else.
There are also some other
difficulties that conflict
with the laws of the UN
in matters like these.
in the decision of the
General Fono in September
1986 it was confirmed that

ka iei he hui o Tokelau
ka malaga ki Niu Ioka
ki te fonotaga a te komiti 24
e talanoa ai ki te lipoti
o te latou ahiahiga ki Tokelau,
iulai 1986 kae ke fakalogologo
foki ki lagona o Tokelau
ki te UNO.
Ko te avanoa na tuku lava
ke filifili he tino mai
na faipule e tokatolu.
Malilie ma filifilia ai loa
ia Fatia Perez,
te faipule Nukunonu
ke fano ki te fono i Niu Ioka
ma talatalanoa ma te komiti 24
e uiga ki Tokelau.
Na malaga fakatahi te faipule
ma te Failautuhi Fakapitoa.
Na toe fakamatala
e te faipule te tulaga
o Tokelau ki te komiti.
Na fakailoa veia
e kehe lava te tulaga
o Tokelau ma ona fakafitauli
e fakafaigata ai ona mulimuli
ki na atiake fakapolitiki
e fai e te UNO
ma atiake aoga
(auala feoaki)
mai na fakalapotopotoga
kua fakapitoa
mo fenua taikokole.
Na takua foki e te faipule
ona ko te kehe o nofonofoga
i Tokelau e tatau ai ke tuku
he tahi takitakiga
ki tagata ke pulepule
e latou te faigamalo
He malo e he fakatupu
fakatauhuai kae ka taumafai
ke fakaogatahi
ma te fakaaganuku.
Ka he toe iei ni va
ma te fakalapotopotoga
ma te Kaufaigaluega Fakamua.
Ko ie nei fakafitauli
nae va na pulepulega
ma te Fono Fakamua.
Ona la ko talatalanoaga
nae fakaauau pea i te va
o pulepulega ma te
kua foia ai ni ietahi vaega

there was a representative of Tokelau
to travel to New York
to the meeting of the C24
when the report were discussed
of their visit to Tokelau,
July 1986 and so that
also Tokelau's opinions
could be told to the UNO.
The opportunity was given to
choose one person from
the three faipule.
They agreed to choose
Fatia Perez
the faipule of Nukunonu
to go to the meeting in New York
and discuss with the C24
concerning Tokelau.
Travelled together, the faipule
and the Official Secretary.
Explained again
the faipule the position
of Tokelau to the committee.
Informed as follows:
Tokelau's status is different
and its problems are special
making it difficult because (it is) behind
in the political developments
which is done by the UNO
and development which works
(roads to go about on)
from the organisations
that have become concerned
with small countries.
The faipule also mentioned
because of the scattered settlements
in Tokelau it is necessary to allow
another kind of leadership
to people so that they can have
power in the government.
It shold be a Government not bringing
about offences but which will attempt
to conform
to the traditional way.
Still there is no relationship
between the village councils
and the Public Service.
These are the difficulties
that separate the decision-making bodies
and the General Fono.
Because then of the discussions
that were carried out in the relationship
Public Service
Some groups of problems have been

ona fakafitauli.
Ke fapukupuku venei atu,
ko te ma ahiahiga
ke fakamautu te iei
o Tokelau ina fonotaga
e talanoagia ai na
matakupu o ia,
ko te tukuatuga ona manatu
fakapitoa ki te komiti
mo te he toe fakakolonea
kae ke fakamauaka
te hokotaga ite va o Tokelau
ma malo Kaufakatahi.
Kua aloakia na fuafuaga
ma kua talia foki e te komiti
te mea e kehe ai ia Tokelau
kae kua atafia mai e tuku lava
kia Tokelau ke fakafehokotahi
ia Niu Hila i te atiakega
ona fuafuaga fakamalo.
Na fakamanuia te ma ahiahiga
ka kikila ki te itu te ia
kae ka tuku ki fuafuaga
a Tokelau ke fakaauau
ni ahiahiga veia i te lumanaki
meamanu la kua uma
te fakamautu o te hokotaga.
C J Perez
Failautuhi Fakapitoa.

solved.
In short it is like this,
it was our two's visit
to firmly establish the existence
of Tokelau in the meetings
where its topics were discussed,

to present the relevant views
to the committee
for the abolishment of colonies
and to make clear
the strong mutual relationship between
Tokelau and the UN.
The arrangements were recognised
and the committee also accepted
the fact that Tokelau is different
and realised that Tokelau should be
allowed to keep up its relationship to
New Zealand in the development of
its governmental organisations.
Our two's visit was blessed
from that point of view
and it will be presented for Tokelau's
consideration whether it will continue
visits like this in the future
since a mutual communication has been
firmly established.
C J Perez
Official Secretary.

Notes

1. This is the name of the meeting house in Fakaofo and also the name of one of the newsletters referred to in Chapter four (*Vainiu mai Fakafotu*).
2. She uses the word *taona*, a disrespectful term which it is improper to use towards one's superiors.
3. See the Introduction for an analysis of 'sides'.
4. See Preface on *teu*, beautifying practices and conflict management.

Bibliography

Barth, F. 1967. 'Economic Spheres in Darfur', in *Themes in Economic Anthropology*, ed. R. Firth. London: Tavistock.

Barth, F. 1971. 'Role Dilemmas and Father–Son Dominance in Middle Eastern Kinship Systems', in *Kinship and Culture*, ed. L.K. Hsu. Chicago: Aldine.

Barth, F. 1992. '"Models" Reconsidered', in *Process and Form in Social Life*, Vol. 1. London: Routledge and Kegan Paul.

Barth, F. 1993. *Balinese Worlds*. Chicago, London: Chicago University Press.

Barthes, R. 1977. 'The Death of the Author', in *Image, Music, Text*, Essays Selected and Translated by Stephen Heath. London: Fontana Press.

Bateson, G. 1958. *Naven*. Stanford: Stanford University Press.

Bauman, Z. 1995. *Life in Fragments*. Oxford: Blackwell.

Besnier, N. 1988. 'The Linguistic Relationships of Spoken and Written Nukulaelae registers', in *Language*, 64: 707–36.

Besnier, N. 1989. 'Literacy and Feelings: the Encoding of Affects in Nukulaelae letters', in *Text* 9: 69–92.

Besnier, N. 1991. 'Literacy and the Notion of Person on Nukulaelae Atoll', in *American Anthropologist*, No. 93, pp. 570–87.

Besnier, N. 1994. 'The Truth and Other Irrelevant Aspects of Nululaelae Gossip', in *Pacific Studies* 17 (3) 1–39.

Besnier, N. 1996. 'Authority and Egalitarianism: Discourses on Leadership on Nukulaelae Atoll', Presented at the Conference on Leadership and Change in the Western Pacific: For Sir Raymond Firth on the Occasion of his 90th Birthday. London School of Economics.

Bloch, M. 1990. 'Language, Anthropology and Cognitive Science', in *Man*, 26, 183–98.

Blom, J.P. and J. Gumperts 1972. 'Social Meaning in Structure', in *Directions in Sociolinguistics*, eds. Gumperts and Hymes. New York: Holt, Rinehart and Winston.

Borofsky, R. 1987. *Making History. Pukapukan and Anthropological Constructions of Knowledge*. Cambridge: Cambridge University Press.

Boulay, J.D. and R. Williams 1984. 'Collecting life histories', in Ellen, R.F. *Ethnographic Research*. London: Academic Press.

Bourdieu, P. 1977. *Outline of a Theory of Practice*. Cambridge Studies in Social Anthropology 16. Cambridge: Cambridge University Press.

Chafe, W. 1979. 'The Flow of Thought and the Flow of Language', in *Syntax and Semantics, Vol. 12, Discourse and Syntax*, ed. T. Givon, 159–81. New York: Academic Press.

Charlot, J. 1983. *Chanting the Universe: Hawaiian Religious Culture*. Honolulu: Emphasis International.

Charlot, J. 1991. 'Aspects of Samoan Literature 2. Genealogies, Multigenerational Complexes, and Texts on the Origin of the Universe', in *Antropos* 86: 217–50.

Cohen, A. 1974. *Two Dimensional Man*. London: Routledge and Kegan Paul.

Comaroff, J. and J. Comaroff, 1992. *Ethnography and the Historical Imagination*. Boulder: Westview Press.

Connerton, P. 1989. *How Societies Remember*. Cambridge: Cambridge University Press.

Crapanzano, V. 1986. 'Hermes' Dilemma: The Masking of Subversion in Ethnographic Description', in *Writing Culture. The Poetics and Politics of Ethnography*, eds. J. Clifford and G.E. Marcus. Berkeley, London: University of California Press.

Danziger, E. 1996. 'Parts and Their Counterparts. Spatial and Social Relationships in Mopan Maya', in Journal of the Royal Anthropological Institute, Vol. 2, No. 1, pp. 67–82.

Duranti, A. 1988. 'Intentions, Language and Social Action in a Samoan Context', in *Journal of Pragmatics* 12: 13–33.

Duranti, A. 1990. 'Politics and Grammar: Agency in Samoan Political Discourse', in *American Ethnologist*, 17.

Duranti, A. 1994. *From Grammar to Politics. Linguistic Anthropology in a Samoan Village*. Berkeley: University of California Press.

Duranti, A. and Goodwin, C. eds. 1992. *Rethinking Context: Language as an Interactive Phenomenon*. Cambridge: Cambridge University Press.

Duranti, A. and E. Ochs. 1986. 'Literacy Instruction in a Samoan Village', in *Aquisition of Literacy: Ethnographic Perspectives*, eds. B.B. Schieffelin and P. Gilmore, pp. 213–32. Norwood: Ablex.

Duranti, A. and E. Ochs. 1990. 'Genitive Constructions and Agency in Samoan Discourse', in *Studies in Language* 14 (1): 1–23.

Eco, U. 1984. 'The Frames of Comic "Freedom"', in *Carnival*, eds. Eco, V.V. Ivanov and M. Rector. Berlin: Mouton.

Eidheim, H. 1971. *Aspects of the Lappish Minority Situation*. Oslo: Universitetsforlaget.

Eidheim, H. 1992. 'Stages in the Development of Saami Selfhood', Working Papers in Social Anthropology, No. 7. University of Oslo, Department and Museum of Anthropology.

Finnegan, R. 1992. *Oral Traditions and the Verbal Arts. A Guide to Research Practices*. London: Routledge.

Firth, R. 1940. 'The Analysis of Mana: An Empirical Approach', in *Journal of the Polynesian Society* 49: 483–510.

Firth, R. 1961. *History and Traditions of Tikopia*. Wellington: The Polynesian Society.

Firth, R. 1985. 'Degrees of Intelligibility, in *Reason and Morality*, ed. J. Overing ASA Monographs. London and New York: Tavistock Publications.

Foucault, M. 1980. *Power/Knowledge: Selected Interviews & Other Writings 1972–1977*, ed. and trans. C. Gordon. New York: Pantheon.

Foucault, M. 1989. *Foucault Live: Interviews, 1966–84*. ed. S. Lotringer, trans. J. Johnston. New York: Semiotext(e).

Fox, J. 1995. 'Austronesian Societies and Their Transformations', in *The Austronesians. Historical and Comparative Perspectives*, eds. P. Bellwood, J. Fox and D. Tryon, pp. 214–25. Canberra: The Australian National University.

Fox, J. 1997. 'Place and Landscape in Comparative Austronesian Perspective', in *The Poetic Power of Place. Comparative Perspectives on Austronesian Ideas of Locality*, ed. J. J. Fox, pp. 1–15. Canberra: The Australian National University.

Friedman, J. 1992. 'The Past in the Future: History and the Politics of Identity', in *American Anthropologist*, No. 94, pp. 837–59.

Friedman, J. 1998. 'Knowing Oceania or Oceanian Knowing. Identifying Actors and Activating Identities in Turbulent Times', in *Pacific Answers to Western Hegemony: Cultural Practices of Identity Construction*, pp. 37–66. Oxford: Berg Press.

Fuglerud, Ø. 2001. *Migrasjonsforståelse Flytteprosesser, rasisme og globalisering*. Oslo: Universitetsforlaget.

Geertz, C. 1973. *The Interpretation of Cultures*. New York: Basic Books.

Gell, A. 1993. *Wrapping in Images: Tattooing in Polynesia*. Oxford: Oxford University Press.

Gell, A. 1995. 'Closure and Multiplication: An Essay on Polynesian Cosmology and Ritual', in *Cosmos and Society in Oceania*, eds. D. de Coppet & A. Iteanu. Oxford: Berg.

Giddens, A. 1979. *Central Problems in Social Theory: Action, Structure and Contradiction in Social Analysis*. Berkeley: University of California Press.

Giddens, A. 1984. *The Constitution of Society*. Berkeley: University of California Press.

Glick, P.B. 1984. 'The Extended Case Method', in *Ethnographic Research*, ed. R. Ellen. London: Academic Press.

Gluckman, M. 1955. *The Judicial Process among the Bartose of Northern Rhodesia*. Manchester: Manchester University Press.

Godelier, M. 1993. 'Is the West the Model for Humankind? The Baruya of New Guinea Between Change and Decay', in *Pacific Islands Trajectories*, ed. T. Otto. Nijmegen: The Centre for Pacific Studies.

Goffman, E. 1959. *The Presentation of Self in Everyday Life*. New York: Doubleday.

Goffman, E. 1974. *Frame Analysis. An Essay on the Organization of Experience*. New York: Harper and Row.

Gordon, R. ed. 1991. *Tokelau. A Collection of Documents and References Relating to Constitutional Development*. Apia: Tokelau Administration, Wellington: Victoria University Printing Department.

Goward, N. 1984. 'The Fieldwork Experience', in *Ethnographic Research. A Guide to General Conduct*, ed. R.F. Ellen. London, New York: Academic Press.

Grønhaug, R. 1974. *Micro-Macro Relations. Social Organization in Antalaya, Southern Turkey*. Bergen: Bergen Occasional Papers in Social Anthropology.

Hale, H. 1846. *Unites States Exploring Expedition [...] Ethnography and Philology*. Philadelphia: Lee and Blanchard.

Handelman, D. 1998. *Models and Mirrors: Towards an Anthropology of Public Events*. Oxford: Oxford University Press.

Hannertz, U. 1992. *Cultural Complexity*. New York: Columbia University Press.

Harvey, D. 1990. *The Condition of Postmodernity. An Enquiry into the Origins of Cultural Change*. Cambridge MA & Oxford UK: Blackwell.

Hastrup, K. 1989. 'The Prophetic Condition', in Edwin Ardener, *The Voice of Prophecy and Other Essays*, ed. Macholm Chapman. Oxford: Blackwell.

Hastrup, K. and K. Ramløv eds. 1988. *Feltarbejde. Oplevelse og metode i etnografien (Fieldwork. Experience and Method in Etnography)*. Copenhagen: Akademisk Forlag.

Hastrup, K. and K. Fog Olwig eds. 1997. *Siting Culture. The Shifting Anthropological Object*. London and New York: Routledge.

Hereniko, V. 1994. 'Clowning as Political Commentary: Polynesia, Then and Now', in *The Contemporary Pacific*. Spring, pp. 1–28.

Hertzfeld, M. 1997. *Cultural Intimacy. Social Poetics in the Nation State*. New York, London: Routledge.

Hoëm, I. ed. 1992. *Kupu mai te Tutolu. Tokelau Oral Literature*. Oslo: Scandinavian University Press/The Institute for Comparative Research in Human Culture.
    a. 'Introduction' (pp. 1–5)
    b. 'Songs and Cultural Identity' (pp. 6–33)
    c. 'Lauga: Tokelau Speeches' (pp. 34–58)

Hoëm, I. 1993. 'Space and Morality in Tokelau', in *Pragmatics*. Quarterly

Publication of the International Pragmatics Association. Vol. 3, No. 2. pp. 137–153.

Hoëm, I. 1994. 'Maui, the Trickster God – a Possible Role Model for Living in a Fictionalised World; An Anthropological Reading of Novels in the South Pacific', in ed. E. Archetti, *Exploring the Written. Anthropology and the Multiplicities of Writing*, pp. 197–230. Oslo: Scandinavian University Press/Oxford University Press.

Hoëm, I. 1995. *A Way With Words*. White Orchid Press, Bangkok, Joint Publication with the Institute of Comparative Research in Human Culture, Oslo.

Hoëm, I. 1995b. *A Sense of Place*. PhD thesis. University of Oslo.

Hoëm, I. 1996. 'The Scientific Endeavour and the Natives', in *Visions of Empire*, ed. D. Miller. Cambridge University Press: Cambridge.

Hoëm, I. 1998a. 'Staging a Political Challenge: The Story of Tokelau te Ata', in *Common Worlds and Single Lives. Constituting Knowledge in Pacific Societies*, ed. V. Keck. Oxford: Berg.

Hoëm, I. 1998b. 'Clowns, Dignity and Desire: on the Relationship between Performance, Identity and Reflexivity', in *Recasting Ritual. Performance, Media, Identity*, eds. F. Hughes–Freeland & M. Crain, London: Routledge.

Hoëm, I. 1999. 'Processes of Identification and the Incipient National level. A Tokelau case', in *Social Anthropology*, Vol. 7, No. 3, 279–95.

Hoëm, I. 2000. 'Aesthetics', in *Essays in Honour of Arne Skjølsvold*, eds. H.M. Wallin and P. Wallin, The Kon-Tiki Museum Occasional Papers, Vol. 5.

Hoëm, I. 2002. 'Contexts and Difference,' in *Oceanic Socialities and Cultural Forms: Ethnographies of Experience*, eds. I. Hoëm and S. Roalkvam. Berghahn: Oxford.

Hooper, A. 1968. 'Socio-Economic Organisation of the Tokelau Islands', in *Proceedings of the Eight Congress of Anthropological and Ethnological Sciences*. Tokyo.

Hooper, A. 1982. *Aid and Dependency in a Small Pacific Territory*. Working Paper 62, Department of Anthropology: University of Auckland.

Hooper, A. 1987. *Class and Culture in the South Pacific*, eds. A. Hooper, S. Britton, R. Crocombe, J. Huntsman, C. Macpherson. Auckland: University of the South Pacific and University of Auckland.

Hooper, A. 1993. 'The MIRAB Transition in Fakaofo, Tokelau', in *Pacific Viewpoint*, 34 (2) 241–64.

Hooper, A. and J. Huntsman. 1972. 'The Tokelau Islands Migration Study: Behavioural Studies', in *Migration and Related Social and Health Problems in New Zealand and the Pacific*, eds. J. Stanhope and J.S. Dodge. Wellington: Epidemiology Unit, Wellington Hospital.

Hooper, A. and J. Huntsman. 1975. 'Male and Female in Tokelau Culture', in *Journal of the Polynesian Society* 84: 415–30.

Hooper, A. and J. Huntsman. 1976. 'The Desacration of Tokelau Kinship', in *Journal of the Polynesian Society* 85: 257–73.

Hooper, A. and J. Huntsman. 1985. 'Structures of Tokelau History', in *Transformations of Polynesian Culture*, eds. A. Hooper and J. Huntsman. Auckland: The Polynesian Society.

Hooper, A. and J. Huntsman. 1992. Chapters 2, 3, 4, 5, 6, and 7, in ed. Wessen, A.F. et al. *Migration and Health in a Small Society. The Case of Tokelau*. Oxford: Clarendon Press.

Hooper, A. and J. Huntsman. 1996. *Tokelau. A Historical Ethnography*. Auckland: Auckland University Press.

Hooper, R. 1987. 'The Discourse Function of Focus Constructions in Tokelauan', paper presented at the 7th New Zealand Linguistics Conference, Dunedin.

Hovdhaugen, E, I. Hoëm, C.M. Iosefo and A.M. Vonen. 1989. *A Handbook of the Tokelau Language*. Oslo: Norwegian University Press/The Institute of Comparative Research in Human Culture.

Hovdhaugen, E. 1992a. 'The Work of Tokelau Women', in *Kupu mai te Tutolu. Tokelau Oral Literature*, ed. I. Hoëm. Oslo: Scandinavian University Press/The Institute for Comparative Research in Human Culture.

Hovdhaugen, E. 1992b. 'Fishing Stories', in *Kupu mai te Tutolu. Tokelau Oral Literature*, ed. I. Hoëm. Oslo: Scandinavian University Press/The Institute for Comparative Research in Human Culture.

Howard, A. 1985. 'History, Myth, and Polynesian Chieftainship: The Case of Rotuman Kings', in *Transformations of Polynesian Culture*, eds. A. Hooper and J. Huntsman, pp. 39–77. Auckland: The Polynesian Society.

Huntsman, J.W. 1969. *Kin and Coconuts on a Polynesian Atoll: Socio-Economic Organisation of Nukunonu, Tokelau Islands*. PhD thesis. Pennsylvania: Bryn Mawr College.

Huntsman, J. 1971. 'Concepts of Kinship and Categories of Kinsmen in the Tokelau Islands', in *Journal of the Polynesian Society* 80: 317–54.

Huntsman, J. 1975. 'The Impact of Cultural Exchange on Health and Disease Patterns: The Tokelau Island Migrant Study', in eds. Y. Chang and P.J. Donaldson, *Population Change in the Pacific Region*, pp. 183–92. Vancouver, Canada: Proceedings of the Thirteenth Pacific Science Congress.

Huntsman, J. 1977. *Ten Tokelau Tales*. Working Paper 47. Department of Anthropology, University of Auckland.

Huntsman, J. 1980. *Tokelau Tales Told by Manuele Palehau*. Working Paper 58, Department of Anthropology, University of Auckland.

Huntsman, J. 2000. 'Fiction, Fact and Imagination: A Tokelau Narrative', in *Oral Tradition* No. 52: 283–315.

Huntsman, J. and A. Hooper. 1996. *Tokelau. A Historical Ethnography*. Auckland: Auckland University Press.

Hviding, E. 1993. 'Indigenous Essentialism? "Simplifying" Customary Land Ownership in New Georgia, Solomon Islands', in *Bijdragen tot de Taal-, Land-en Volkenkunde*, 149: 802–23.

Hviding, E. 1994. '"Island Cultures" and "Cultural Islands"', Paper Presented at the Basel Conference of the European Association for Oceanists.

Hylland Eriksen, T. 1993. *Ethnicity and Nationalism. Anthropological Perspectives*. London: Pluto Press.

Hylland Eriksen, T. 1993. *Små Steder – Store Spørsmål. Innføring i Sosialantropologi*. Oslo: Universitetsforlaget.

Irvine, J. 1982. 'Language and Affect: Some Cross-Cultural Issues', in *Contemporary Perceptions of Language: Interdisciplinary Dimensions*, ed. H. Byrnes, pp. 31–47. Washington DC: Georgetown University Press.

IWGIA document. 2001. *Challenging Politics: Indigenous People's Experiences with Political Parties and Elections*, No. 104.

Jackson, M. 2002. *The Politics of Storytelling. Violence, Transgression and Intersubjectivity*. Copenhagen: Museum Tusculaneum Press.

Kapferer, B. 1969. 'Norms and the Manipulation of Relationships in a Work Context', in *Social Networks in Urban Situations*, ed. J. Clyde Mitchell. Manchester: Manchester University Press.

Keating, E. 1998. *Power Sharing. Language, Rank, Gender, and Social Space in Pohnpei, Micronesia*. New York, Oxford: Oxford University Press.

Keating, E. 2000. 'Moments of Hierarchy: Constructing Social Stratification by Means of Language, Food, Space, and the Body in Pohnpei, Micronesia', in

American Anthropologist, Vol. 102, No. 2, June, pp. 303–20.

Keesing, R.M. 1989. 'Creating the Past: Custom and Identity in the Contemporary Pacific', in *The Contemporary Pacific* Vol. 1 , Nos. 1 and 2, pp. 19–42.

Keesing, R.M. 1992. '"Earth" and "Path" as Complex Categories. Semantics and Symbolism in Kwaio Culture', in *Cognitive Aspects of Religious Symbolism*, ed. P. Boyer. Cambridge: Cambridge University Press.

Krupa, V. 1982. 'The Polynesian Languages', in *Languages of Asia and Africa*, Vol. 4. London: Routledge and Kegan Paul.

Labov, W. and J. Waletsky. 1968. 'Narrative Analysis', in A Study of the Non-Standard English of Negro and Puerto Rican Speakers in New York, ed. W. Labov, pp. 286–338. New York: Colombia University Press.

Lavie S. and T. Swedenburg eds. 1996. *Displacement, Diaspora and Geographies of Identity*. Durham & London: Duke University Press.

Larsen, T. 1989. 'Kultur og Utvikling', in *Hvor Mange Hvite Elefanter? Kulturdimensjonen i Bistandsarbeidet*, ed. T. Hylland Eriksen. Oslo: Ad Notam.

Lefebvre, H. 1991. *The Production of Space* (translated by Donald Nicholson–Smith). Oxford: Blackwell.

Lévi-Strauss, C. 1966. *The Savage Mind*. London: Weidenfeld and Nicolson.

Levy, R.I. 1973. *Tahitians: Mind and Experience in the Society Islands*. Chicago and London: University of Chicago Press.

Levy, R.I. 1984. 'Emotion, Knowing, and Culture', in *Culture Theory: Essays on Mind, Self, and Emotion*, eds. R.A. Shweder and R. LeVine. Cambridge: Cambridge University Press.

Lieber, M. ed. 1997. *Exiles and Migrants in Oceania*. Honolulu: University of Hawaii Press.

Lister, J.J. 1892. 'Notes on the Natives of Fakaofu. (Bowditch Island). Union group', in *Journal of the Anthropological Institute of Great Britain and Ireland* 21: 43–63 .

Lyons, J. 1968. *Introduction to Theoretical Linguistics*. Cambridge: Cambridge University Press.

Macgregor, G. 1937. *Ethnology of Tokelau Islands*. Honolulu, Hawaii: Bernice P. Bishop Museum Bulletin 146. New York: Kraus Reprint Co., 1971.

Macpherson, C., P. Spoonley and M. Anae (eds.) 2001. *Tangata o te Moana Nui*. Palmerston North: Dunmore Press.

Mageo, J.M. 1998. *Theorizing Self in Samoa. Emotions, Genders, and Sexualities*. Ann Arbor: The University of Michigan Press.

Marcus, G.E and M.M.J. Fisher. 1986. *Anthropology as Cultural Critique: an Experimental Moment in the Human Sciences*. Chicago and London: University of Chicago Press.

Matagi Tokelau. 1990, 1991. Eds. Hooper and Huntsman. Office for Tokelau Affairs: Apia and Institute of Pacific Studies, USP: Suva.

Maude, H.E. 1968. *Of Islands and Men. Studies in Pacific History*. Melbourne, London: Oxford University Press.

Mauss, M. 1954. *The Gift. Forms and Functions of Exchange in Archaic Societies*. London: Routledge & Kegan Paul.

Meleisea, M. 1987. *The Making of Modern Samoa. Traditional Authority and Colonial Administration in the Modern History of Western Samoa*. Suva: Institute of Pacific Studies of the University of the South Pacific.

Moore, S.F. 1975. 'Epilogue: Uncertainties in Situations, Indeterminacies in Culture', in *Symbol and Politics in Communal Ideology*, eds. S.F. Moore & B. Myerhoff. Ithaca: Cornell University Press.

Moore, S.F. 1984. 'Explaining the Present: Theoretical Dilemmas in Processual Ethnography', in *American Ethnologist*, Vol. 14, pp. 727–31.

Morton, H. 1996. *Becoming Tongan: An Ethnography of Childhood.* Honolulu: University of Hawaii Press.

Mosel, U. and E. Hovdhaugen. 1992. *Samoan Reference Grammar.* Oslo: Scandinavian University Press/The Institute for Comparative Research in Human Culture.

Newell, J.E. 1895. 'Notes, Chiefly Ethnological, on the Tokelau, Ellice and Gilbert Islanders', in *Australasian Association for the Advancement of Science*, Vol. 6, pp. 603–12.

Ochs, E. 1988. *Culture and Language Development. Language Acquisition and Language Socialization in a Samoan Village.* Cambridge: Cambridge University Press.

Ochs, E. and L. Capps. 1996. 'Narrating the Self', in *Annual Review of Anthropology*, Vol. 25, pp. 19–43.

Ochs, E. and L. Capps. 2001. *Living Narrative. Creating Lives in Everyday Storytelling.* Cambridge Mass. & London: Harvard University Press.

Otto, T. 1992. 'The Paliau Movement in Manus and the Objectification of Tradition', in *History and Anthropology*, Vol. 5, Nos. 3–4, pp. 427–54.

Pacific Studies. 2002. *Constructing Moral Communities: Pacific Islander Strategies for Settling in New Places.* Vol. 25, Nos. 1–2.

Parkin, D. 1982. 'Introduction', in *Semantic Anthropology.* London & New York: Academic Press.

Pasilio, T.M. ed. 1992. *Nuanua of Tokelau. A Collection of Poems by Young Writers From Tokelau.* Apia: Office for Tokelau Affairs.

Perez, C. and C. Giese. 1983. 'Tokelau, Micro-Politics', in eds. *Politics in Polynesia* (Politics in the Pacific Islands; Vol. 2). Suva: Institute of Pacific Studies of the University of the South Pacific.

Prior, I. and J. Stanhope. 1980. 'Epidemics, Health and Disease in a Small, Isolated Environment', in World Development 8: 995–1016. Pergamon Press.

Rappaport, R. 1979. 'Aspects of Man's Influence on Island Ecosystems: Alteration and Control,' in *Ecology, Meaning and Religion.* Berkeley: North Atlantic Books.

Ree, J. 1990. 'Funny Voices: Stories, Punctuation, and Personal Identity', in *New Literary History*, No. 21: 1039–58.

Report of the United Nations Visiting Mission to Tokelau, 1994.

Ricoeur, P. 1981. *Hermeneutics and the Human Sciences.* Cambridge: Cambridge University Press.

Rosaldo, M.Z. 1980. *Knowledge and Passion: Illongot Notions of Self and Social Life.* Cambridge: Cambridge University Press.

Rosaldo, M.Z. 1983. 'The Shame of Headhunters and the Autonomy of Self', in *Ethos*, No. 11, pp. 135–51.

Rosaldo, M.Z. 1984. 'Towards and Anthropology of Self and Feeling', in *Culture Theory: Essays on Mind, Self, and Emotion*, eds. R. Shweder and R.A. LeVine, pp. 137–57. Cambridge: Cambridge University Press.

Said, E. 1978. *Orientalism.* Penguin Books.

Sahlins, M. 1985. *Islands of History.* London: Tavistock.

Sahlins, M. 1993. 'Goodbye to Tristes Tropes: Ethnography in the Context of Modern World History', in *Assessing Cultural Anthropology*, ed. R. Borofsky, pp. 377–93. New York: McGraw–Hill.

Sallen, V.G. 1983. *Tokelau Scholars in New Zealand: Experiences and Evaluations.* MA thesis. Auckland: University of Auckland.

Sallen, V.G. 1998. *Tupulaga Tokelau in New Zealand.* PhD thesis. Auckland: University of Auckland.

Senft, G. 1987. 'Rituelle Kommunikation auf den Trobriand Inseln', in *Zeitschrift für Literaturwissenschaft und Linguistik*, Vol. 65, 105–30.

Senft, G. 1991. 'Prolegomena to the Pragmatics of "Situational–Intentional" Varieties in Kilivila Language,' in *Levels of Linguistic Adaption*: Selected Papers from the 1987 International Pragmatics Conference, ed. J. Verschueren, pp. 235–48. Vol. ll. Amsterdam: Benjamins.

Senft, G. ed. 1997. *Referring to Space. Studies in Austronesian and Papuan Languages*. Oxford: Clarendon Press.

Shore, B. 1982. *Sala'ilua: A Samoan Mystery*, New York: Columbia University Press.

Shore, B. 1989. 'Mana and Tapu', in *Developments in Polynesian Ethnology*, eds. A. Howard and R. Borofsky, pp. 137–73. Honolulu: University of Hawaii Press.

Spitulnik, D. 1997. 'The Social Circulation of Media Discourse and the Mediation of Communities', in *Journal of Linguistic Anthropology*, Vol. 6, No. 2, pp. 161–87.

Spitulnik, D. 1999. 'The Language of the City: Town Bemba as Urban Hybridity', in *Journal of Linguistic Anthropology*, Vol. 8, No. 1, pp. 30–59.

Street, B. ed. 1993. *Cross-Cultural Approaches to Literacy*. Cambridge: Cambridge University Press.

Summerhayes, G. 2000. *Lapita Interaction*. Canberra: The Australian National University.

Te Vakai, June 1987. Apia: Office for Tokelau Affairs.

Tokelau Dictionary [TD]. 1986. Apia: Office of Tokelau Affairs.

Thomas, A. 1986. *The Fatele of Tokelau: Approaches to the Study of a Dance in its Social Context*. MA thesis. Wellington: Department of Anthropology, Victoria University of Wellington.

Thomas, A., I. Tuia and J. Huntsman eds. 1990. *Songs and Stories of Tokelau; an Introduction to the Cultural Heritage*. Wellington: Victoria University Press.

Thomas, N. 1995. *Oceanic Art*, London: Thames and Hudson.

Tonkin, E. 1992. *Narrating Our Pasts. The Social Construction of Oral History*. Cambridge: Cambridge University Press.

Toren, C. 1990. *Making Sense of Hierarchy: Cognition as Social Process in Fiji*. London: The Athlone Press.

Toren, C. 1994. 'All Things Go in Pairs, or the Sharks Will Bite: The Antithetical Nature of Fijian Chiefship', in *Oceania*, Vol. 64, No. 3.

Turner, V. 1967. *The Forest of Symbols. Aspects of Ndembu Ritual*. Ithaka and London: Cornell University Press.

Turner, V. 1992. *The Anthropology of Performance*. New York: PAJ Publications.

Tyler, S.A. 1986. 'Post-Modern Ethnography: From Document of the Occult to Occult Document', in *Writing Culture. The Poetics and Politics of Ethnography*, eds. J. Clifford and G.E. Marcus. Berkeley, London: University of California Press.

Vainiu mai Fakafotu, 1992, Newsletter No. 19, September–October, Fakaofo, Tokelau.

Valentine, D.E. 1994. 'The Individual In Terror', in *Embodiment and Experience. The Existential Ground of Culture and Self*, ed. T.J. Csordas. Cambridge: Cambridge University Press.

Valeri, V. 1985. 'The Conqueror Becomes King: a Political Analysis of the Hawaiian Legend of 'Umi,' in A. Hooper and J. Huntsman (eds.) *Transformations of Polynesian Culture*, Auckland: The Polynesian Society.

Van Velsen 1967. 'The Extended-Case Method and Situational Analysis', in *The Craft of Social Anthropology*, ed. A.L. Epstein. London: Tavistock.

Venbrux, E. 1995. *A Death in the Tiwi Islands*. Cambridge: Cambridge University Press.

Voren, A.M. 1993. Parts of Speech and Linguistic Typology. PhD thesis. University of Oslo.

Wendt, A. 1973. *Sons for the Return Home*. Longman Paul.

Wessen, A.F. et al. (Ed.) 1992. *Migration and Health in a Small Society. The Case of Tokelau*. Oxford: Clarendon Press.

Wierzsbicka, A. 1992. *Semantics, Culture and Cognition: Universal Human Concepts in Culture-specific Configurations*. New York: Oxford University Press.

Wilkes, C. 1845. *Narrative of the United States Exploring Expedition During the Years 1838, 1839, 1840, 1841, 1842*, Volume V. London: Wiley and Putnam.

Williksen–Bakker, S. 1994. 'The Moulding of Identity in South Pacific Poetry and Prose. The Mode of Mimesis: A New Way of Addressing the Issue in Fiji', in *Exploring the Written. Anthropology and the Multiplicity of Writing*, ed. E.P. Archetti. Oslo: Scandinavian University Press.

Index